CONTENT WARNING

This story, including earlier writings about the 1967 Gordonvale flood and 1970 Search and Recovery mission on Bell Peak North, has views, images, expressions, opinions, assumptions, language, and references to Indigenous Australians and others, no longer living, that a reader might find offensive or disturbing. No offence or disrespect is intended for any person, living or dead. Should the words or images cause sadness or distress, or trigger memories, particularly for survivors of past abuse, violence, or childhood trauma, please seek immediate support and counselling.

A copy of this publication can be found in the National Library of Australia and State Library of Queensland.

Author: Neil Raymond Bradford
Title: Four Days, Three Nights on Bell Peak North: My Story
ISBN: 9780648430506 (paperback)
Imprint: Independently published
Subjects: Bradford, Neil Raymond.
             Hill, Patrick John.
             Drummond, Stewart Rutherford.
             Search and Rescue operations -- Queensland -- Bell Peak North (Mountain) -- Anecdotes.
             Aircraft Accidents -- Queensland -- Bell Peak North (Mountain) -- Anecdotes.
             First Responders -- Queensland -- Bell Peak North (Mountain) -- Family History -- Autobiography.
             Aircraft Accident Victims -- Queensland -- Bell Peak North (Mountain) -- History -- 1970.
             Cessna 402 (Private plane) -- Queensland -- Bell Peak North (Mountain) -- History -- 1970.
             Mountains -- Queensland -- Bell Peak North (Mountain) -- History -- 1970.
             Police, Rural -- Queensland -- Gordonvale -- Family History -- Autobiography.
             Floods -- Queensland -- Gordonvale -- History.
             Mackay (Qld.) – History.
             Gordonvale (Qld.) -- History.
             World War, 1939-1945.
             Australian.

Cover Design: Neil Raymond Bradford

Front Cover Image: Author at the Gordonvale Police Station in 1971 (Private Source)

Back Cover Image: Robert James (Bob) Wallace at the crash site in 1970 (Courtesy of Patricia Wallace)

Published by Neil Raymond Bradford at neilraymondbradford@gmail.com of Birtinya, Queensland, Australia.

FOUR DAYS, THREE NIGHTS ON BELL PEAK NORTH

MY STORY

NEIL RAYMOND BRADFORD

BOOKS BY NEIL RAYMOND BRADFORD

Voices from The Past: Law Enforcement on the Central Highlands
Oxley-Gatton Murders: Exposing the Conspiracy
&
Jack the Ripper: His Australian Murders

Dedicated to the memory
of
Madge & Wally Pannell

Rest in Peace

ACKNOWLEDGEMENTS

Foremost in my mind, I would like to thank my wife, Patricia, who, during my 31 years' service in the police force, accompanied me all over Queensland. Without her support and dedication, I would not have undertaken that journey. The same goes for our sons, Mark, and Christopher, who became young men, other parents would be proud to call their own. The moves and changes did not deter their ability to achieve and achieve they did. Lastly, but not the least, without the encouragement and faith of my late mother-in-law, Madge Pannell, I would not have embarked on what I now look back on as a rewarding career.

CONTENTS

CONTENT WARNING..i

COPYRIGHT ii

ACKNOWLEDGEMENTS...vi

INTRODUCTION 1

1   EARLY BEGINNINGS...3

2   TOUGH TIMES...31

3   NEW BEGINNING 60

4   GORDONVALE FLOOD.......................................88

5   WALL OF SILENCE.. 112

6   FATAL FLIGHT.. 126

7   SEARCH AND RECOVERY 137

8   FORGOTTEN HEROES....................................... 153

9   MISSION IMPOSSIBLE 169

10 SAFELY EXTRACTED.. 177

11 GREEN MAFIA 187

12 FALSELY ACCUSED 200

13 THE JOKE... 230

14 GAME OVER 249

CONCLUSION.. 275

ABBREVIATIONS.. 280

ENDNOTES 282

BIBLIOGRAPHY 295

INDEX 300

INTRODUCTION

Born into humble beginnings, subjected to child abuse at nine through to thirteen years, and denied an education, but having the desire and ability to achieve, whether it be in sport, work, education, or any other endeavour, sent me down the path of policing when corruption was flourishing in Queensland.

Extremely pleased with my acceptance into the Queensland Police Force (QPF), married and with a child on the way, while serving as a Probationary Constable, I drew a line between *right* and *wrong* in the sand, not to be stepped over, even if it meant offending colleagues.

It was the *right* and *proper* thing to do, but one thing led to another, and colleagues subjected me to a *wall-of-silence*, which was *daunting* and *confronting*, but it was the complete opposite when it came to how the community accepted and treated me.[1]

Those circumstances had advantages, as I was never interested in *long-term relationships*, except for someone with whom to share life with me, achieve an education denied to me, and being there and doing the best I could for a young family, completely opposite to my upbringing, was more important.

Several years later, instead of being *debriefed* and acknowledged for the excellent work done, what I endured over four days and three nights recovering the pilot and his passenger killed in a light aircraft accident on Bell Peak North of the Malbon Thompson Range, south from Cairns in Far North Queensland, was suppressed by the *wall-of-silence*.[1,2]

It was a defining moment in anyone's policing career, but when my excellent work and devotion to duty were not acknowledged, I remained at the summit of Bell Peak North with what I endured there over four days and three nights confined for the next forty years in the subconscious of my mind.

Adding insult to injury, the year following the fatal plane accident, my colleagues accused me, as well as my wife, of leaking sensitive information about the alleged activities of police, *on* and *off* duty, to a person who lodged complaints against them, identified as the reason for the *wall-of-silence*.[1]

Although admonished from any wrongdoing, which was the year after my transfer in disgrace to another police station, it was common for a colleague to call me either a *dog* or refer to me as someone in the police force not to trust, despite them not known anything about me.[3]

Going back to Cairns a decade later as a Sergeant, I often found myself looking up at the summit of Bell Peak North to discover that I was still on the mountain, enduring what I did there over four days and three nights.

After the Fitzgerald Commission of Inquiry into *possible illegal activities and associated police misconduct*, then stringent vetting by the Criminal Justice Commission (CJC), I was selected and promoted to the rank of Inspector, only to be demoted back to the rank of Senior Sergeant, two years later, over a report that was altered without my knowledge and permission.[4,5]

Eighteen years on from my demotion, which was 40 years after the fatal aircraft accident on the Malbon Thompson Range, I broke my silence and *The Weekend Post* published the article *Four days, three nights on Bell Peak North*.[6]

After publishing of that article, I came down from Bell Peak North on the Malbon Thompson Range!

More importantly, this story is about how an *autistic* person achieved so much in sport, work, education, or other endeavours, cynics believed were impossible.

Others have published their *versions* or *memories* of what they did as civilians during the Search and Recovery mission on Bell Peak North, purporting that they were the *principles*, but that is not what happened.[7,8,9]

About my life, here is my *version* of what happened before, during, and after the mission over four days and three nights on Bell Peak North.

1

EARLY BEGINNINGS

Born in 1946 at Mackay, Queensland, Australia, and the third eldest of ten children registered at birth to Arnold Bradford and Margaret Isabella Bedford, apart from almost two years away at Margate on the Redcliffe Peninsula, Queensland, and Limevale on the border of Queensland and New South Wales, my upbringing until 19 years was in the Mackay district.[1]

Throughout those years, it appeared not only to me, but also to others, so it seemed to me at the time, that Arnold was not my father, and honestly, his interaction with me, which was unlike what he had with my eldest brother, four years older than me, sowed that seed in my mind.

Any other worthwhile comparison with a brother, or sister, for that matter, is difficult to make.

The next brother was five years younger, and the other two were born seven and nine years after me. Then, of the sisters, one was born before, another following me, and the others 11, 13, and 18 years after me.

So, during those first 19 years of my life, often it felt as if nurses had mixed up the cribs at the hospital, and the wrong family took me home.

However, prior to authoring this story, an Ancestry DNA test proved, beyond reasonable doubt, that Arnold was, in fact, my biological father, putting to rest the doubts in my mind that haunted me for so many years.[2]

What compounded those doubts is the fact that despite having four brothers and five sisters, I grew up as an *only child*, as my *thoughts* and *behaviour*, and *abilities* and *capabilities*, whether it be in *sport* or *education*, as well as my *direction in life*, were *different* to my siblings.

Often, my siblings, older and younger, even my parents, occasionally, referred to me as being *odd* or *dumb*, and that I was *always up to something.*

Furthermore, whenever anything happened, others never accepted that I was being *truthful,* and that what happened, was *unintentional* and beyond my control.

How I *coped* or *responded* to *situations* and *circumstances* in which I found myself, was the complete opposite to those of my parents and siblings.

I could have accepted that I was a *worthless* individual, but my brain, *constantly working overtime,* made me think of them as being *stupid* or *idiots.*

Then, their way of being *friends* one day, and *enemies* the next, did not interest me, as *consistency in conduct and behaviour* was more important to me.

Even the presents on a birthday or at Christmas were entirely *different* to my siblings, as their gifts were common to children of their age, whereas mine made *use of the mind,* such as *completing complicated puzzles* or *building with a Meccano set.*

Siblings even had difficulty playing with my presents, such as a scooter.

Lacking the same *abilities* and *coordination,* my older sister failed to slow the scooter's rapid descent of a hill, simply by applying a foot to the brake at the rear.

Crashing headlong into a crop of sunflowers at the side of the road, getting up with only scratches and bruises, my sister discovered that she was allergic to those flowers, suffering a rash then and afterwards from those flowers.

Then, preferring to wait and see what others were doing, when I got the urge to play, the game was over!

I was more comfortable doing things by myself, rather than interacting with siblings, or others, as well as I had medical issues, such as sensitivity to *light* and *sound,* not shared by siblings.

It was not a matter of being *shy* or *bashful,* as often alluded to by others, but a matter of being *comfortable* in the *surroundings* before *interacting* with others.

Playing a game at school, such as *Ring-a-ring o' roses*, was *silly* and *ridiculous*, as I could not see the sense of forming a ring with other children, dancing within a circle around a person standing in the centre of the ring, while singing –

> *Ring-a-ring o' roses,*
> *A pocket full of posies,*
> *A-tishoo! A-tishoo!*
> *We all fall down,*

curtsying after the final line, and then everyone *flopping* to the floor, with the last to fall, replacing the one in the middle.[3]

Instead, being the first over the finish line in a sprint of fifty to one hundred yards or smashing the ball in rounders out of the playground was more rewarding.[4]

In the absence of a current diagnosis, and without my parents telling me before they passed on, there is more than sufficient evidence, outlined herein, for me to say that I am *autistic*.[5]

Believing there is no use saying one thing and meaning another, I will tell it as it happened, how what I experienced during those early years of learning, shaped me into the person I became.

Hopefully, others will understand that I loved my parents for bringing me into this world, but I did not love them for the *pain* and *suffering* endured during my childhood, and for the *hurtful* things done and said to me as an adult.

If they were still alive, they might say otherwise!

While penning those few words, tears welled in my eyes, as neither knew how much I loved them, despite what they did to me throughout my life.

If I had my time over, I would like the same parents, but with things done differently, including my dealings with family matters, which would not have been an easy task, as things to me are *black* and *white*, with *grey* being difficult to determine.

After my parents married, my father worked mostly away from home during the crushing season of about six months, cutting and loading sugarcane by hand, mainly in the Sarina district, south from Mackay, returning home, when transport was available, for a weekend.

During his absences, my mother lived with an older brother and sister in a two-bedroom cottage built by my father on the dairy farm known as *Eureka* at Andergrove, northside of Mackay, owned by my grandfather, Cecil Herbert (Pop) Bedford.[6]

Others call it *Fernleigh Dairy*, but that was the name of the business and not the dairy farm.

Adding to the intrigue about my parentage, it surprised me when told by my mother that I had been born at the Cromer Private Hospital.[1]

All siblings, apart from the youngest, because my mother was going through menopause and expected complications, were born at the Mackay District/Base Hospital.[1]

"Why was I born in a private hospital," I asked my mother, who responded, "Not everything was right!"

"What do you mean?"

"After you were born, lights and sounds bothered you, and you didn't sleep soundly!"

"And …"

"Well, they assessed your eyes and ears when you were two years in the Lister Private Hospital."

"What was the diagnosis?"[5]

"I don't remember," said my mother, but I suspected she did.

This conversation, dragged out of my mother, came about after she read an article in the newspaper that, along with other police officers, I had attended a report of a prowler at the Cromer Private Hospital, converted by then into a female hostel in Shakespeare Street at Mackay.

"I have memories of waking up at night, standing on the top step, and you behind me."

"Yes, that happened often."

"Why didn't you say something to me, instead of just allowing me to go back to bed?

"I was told that it would frighten you and give you nightmares."

"Who told you this?"

"The doctor who examined you at the Lister Hospital."

I should have continued, but after dragging things piece-by-piece out of my mother, the conversation ended there.

At the time of the diagnosis in 1948, my father's younger and only sister, Marjorie May (Marj) Petersen, formerly Bradford, was a nurse at the Lister Private Hospital.[5]

"You were a beautiful baby," said Aunt Marj, "when I nursed you in the Lister Private Hospital!"

Stunned by that comment, "I wasn't aware that you nursed me in hospital," I responded.

"Neil," continued Aunt Marj, "you know that you are *different* to your brothers and sisters?"

"Yes," I responded, "I speak differently to them!"

Becoming frustrated, "No, that is not what I am trying to tell you," Aunt Marj said, adding, "You …," before abruptly ending the conversation.

I knew there was something important that my aunt wanted to tell me, but I was then in denial, so I jokingly change the conversation to *speaking differently than my siblings.*

Decades later, I had a similar conversation with her, before she passed away, and I was still in denial and made the same joke about *speaking differently to my siblings.*

Sorry, Aunt Marj, I should have listened closely to what you had to say!

Putting things into perspective, Doctor Paul William Hopkins was the attending doctor at my birth in 1946 at the Cromer Private Hospital.[1]

Prior to then, Doctor Hopkins was the medical superintendent of the Mackay District Hospital until he resigned in 1928, which was two years after he took over the private practice of Doctor H. L. Ashton-Shorter at 29 Brisbane Street, Mackay, known today as the Paul Hopkins Medical Clinic.[7,8]

In January 1948, *owing to an acute shortage of trained nursing staff and the introduction of the 40-hour week,* the Cromer Private Hospital ceased to exist.[2]

That year, Doctor Hopkins was the family's private doctor, so it makes sense that he conducted the diagnosis at the Lister Private Hospital, which is where he treated private patients after the closure of the Cromer Private Hospital.[5,9,10]

In 1953, Doctor Duncan Robertson, who became the family's doctor, and who operated on me, ten years later, joined the private practice with Doctor Hopkins.[8]

Seventeen years after the diagnosis at the Lister Private Hospital, I had a chance meeting with Doctor Hopkins, but he did not say anything to me about *autism*, as I was at the practice to see Doctor Robertson for another matter.[11]

So, there were opportunities for someone to say something to me, but everyone kept me in the dark.

It hurts, even today, that my parents never sat down and discussed the medical condition with me. If they had, and if it was before I made application to join the police force, I might not have embarked on the greatest journey of my life!

The first home for me, was a sugarcane cutter's barracks cladded with corrugated-iron and a rammed-earth floor on a farm where my father cut and loaded sugarcane by hand at Loloma, near Koumala, south from Mackay.[1]

That change of living conditions, albeit temporary, was after a son, and my half-brother, was born the previous year to the wife of one of my father's older brothers.

How do I know that to be correct?

While others thought I did not understand what they said, which was during the extended Bradford family of twelve boys and one girl gathering on New Year's Day at an uncle and aunt's home on the outskirts of Mackay, I overhead that heated conversation between the uncle in question and my father.

Being the aggrieved party, the uncle remained, and my father and his family banished from the festivities, which was not the last time that happen.

Sober, he was a good man, but when drunk, I despised him, as he did things in my presence that did not fit in with my *black-and-white* approach to life.

In my earliest memories of him, my father was a mysterious person, disappearing and reappearing at irregular intervals.

Now that I know more, he was a seasonal worker, going from one job to another, away from home, which changed often, as we moved from one dilapidated house to another, never being in the same place for any length of time.

Despite those upheavals, along with my siblings, we were well-clothed, as seen in the first two photographs at the end of this chapter, and there was always food on the table, as my mother was an exceptional cook.

At the end of the harvesting season, my father found alternative work around Mackay.

Going into town to do shopping, my mother would leave me in a child-minding centre at the rear of what is now the old Town Hall in Sydney Street, Mackay, and take my siblings with her.[12]

I must have been a problem child, but it did not seem that way to me!

I was never unduly perturbed, and instead of playing *silly* games with other children, I would explore my surroundings, or sit and ponder what to do once I got out of there.

And that is how it was, during my adolescence, and into early adulthood, enjoying my own company, more than the company of others, including my siblings.

The very beginnings of my life, overall, was full of contentment and adventure, particularly when the family relocated during 1951 from Mackay to Brisbane.

That move was soon after my father joined the Permanent Air Force (PAF) at the Royal Australian Air Force (RAAF) base, Amberley, which is on the outskirts of Ipswich, south-west from Brisbane.[13,14]

Arriving in Brisbane, which was while my father was training and living in barracks at Amberley, along with my mother and four siblings, we lived in a flat overlooking the Pacific Ocean at Margate Beach on the Redcliffe Peninsula.

We had an unobstructed view of the sand dunes on Moreton Island, referred to by us as the *White Cliffs of Dover*, having in mind a song of a similar name sung regularly by Vera Lynn during and after the Second World War.[15,16]

Oh, Vera, how I miss you enchanting voice, heard regularly in those times!

With Vera's songs resonating in our young minds, along with my older brother and sister, it was easy for us to believe that Australia was still at war with Germany and Japan, particularly after a squadron of Lincoln bombers from the RAAF base at Amberley, flew over Moreton Bay.[14,17]

This was around the eighth anniversary of the sinking of the *Centaur* at about 4.00 am on May 14, 1943, east of the Cape Moreton Lighthouse on Moreton Island, and approximately fifty miles east north-east of Brisbane, in which only 64 out of the 332 on board survived the sinking.[18]

Australians were deeply shocked at the loss of the *Centaur*, and Japan sinking an Australian Hospital Ship (AHS) became a symbol of the country's determination to win the war against a callous and brutal enemy.[18]

Those childhood imaginations were less than six years after the Second World War, and during assessment of the air-raid siren on the street at the front of our flat to see if it was still in good working order.[19]

Hearing the siren at dusk for the first time, along with my older brother and sister, we ran inside the flat and asked what was happening.

"It means that the bears are about to come out," our mother replied, "so it is time for children to come inside, otherwise they might be eaten."

We obeyed our mother, until we saw other children not doing the same, quickly realizing that she fooled us into coming inside early.

That humour, combined with her cooking abilities, are the fond memories I have of my mother.

While my older brother and sister continued their schooling at the Humpybong State School, only a short distance from the flat, I attended for two days during the week, quite possibly under a pre-school arrangement?[20,21]

At least, that is what I thought happened, as it might have been the case that I went of my own accord, and the teachers, knowing something about me being *autistic*, allowed me to come and go as I pleased!

Being adventurous, my older brother took the round galvanized bathtub from the flat, down to the shore of the Pacific Ocean, and using a slat from the side of a wooden apple case, he began paddling towards the *White Cliffs of Dover*.

Calling out with my older sister, for him not to leave us, our frantic screams turned to laughter when a wave upturned the tub, washing the would-be mariner back to shore.

When granted leave, my father lived with us in the flat at Margate Beach.

Those were good and happy times, seeing my mother enjoying a glass of lemonade with a splash of beer, called a *Shandy*, and my father in the public lounge of the Belvedere Hotel at Woody Point, singing with others around the piano.[22]

I do not remember my parents arguing then, despite my father drinking too much, and they were happy, even though separated while he was training. And there was a direction in their lives as a permanent posting in the future offered the opportunity of the family being together again.

Going so well, the world of my parents spun out of control when it was decided that my father was *unfit for service due to a disability existing prior to enlistment.*[13]

Five months into his training, my father was disappointed when discharged from the PAF.[13]

Having injured a knee while playing rugby league in his younger days at Mackay, he aggravated the same injury during a game of rugby union for the PAF.

With insufficient money to get us back to Mackay, we moved to Limevale, about two hundred and eighty-six kilometres south-west of Brisbane, where my father worked in a lime mine.[23]

Being six the following year, my schooling began at the Limevale State School.[22]

It was extremely cold at Limevale, and I remember blankets placed on the bed base, and mattress laid over us, kept us warm during winter.

That might seem stupid, but it worked!

With the tap water freezing overnight, it was necessary to leave pots of water on the wood stove, thawed in the morning for a cup of tea and drinking water.

Not catching anything on a line in Oaky Creek, we used galvanised wire netting to drag a waterhole. The size and number caught, surprised everyone, but our satisfaction quickly turned to disappointment when the fish turned out to be *European Carp* with too many fine bones for young children to eat.

Other boys, same age as my older brother, earned pocket money from trapping and skinning rabbits, as well as foxes, if caught in a trap.

Unlike my older brother, who was prone to being nauseous, I learnt how to kill and skin an animal, not something I should have done so young.

Emotion then was not ever-present, but when allowed to have a pet, and they showed affection, things changed for me, and I accepted responsibility for the welfare and wellbeing of others, and not just for myself.

Going to the pictures one night at a theatre in Texas, when an inebriated ringer lost a ten shillings' note from a trousers pocket, I quickly picked it up and ran to my parents, telling them what I had found.

Having seen what happened, my parents told me to give the note back to the man, which I did, reluctantly, and he thanked me for being honest, words that stuck thereafter in my mind, and a lesson well learnt.

Work at the lime mine paid well, and soon my parents had sufficient money to get us back to Mackay, even enough to buy the first vehicle I remember them having.

The vehicle was a second-hand *Whippet* utility that had a canvas canopy over the front compartment, but nothing covering the rear tray.

At the end of this chapter, there is a photograph of a larger utility owned later by the family, which had the same configuration of a canvas canopy over the front compartment and nothing over the rear tray.

Every two years, except for the last born, the family got larger, and a utility is how we got around.

The adults and youngest were in the front compartment, with the older children in the rear tray, until the eldest started moving out on their own, and the size of the family decreased.

Huddling together when it was raining or bitterly cold, just like chickens do in the fowl house, teeth often chattering, the days and nights in the rear tray were miserable, to say the least!

In late 1952, during the school holidays, we left Limevale and returned to Mackay.

Together with my older brother and sister, and the family's possessions, we sat, ate, and slept in the rear tray during the entire journey, while our younger sister and brother were in the front with our parents.

Making our way slowly through Cunninghams Gap on the Great Dividing Range, around one hundred miles from Limevale, the foot brake started failing.

Doubling the clutch to select a lower gear, my father then applied the handbrake, same time with the foot brake, slowing the utility slightly, but not sufficiently enough on the descent down the steep and winding road.

Thrown around like rag dolls in the rear tray, unlike my older siblings, screaming at every jolt, my attention was on my father, admiring his coolness and action taken to see us safely to the bottom of the range.

Not a procrastinator, and always calm and collected, that one instance of how to respond under pressure, made me decide that I would follow my father's example.

Throughout the journey, apart from relieving ourselves, we only stopped at the side of the road for my father to have a rest, and when refreshed, we continued onwards to Mackay.

Arriving at Carmila, rain by that time going from showers to torrential downpours, and floodwater flowing over the causeway of a creek, brought us to a stop.

There was a way to the other side, but we did not have enough money to pay an enterprising farmer to tow the utility across the causeway.

Assessing the depth of the water and being satisfied that the utility would stay upright in the current, my father began driving to the other side.

About halfway across, however, the driver's side front wheel went over the edge of the causeway, and under the water, and at the same time the passenger's side rear wheel left the causeway, raising that side of the rear tray into the air.

Giving the appearance that the vehicle was about to slide sideways into the depths of the creek, my father yelled out for everyone to remain still.

Opening his door and stepping out, my father disappearance

in the water.

Well, do I remember his hat floating downstream!

It was a profoundly serious situation, but I was more concerned by the progress of the hat, bobbing along in the floodwater, rather than our predicament.

Then, unlike my siblings in the rear tray, who were fretting, even though I could not swim, I knew that I would find a way out of that predicament.

And that is how it was when, as a police officer, I went to a brawl in progress, not fearing anyone or anything, as I was always confident that I would overcome any adversity.

Surfacing, "Don't anyone move," urged my father, obviously realising that our situation was dire, which snapped me back to reality.

Once again, despite his failings, as perceived by me, this was his strongest attribute, being able to assess a situation quickly and take appropriate action to prevent or deal with an accident or disastrous situation.

The horrified farmer, remorseful for not saying anything about how close the edge was to the crossing, after helping my father carry everyone, including my mother, to the bank, towed the utility to the other side.

Surviving two serious incidents, and thankful that we were still alive, we arrived during the afternoon that day on the dairy farm of Pop Bedford at Andergrove.

My grandmother, Alice Rebecca Bedford, formerly Riseham, passed away before anyone in my family was born.

Upon our arrival at Andergrove, my mother's older sister, Iris Neta Annie Bedford, who married William Henry (Bill) Turner, and their six children, were living with Pop.

There was always a spare mattress in the extended family, and it was common in those times to sleep on the floor. That is how it was upon our arrival, and how it remained until Pop, having sold *Eureka*, and Uncle Bill, moved the herd to another dairy on Heaths

Road at Glenella.

The next school I attended was the Andergrove State School, located on the southern side of the road to the former dairy farm of *Eureka*.

Sitting on the timber surround of a sandpit, no intention of getting involved in the *silly* game they played, someone threw sand into the eyes of a girl from my class.

In his office, the Head Teacher accused me of throwing sand in the girl's eyes.

When he told me to bend over for a smack on the backside with a ruler for the transgression, "No," I exclaimed, "you're not going to hit me!"

Sidestepping the *bully* to show later prowess as a rugby league player, I ran quickly to the door, dodging and weaving as I outran him to the gate.

This was the first time that I challenged authority for something that I did not do, and it would not be the last time over more than 70 years of my life.

If I had done the crime, I would gladly pay the penalty, but I did not do the crime!

Moreover, it was from that one incident, that I realised I had the gift of athleticism, not only for running, but also for other sporting activities, which came naturally to me, rather than achieved through training.

Anyhow, arriving home, "Why aren't you at school," my mother asked.

"The teacher wanted to smack me on the bum for something I didn't do," I replied, proudly adding, "and he couldn't catch me when I ran away."

Years later, my mother told me that she had to write a letter to the Board of Education for my return to school, giving an assurance that I would behave.

Alarm bells rang in the 1970s, but I did not pursue what is now obvious to me, and that is I am *autistic*.

In fact, now that I know who I am, it feels as if I have led a double life!

It is possible that I had disruptive behaviour in early years, but by the time of the incident with the Head Teacher at Andergrove, I had an inferiority complex, and I began challenging others, when wrongly accused.

There was never any intention to be disruptive, but sometimes the smell of liquid, like phenol, used for cleaning the timber floors at the schools, made me nauseous, sometimes causing me to become disorientated.[24]

Nowadays, if a scent or perfume does not pass my smell test, it stays on the shelf!

And pain is something that I did not endure well in my younger days, which was the compelling reason I would not let the Head Teacher smack me.

While driving the old utility at night across the Forgan Bridge over the Pioneer River at Mackay, near the Cremorne Hotel, my father ran over and killed an intoxicated man asleep in a hollow on the Barnes Creek Road.

Bystanders did their best, but they failed to hold me back, as I was then capable of mustering extraordinary strength, in certain situations.

Squirming to the front, it was the first dead body I would see in my lifetime, as a police officer at the scenes of accidents, suicides, and murders.

Having *eidetic memory* capability, a *mental image snapshot* takes me back to that night.[25]

Unfortunately, the street lighting at the scene of the accident was poor, and the headlights of the old utility were about the same, resulting in the deceased not being clearly visible in the hollow of the road.

The finding of death was a *consequence of misadventure*, was of no comfort to my father, as he often suffered flashbacks, mainly when intoxicated.

I do not suffer flashbacks, but I can recall *mental image snapshots* without suffering mentally.

For instance, a detective approached me during the 2010s to give evidence in a trial, about a stepfather in the 1970s sexually interfering with his young stepdaughter at Gordonvale.

When the stepfather arrived home from work in Western Australia, the mother withdrew her statement, and without any other witness or medical evidence to support the evidence of the young girl, the CIB decided not to prosecute.

I recalled a vivid image of the young female, particularly the expression on her face, that *no one believed her*, and supplied an exact description of the four-leg bathtub in which the sexual interference took place.

Unfortunately, my evidence arrived too late, and after requesting the prosecutor to thank me, the judge told the court that if the evidence had been prompt, the trial would have continued, instead of her dismissing the charge.

After the fatal accident, I became aware of arguments between my parents, particularly when my father arrived home drunk, mostly at night, and failing to give a satisfactory account of where he had been, and what he had done.

Although heated at times, under no circumstance did my father every hit my mother, even when my mother hit him!

Upon returning from Limevale to Mackay, I saw a change in my mother's demeanour, like postnatal depression, after the birth of the other siblings.

Wrapping the pillow around my ears at night during those arguments, I drowned out the *sound* sensitivity suffered on those occasions.

This is when I began drifting away from my parents!

At seven years of age, soon after getting into a rowboat at Alligator Creek, south from Mackay, without any warning, as to what he was about to do, my father threw me into the crocodile and shark infested saltwater.

Reflecting on what happened then, and later, it might have been the case that my father tried to do me a favour and decided to end my life early.

That is how it appeared to me when I was young, as sometimes what he did, could have resulted in death, but I always escaped with only bruises and scratches.

For instance, he got me to lay on top of sticks of sugarcane loaded into the rear tray of a utility, holding the sticks together with my outstretched arms, as he drove from one paddock to another.

I protested, but my father told me to do as asked, and instead of driving slowly to the other paddock, he drove quickly over bumps and through dips in the road, spilling the sugarcane out of the back of the utility.

Having natural ability, I kept rolling when I hit the ground, sufficiently away from where the sugarcane landed, and I avoided death or severe injury.

It was all right for my older brother to go fishing with him in Alligator Creek and believing that I also should go on those trips, I pestered until my father capitulated.

Sinking quickly to the bottom, water beginning to fill my lungs, I managed to kick myself off the muddy creek-bed and instinctively learnt how to dog-paddle, making it to the surface, and then safely back to the boat.

Clinging to the side of the boat, coughing and spluttering, "If you want to come fishing with me," said my father, "you had to learn how to swim!"

I did not look into my father's eyes, avoiding eye contact with others, even today, so whether he was angry or not, is unclear. What he did, however, was intentional, and it made me wary of him from thereon.

Establishing that I could swim, whereafter I became very proficient in freestyle, backstroke, breaststroke, and butterfly, without any tuition, my father allowed me to go fishing in the boat.

While they talked freely with each other, my father and brother never included me in their conversations then, or later, and I was handed an old cord line on that first fishing trip and made to fish near the bank.

Catching a large cod, followed by another, my father turned the boat around, making me fish in the middle of the creek, while my father and older brother fished against the bank.

Suddenly, I was pulling in bream after bream, while they did not even get a bite, earning me the nickname of *Arsey Joe*, which was shortened to *Joe*, and the name by which I became known in the family.[26]

Thereafter, during school sports at the Alligator Creek State School, despite winning a footrace over fifty yards, I was disqualified for not breaking the finishing tape.

Being concerned that no one was with me, when I glanced around to see where they were, I tripped over and slid along the grass under the tape and was disqualified.

Try explaining that decision to a child not then seven years of age, who is *autistic*!

At the end of this chapter, there is a photograph of me attending the school sports.

Three years later, while walking barefooted to school, which was the complete opposite to how I was dressed when younger, I kicked a stone and suffered a blood blister to the ball of my right foot.

Instead of seeing a doctor when a lump developed in my groin, I was taken during the evening of that day to the ambulance centre in Mackay where a bearer lanced the blister, then bathed and bandaged my foot.

This was at the time when my older brother had gone to work for a farming family at West Plane Creek, near Sarina, returning home, now and again, on a weekend.

Unlike my older brother and sister, who continually ran to our mother and told her what our father had done, I did not believe in doing anything of the kind, saying nothing, when interrogated by my mother.

After treatment at the ambulance centre, we should have gone home. That did not happen, and my father went to a nearby hotel and borrowed money from the publican, buying rounds, not only for himself, but also for a group that included females drinking in the public lounge.

Going inside the hotel for the umpteenth time to ask if we could go home, the publican directed me to the courtyard at the back of the hotel where I came across my father having intercourse with one of the females.

He saw me there, but we never spoke about that incident, either then or later in life.

Something that I would investigate later as a police officer, this was my first exposure to prostitution, which disgusted me, as it involved my father.

After the 10 pm closing time, arriving home on the outskirts of Mackay at Paget, I went to bed, and there was the usual argument between my parents.

In the morning, I did not say anything when interrogated by my mother, even after a flogging with a cut-down broom handle, which was excruciatingly painful, and made me cry.

I have no doubt in my mind that my mother used *pain* sensitivity to have me submit to her rule, but instead, it made me more strong-willed.

In retrospect, there is no doubt in my mind that my parents were not capable of looking after an *autistic* child, and, obviously, I was to them a burden on the family!

Around the time of the blood blister, I suffered frequent bouts of feeling unwell and tiredness, others often inferring that I could sleep on a barbed-wire fence.

Other symptoms included excruciating headaches, and difficulty establishing long-term relationships with others, including my siblings.

I had difficulty with small talk, and what interested me, was the complete opposite to what others wanted to discuss, and I became alienated and excluded, and that is how it is, even today.

Moreover, I lived then in a world of my own, not allowing anyone through the front door, including my siblings, because others were in the habit of being friendly one moment and unfriendly the next, quickly turning on me.

So, I would go missing on a bicycle, exploring the countryside, including walking in the mangroves of saltwater creeks, infested with crocodiles, until I had enough of that activity.

Arriving home, when questioned where I had been, I would simply turn around and walk away without answering, no doubt frustrating my parents, who gave up on me, resulting in me going and coming when I pleased to do so.

Occasionally, when I did play with others, and something went wrong, they would blame me, like what happened at Andergrove, even when it was not entirely my fault.

Playing a game of rounders with my older sister and children from the neighbourhood, I swung the stick used as the bat in a game of rounders to hit the tennis ball, and during the backswing, I almost knocked out the eye of a younger brother.

This was after told to come inside, and unbeknown to me, and without any warning from my sister, who threw the ball, or any of the fielders, my younger brother had wandered away from a younger sister, looking after him, and was standing behind me.

Even today, I am remorseful and can feel the pain suffered by a sibling at my own hands, but I still do not feel entirely guilty for what happened, as the others urged me to continue playing, and I did so when my sister threw the ball.

And neither did I have eyes in the back of my head to see my brother standing there!

Nevertheless, snatching the stick from my hands, my mother mercilessly bashed me to the ground, even hit me around the head, and kicked me in the stomach and kidneys, until she was satisfied that I had suffered an injury, same as my sibling.

Even though my older sister threw the ball, my mother deemed that I was solely responsible for the terrible injury suffered by a sibling.

That night, I went to bed, same as before and thereafter, without supper.

Others, particularly relatives, saw those merciless floggings, and two female cousins, in later life, told me that what they witnessed was horrifying to them.

Despite having a low threshold, the more pain inflicted, the more determined I became that I would never divulge anything, such as the wayward behaviour of my father, which appalled and disgusted me, as I was not and would never be a *dobber*; a person who informs on someone.[27]

In time, however, after I joined the police force, others accused me of doing exactly that, which was the complete opposite to my personality profile.

On Friday of the week that I hit my brother with the bat and injured his eye, my parents went shopping for groceries with the other siblings, leaving me with my older brother, who was home for the weekend.

Suffering a bout of tiredness, I went to sleep and woke to the sound of a loud explosion!

Before then, I went with my older brother to the Princess Theatre in Mackay to see a particular movie, while our parents and the rest of the family saw another at the Civic Theatre.

Leaving me alone outside the toilets, my older brother thought I was awake, but he should have known better, as I walked and talked in my sleep.

Soon after, I wandered away from the toilets and woke as I was about to board a bus, running thereafter up and down the streets, sobbing uncontrollably, until some kind taxi drivers stopped and comforted me.

It so happened that my parents and other siblings walked past around that time, and after thanking the taxi drivers, the family came across my older brother, running up and down the streets, calling out to me.

For years, because I am *different*, it seemed to me that the wrong family took me home, but DNA dispelled those doubts.

While I walked and talked in my sleep, I did not sleep with my eyes open, same as my father, but others do, such as a son, and at least a granddaughter.

Soon after arriving home from the hospital, my wife, Patricia, came to me crying, which made me ask, "Why are you crying?"

"He's dead – his eyes are wide open," said Patricia.

Finding our son asleep on his back in the cot, eyes widely opened, "Sorry," I apologised, "I forgot to tell you that my father often slept with his eyes open."

And, yes, he was asleep, and it was not the last time that he would give his mother a fright, until it became common for her to see him that way.

Woken by the loud explosion, I asked my older brother, "What happened?"

Holding a beer bottle, "You told me the kerosene was in this bottle," my brother declared.

Checking the overhead cupboard, "No, not that one, that is the Metho bottle," I responded. "The kerosene is in the other bottle here in the cupboard!"

Stuttering, as he did when excited, "But you told me it was in this bottle," said my brother.

Sure, I have no doubt that while asleep I did say where to find the kerosene in the same size and type of bottle kept in the cupboard beside the methylated spirits.

Always professing that he was brighter and smarter than me, I would have expected him to smell the contents, but he did not do that, and he poured the methylated spirits over and then lit the kindling in the wood stove, resulting in the explosion!

Soot all over the kitchen floor, and the chimney and top of the stove blown off, horrifyingly greeted my parents and other siblings when they arrived home.

Rather than admit that it was his fault for not smelling the contents of the bottle, my brother laid the blame on me for telling him, while I was asleep, that it was kerosene in the bottle, readily accepted by my mother.

When my mother urged that he should do something about my destructive behaviour, after seizing me by the throat, my father, drunk as usual, lifted me and pinned me against the kitchen door, legs off the floor and dangling.

Then, with a fist cocked in front of my face, "If you want me to do it," said my father, angrily, "I will smash his head in now?"

Once again, it was obvious to me then, and more so now, that my parents believed, because of my *autism*, that I was a burden on the family.

And it is also obvious to me now that they had discussions about what to do with me.

The murderous action of my father, brought on hysterical screaming and crying from my siblings, particularly the younger ones, and my mother shrieked at my father to stop what he was doing, and, fortunately for me, he did.

After my father released his grip, I fell in a heap on the floor, gasping for air, and I was sent straight to bed, still crying from the experience, and without any supper.

Not once did my older brother accept any blame for what he did to the stove; it was all my fault!

At the end of this chapter, there is a photograph of me sitting of the sidestep of a utility with three siblings, taken just before that incident.

Having gone previously with my mother to pick him up from the watchhouse, I thought that my father was incarcerated overnight for *drunkenness*, only to discover after I made application to join the police force, that he was arrested and charged with *going armed so as to cause fear*.[28]

Failing to disclose in the application that my father had a criminal conviction, the processing officer considered that I had been untruthful, but two later colleagues, then serving in the police force, came forward and vouched for my honesty.

Moving to Glenella, on the outskirts of Mackay, which was after that criminal conviction, the family occupied another rundown house, infested with snakes and rats.

Not only was the yard overgrown, but also creeping vines were all over the roof that leaked when it rained.

When it came to getting rid of the snakes, our saviour was a Great Dane-Kangaroo crossbred dog named *Pluto*, ridden like a horse by a younger brother.

Coming home drunk again, late at night, after an argument with my mother in their bedroom, my father threw his pay packet out through the window. Quietly going out into the yard, I recovered the pay packet, notes, and coins therein, which was handed to my mother the next morning.

On my father's death bed in 1998 at Mackay, gathered around him with all siblings, "Now that we are all here," announced our mother, "there is something that you all need to know."

While we waited anxiously, after her eyes met with either our father or eldest brother, my mother told the story about *Pluto* not eating the pay packet and money.

Over a beer later with a younger brother at the Shamrock Hotel, we agreed, before pausing, that our mother was going to announce that one of us was not our father's son, as had been rumoured for years, but instead, she told the alternative story about the pay packet.

Because I was at the centre of what my mother told others, there is now no doubt in my mind that my mother was about to tell my siblings, that I was diagnosed and suffered from *autism*, when another stopped her from doing so.

After spending years of my adult life away from Mackay, and with the family together, my mother obviously thought that it was a suitable time to let everyone know.

Once again, why my parents, instead of subjecting me to child abuse, never sat down and explained the medical condition to me, beggars' belief!

**Author in the arms of his mother and
siblings at Mackay in 1947**
(Private Source)

**Author (left) and siblings at Limevale
in 1951**
(Private Source)

Permanent Air Force (PAF) at Amberley in 1951
Arnold Bradford, third from the left, front row
(Private Source)

Lincoln bombers at Amberley RAAF Base in 1951
(Courtesy of National Library of Australia, ID 6846251)

**Author (left) and siblings at Alligator
Creek School in 1952**
(Private Source)

**Author (third from left) and siblings at
Paget in 1956**
(Private Source)

2

TOUGH TIMES

In 1957, my parents admitted that they were unable to provide for their ever-increasing family, then numbering seven children still living at home, with the eldest working elsewhere. Fortunately, older brothers of my father, then established sugarcane farmers in the Mackay district, came to their assistance and went guarantors for them to buy a rundown sugarcane farm at Karremal Siding, near Koumala.

This was the chance for which my parents yearned, and even though only 12 years of age, I vowed to do whatever I could to make this happen, providing a better life in the process for my younger siblings.

By this time, my older brother had moved from West Plane Creek, where he had been employed, and was working and living on the sugarcane farm of my father's brother, James (Slim) Bradford, at Shinfield, near Sarina.

With a booming voice heard throughout whenever he jovially walked into a hotel, Uncle Slim passed away at 54 years from bowl cancer.

Not long before he passed away, I saw him in hospital.

While the nurse believed he had swallowed the tablet, Uncle Slim, after she left, took the tablet out from under his tongue and put it with others in a drawer.

"I'm not going to be a *junky* when I get out of here," explained Uncle Slim.

A kind and gentle person, Uncle Slim showed more interest in me than my siblings, causing me to believe that I had done something wrong, rather than the interest being associated with my medical condition.

That interest from relatives and family friends, did intrigue me, and now that I know more, they expected, more than likely, an adverse reaction from me to something, but mostly I sat in deep tho-ught, often referred to as the *quiet one*.

I did have difficulty then, and still do, joining a discussion with others, as mostly anything that I say, is usually incorrect, untruthful, or not what others want to hear, which, invariably, shuts me down in a conversation.

It is like being an alien from another planet, trying to mix in with the locals on earth!

While my older sister, then 13 years, stayed at home to help my mother, never going to school again, I was responsible at first for the safety of the school-age siblings travelling by railmotor to school in Koumala.

Not only did my older sister and I have that responsibility thrust upon us at an early age, but our father had us help him with the farm work.

Our older brother, who continued working for Uncle Slim, only came home for short periods, and when he did come home, he hardly did anything, as he had to rest up, according to our mother, before going back to work.

Robbed of our youth, the three of us matured too soon, rather than having the opportunity to enjoy our teenage years with others of the same age.

Life on the farm, however, was better than moving constantly from one place to another, and the advantages began to outweigh the disadvantages.

It soon became obvious that the Head Teacher at the Koumala State School did not like me.

Scolding me for not looking directly at him while he was talk-ing to me, doing so, he then gave me *six-of-the-best* for the way I look-ed at him.

Years later at Brisbane, when a police colleague asked if I was listening to him, when I looked in his direction, "Don't look at me that way," he responded.

And a female colleague in security at the Brisbane Airport

screamed, "He's looking at me with that *death stare*!"

Try though I may, I have not mastered how I should look at others, as it is a matter of perception on the part of others that I am doing something to annoy them, showing how ignorant others can be towards another.

When the younger siblings were confident of travelling to and from school without me, my father kept me home for up to three days during a school week to work on the farm.

After walking on the wall near Beijing in 2000, I can say that there is a much smaller version along the foothills at the back of the farm, referred to as our *Great Wall of China*, constructed from the rocks removed from the paddocks.[1]

With a trailer behind the tractor, we would load the rocks from the paddocks and tow the trailer to unused land along the foothills where the unloaded rocks became our wall.

It was extremely demanding work for a 12-year-old, but I did what I was asked, as being the eldest son at home, I thought that it was my duty to do so.

A small crop of sugarcane was available for harvesting, and before planting for the next season, my father also decided to remove the dead trees from the paddocks, as well as ringbark all trees on the fringe of paddocks.

I had seen my father do this when we lived on Pop's old dairy farm at Andergrove. So, I knew what I had to do, as well as I came from an extensive line of woodcutters in England and Australia, and what I did, came naturally to me.

It was demanding work ringbarking the trees, same as what we did with the rocks, but we killed off the roots encroaching on the paddocks to increase the yield of next-year's crop.

We then used a crosscut saw on the smaller dead trees, cut them into blocks of wood for the stove, and burnt down the larger trees, as well as the root systems, turning the harrows upside-down to spread the ash all over the paddocks.

While we removed all rocks aboveground, those underground

remained until they came to the surface.

After several disagreements of what to do, upon the planter's progress being halted by a large underground rock, once too often, causing the front of the tractor towing the planter to rise from the ground, "You can do it yourself," said my mother, as she stormed off out of the paddock and back to the house.

Without any tuition, after hearing their discussions and seeing what my mother did, I got on and drove the tractor for the planting that year, as well as for other work on the farm.

Providing additional income during the first year, my father was the liftman at Karremal Siding to unload cut sugarcane of all farmers from their trucks and tractor-drawn trailers into railway wagons, delivered thereafter for crushing at the Plane Creek Sugar Mill in Sarina.

We only had a small crop of sugarcane to harvest, and as it was unlawful to cut on weekends, my father kept me home during the school week to do what he could not do.

So, without any tuition, I loaded the cut sugarcane, once a day, two to three times a week, onto the truck and left it near the farm-house for my father to collect and take to the Karremal Siding during his lunch break.

Although I only attended two or three days during the school week, I always caught up quickly and was placed, by this time of my schooling, from first to third in the class, sitting between Patty Hill and Mary Ahern to stop them from talking.

I had other daily chores to do, one being to fetch the five dairy cows in the afternoon, let out into the *long paddock* after milking in the morning.[2] If I did not see them on the way home by railmotor, the search would commence from Karremal Siding, south to Mount Christian, and sometimes around the back of the hills on the farm to Turnors Paddock.

The cows knew when it was time to come home, but something waylaid them at times.

Giving up after several hours of searching, I arrived home one day after sundown without the cows to find all the family, sitting around the table having the evening meal.

When told I came home without the cows, after kicking me in the backside for back-chatting, about also being hungry, my father sent me to look again, even if it took me the rest of the night.

Around 8.30 pm, I found the cows, one with a calf, stalked by a pack of dingoes.

So, with the calf in the midst, I kept the small herd together and made it safely back home.

The dingoes were not the only danger, as I walked through the tall *Guinea* grass, mostly above my head, without any protective clothing, such as shoes.[3]

Seen often lurking in the grass, and almost bitten previously by one, was the *Coastal Taipan*, the third-most venomous land snake throughout the world.[4]

Having heightened senses from *autism*, the hair stands up on the back of my neck, providing me with an early warning that danger is near.

From an early age, often scoffed at by others, who do not have that ability, the warning sign has saved me from impending death or injury.

"I saw you first," is what I would say to the *Taipan*, arched and ready to strike!

If bitten, my chances of survival would have been very slim, and no doubt others would not have found my body until daylight of the next day.

After securing the cows in the milking pen, the others had already retired, my meal being cold and left on the table. The bath water also was cold, and after a quick wash, it was about 9.30 pm when I got into my bed.

If going to school the following day, the homework not done the night before, I would finish in the morning while waiting for the railmotor at Karremal Siding.

Starting out as an introvert, I progress quickly to extroversion, as soon as surroundings become clear, and I was looking forward to giving a presentation for the first time to the class.

Walking confidently to the front of the class, upon turning towards fellow students, I froze when our eyes met, forcing me to look away quickly.

"What's the matter with me," I thought, and then my neck became ridged as a rock, vision became blurred, perspiration flowed freely, had difficulty breathing, became light-headed, and was unable to utter a word.

Abruptly, I went back to my seat, which shocked and surprised the teacher, and fellow students, never to give that presentation, or any thereafter while at school.

Even today, the only way I can talk in front of others, is not to look at them, sometimes perceived by others as being offensive or disrespectful.

However, when the situation and surroundings were clear, I never had any difficulty taking command and control of an incident as a police officer, giving concise orders or instructions to others present.

In fact, it was common for others in charge of those situations to seek clarification from me as to what to do next, particularly when it came to complex situations.

Riding a horse up into the hills at the back of the farm, after a severe flogging, I often contemplated hanging myself, using the reigns of the bridle as a rope.

At the end of this chapter, there is a photograph of the horse and how I rode into the hills behind the farm, as well as another of me about to go mustering.

I had stopped crying by this time, but I was visibly shaken and upset by the way my younger siblings, encouraged by our mother, would follow me, mimicking every word I uttered, or move I made, so much so that I had to escape out of a concern that I might hurt a sibling.

Instead of exploding, as I did earlier in my life, and without any treatment or encouragement from others of how to control my outbursts and sometimes destructive behaviour, I learnt to walk away.

It was on the first occasion of riding into the hills that I heard Aboriginal people, existing only in my mind, talking to each other as they hunted kangaroos in the countryside below, as outlined in *Voices from The Past: Law Enforcement on The Central Highlands*, stopping me from ending my life.[5]

After fastening the bridle to an overhanging branch, making a noose with a reign, upon being calmed by the Indigenous people, I would take the bridle down, and then head home on the horse, never to be asked by my parents as to where I had been, or what I had been doing.

One moonless night, around this time, after narrowly avoiding a crocodile on a previous occasion, as it slid down the muddy bank into the water, I swam over another in the side-creek known as *Tedlands* in Rocky Dam Creek, near Koumala.

Why did the crocodile not take me is a mystery?

"Well," may you ask, "why were you swimming across the creek infested with crocodiles on a moonless night?"

My father told me to do so, and up to that point in my life, I had not stood up to him. However, a recent growth spurt made me taller than him, and when pushed once too often, I did stand up to him that night.

Without a boat, I swam across *Tedlands* at high tide with a rope and pulled across a fishing net. Securing the net to a mangrove tree, I then swam back to where my father was on the other bank, drinking from a large bottle of beer.

In addition to providing a starving family with food, my father sold part of the catch to the publican to settle outstanding debts that he owed.

Years before my time, Mary Tuckett, ten years, and her younger sister, Thelma, six years, went missing in 1933 while riding double-banked on a horse across Alligator Creek at Pindi Pindi, north from Mackay.

Thelma died from drowning in the murky stream.

When the initial search failed to locate Mary's body, it became evident that something more than accidental drowning caused Thelma's death.

Based on that suspicion, Constable Jack Gallagher of Koligo, used poison baits to kill a crocodile in Alligator Creek, and he found Mary's decomposing body in its stomach.[6]

At the end of this chapter, there is a photograph of the crocodile that killed Mary and Thelma Tuckett.

Eighteen years after that tragedy, employees from the Tedlands' cattle property destroyed a nest of seventy crocodile eggs in Rocky Dam Creek, and residents of nearby Mount Christian heard the roaring at night of a monster crocodile.[7]

In the same locality, also at night, I saw bull crocodiles fighting over a female, roaring one moment like a bull, and yipping the next like a dingo, as branches of saplings broke off, or the saplings were knocked over.

Furthermore, the shooting of a monster crocodile measuring thirty-two feet and nine inches in length at Mackay *was substantiated by the Australian Encyclopedia in which J. D. Ogilvy, then curator of the Brisbane Museum, [was] given as the authority for stating the reptile was shot and killed in the Pioneer River.*[7,8]

In fact, during the 1970s, when I was a police officer at Mackay, I saw a photograph on a wall of the Leichhardt Hotel, of the shooter and rifle in his hands, with the crocodile, and others standing around or on top of the dead reptile.[9]

Crossing back over to where my father was sitting on the opposite bank, "Joe," he said, "if you had been in the Olympics, no one would have caught you!"

Swimming over the crocodile, it simply *popped* under the water as if it also got a huge fright, prompting me to take off and swim as fast as I could, my frantic strokes clawing through the mud as I made my way to safety of high ground on the bank.

Possessing an *eidetic memory* allows me to recall vividly what happen, even feel the bumps on the back of the crocodile as I swam over it.

If the crocodile had come after me, the next move would have been for me to climb a tree, but it did not, leaving me alone on the bank, terrified and shaken, jumping at each splash made near me by fish and prawns.

My father told others that it was not a crocodile, but a log that I swam over!

At low tide, it was time for me to swim back across the creek to untie the nets.

I did that for the net across where I swam over the crocodile, but suffering from a loss of nerve, and concerned that my time might be up, I refused to do the same for the net at the mouth of the side-creek known as *Tedlands*.

At the end of this chapter, there are overhead images of where we put the nets across the creek.

"I will throw you into the water," said my father, unsteady from the beer that he had consumed.

The threat, however, did not budge me, and when he stepped towards me, I adopted a southpaw boxer's stance and defiantly said, "You can do it yourself!"

After cursing me, my father swam across the creek and untied the net, almost drowning in the process when a button on his shirt became entangled.

Experiencing that growth spurt, which was around 13 years, I was five feet and six inches tall (168 cm) and weighed nine stone and six pounds (60 kg), and suffered increased bouts of feeling unwell, tiredness, legs swelling to twice their normal size, face became puffy, and eyelids almost closed.

Soon after the incident with the crocodile, when I said that I was sick and could not do any chores, my mother brutally bashed me to the ground with a stick used for stirring the clothes in the copper, and while on the ground, she kicked me in the head, kidneys, and stomach.

Try though she may, infuriated that she could no longer make me cry, she would hit harder and more often than previously, but I still did not cry.

There comes a time in one's life, when enough is enough, forcing one to make a stand!

I am not proud of what I did, but standing up quickly, I snatched the stick from my mother's hand, raised it above her head and said, "If you hit me again, I will kill you!"

It is only in later years that the tears have flowed, particularly after the death of my eldest son.

If my mother had tried that day to assert her authority over me, there is no doubt in my mind that I would have gone through with the threat, resulting in the demise of my mother, and me charged with murder.

What I did that day, however, had the desired effect, leaving my mother pale and shaken, never for her to hit me again, or my father, for that matter.

Instead of physical abuse, both resorted to verbal abuse from thereon, such as my father telling others that bruises on his wrists were from handcuffs that I put on him.

Having had too much to drink, and taking him home while I was off duty, he started bashing into a younger brother, driving at the time, so I took hold of the left wrist, and the brother seized the other with his left hand, resulting in the bruises.

That, however, did not stop the family from believing my father, resulting in my older brother saying, "Don't every put handcuffs on our father again!"

He wanted to fight, but when I stepped towards him and said, "Bugger off," he quickly retreated.

Suffice to say that after standing up to my mother, it was then that I began to take control of my life, but not until I overcame a serious health scare.

After composing herself, following the threat that I made, and obviously feeling remorseful, "Neil," exclaimed my mother, "your legs are swollen!"

"So is my face puffy, and eyes almost closed," I responded, adding, "I have been telling you that I am unwell, but you haven't listened to me!"

Left with welts on the lower legs, and despite the pleadings of my older sister to do something immediately, my parents decided instead that they would wait until the marks were no longer visible, and then they would take me to a doctor.

When the welts were no longer visible, a doctor at Sarina, after examining me, and evaluating my urine, arranged for my immediate admission to the Mackay Base Hospital.

It is possible I tested positive for the first time with Porphyria Cutanea Tarda (PCT), which is an acute form, but the records of the doctor and hospital are no longer available, so I do not know if that was the case.[10]

A niece suffers from *Asperger's syndrome* and a grandchild has *autism*, both of whom experience *difficulties in social situations* with others.[11]

Not having sufficient for petrol to get me to Mackay, and him back to the farm, my father went to a nearby hotel and borrowed money from the publican.

Only one glass is all that it took, and instead of filling the car with petrol and take me to the hospital, my father soon forgot about my predicament.

Fortunately for me, another of my father's brothers, Albert Edward (Ned) Bradford, walked into the hotel.

When told about my health concern, Uncle Ned drove me into Mackay and provided the details for my admission, which, because of my size then, was in the Men's Ward at the hospital.

My father never looked after me, but there were paternal uncles, who continually watched over me, particularly while riding in rodeos and playing rugby league.

I was curious then by their attention, appreciated immensely by me, and now it is obvious to me that they knew of the diagnosis in the Lister Private Hospital.

Another of my father's brothers, Stanley Septimus (Stan) Bradford, along with Uncle Ned, were the only visitors I had in the Mackay Base Hospital.

Recovering from the illness in six weeks, John Lenning, son of a neighbouring farmer, booked me out of hospital and took me home to Karremal Siding.

Arriving home, I learnt that my older sister was, in fact, bitten by a snake while fetching the milking cows from where they were feeding in tall *Guinea* grass.

Fortunately, it was non-venomous, more likely a yellow-bellied black tree snake, otherwise she might not have survived the bite, if it had been the dreaded *Coastal Taipan*.[4,12]

While my mother was in the Mackay Base Hospital, having another sibling, my father arrived home late at night, extremely intoxicated, so much so that I heard him heaving up through the bedroom window.

Afterwards, in the early hours of the morning, I woke to my older sister screaming, "Get off me!"

Rushing into the bedroom, when I found him on top of my older sister, our younger sister lying mortified beside her, I yelled out to my father, "What is going on?"

When our eyes met, and no doubt seeing me with an aggressive stance, my father went back to his bed.

Later that day, when asked what happened, I treated my father with contempt, and did not say anything, which is the way I usually react to confrontations.

If I do say something, others usually turn things around and say that I am lying or being argumentative.

I, however, gave my father the benefit of the doubt, as his scruples known to me then, despite him having extramarital affairs, did not include incest.

Being who I am, personality wise, I never forgave my father for what he almost did that night.

When the time was right, my older sister and I told our mother what happened, and she accused us of being untruthful, with our younger sister agreeing that nothing happened.

From thereon, my older sister and I became lepers through the family treating us as being untruthful and not to be trusted under any circumstance.

Over time, however, the younger siblings have departed from those ways.

In 1958, I came second in a footrace over seventy-five yards and then first for one hundred yards in a time of 12.8 seconds at the Sarina and District All School Sports.[13,14]

Winning my first trophy, which was the coveted C. A. Cumming's Cup, I ran into the hotel to show my father, only for him to tell those drinking with him, that his eldest son was a much better athlete.

And that is where he had been all day, and at other sporting events, unlike his older brothers, Uncles Ned, and Stan, who were officials, not only at the school sports, but also at the rodeos in which I competed.

In fact, none of my siblings had the same athletic abilities that came to me naturally, and I played sports with cousins, rather than a sibling.

The following year, soon after my release from the hospital, the placings achieved at the same sports were, as follows:

- **Second** (one hundred yards' footrace).
- **First** (senior high jump).
- **First** (senior broad jump).
- **First** (one hundred yards' open hurdle).
- **Captain** (one hundred yards' winning relay team).[15,16,17,18]

At the end of this chapter, copies of those certificates will be found.

During my time playing rugby league, rather than my parents being at the games, there was another of my father's brothers, George Edward (Bunny) Bradford, who, together with Uncles Ned and Stan, watched over me.

In fact, while playing in an Under-19 team, Uncle Ned appeared out of nowhere and assisted when I suffered an injury, above and below an eye, requiring treatment at a doctor's surgery.

Those uncles watched over and protected me, but I never got to thank them properly!

Obviously hearing how I swam the nets across *Tedlands*, apart from John Lenning watching over me to ensure that I did not do anything like that again, two of our farmers, Albert Carr, and Bob Lamb, took an interest in me.

And the reason I did what my father asked me to do, is because I thought my older brother in the past had done something of the like kind, and I thought, being the eldest son at home, that it was my duty to continue the tradition.

In later life, my older brother admitted that our father never asked him to do what he requested of me, and he told me that I was *stupid* for handing over money earned to our parents, as he and my older sister put their money into bank accounts.

I blame this on a lack of communication and socialization during those early years with my older brother and sister, combined with an expectation instilled by my parents that I had to emulate what they did.

I was a *deep thinker*, and when my mother sought clarification for the first time from me, about something that I did, I responded, "I thought ...," and she cut me off with the question, "You know what thought did?"

Naively, "No," I responded.

"He thought, he shit himself!"

That explanation then, and later, made no sense to me, as I did not see myself as a lemming following others in a headlong rush to destruction, such as jumping off a cliff.

I had a mind, and I would use it, despite what my mother said!

Capable of solving problems quickly, I would not do anything willy-nilly, just because someone told me to do so, as I needed to know the outcome before I leapt headlong into something.

That might seem contradictory, since I swam nets across a crocodile-infested creek, and did something that could have ended my life, but I stopped and stood up to my father when I determined it was too dangerous to continue.

Similarly, I submitted to the beatings from my mother, until I was certain in mind and body that I was capable of resisting, and I rebelled.

Moreover, it was a matter of being clear in my mind, about the dangers, and then deciding whether to take the risk, which could result in death or injury, such as later riding of bucking bullocks and horses at rodeos.

When we did get a boat, which was previously a 14-foot bondwood sailboat, I would row against the strong tidal currents in the Mackay area, while my father sat on the rear seat, swigging on a large bottle of beer.

Getting the boat off the truck and launching it in the water during high tide was easy for me and my father. However, removing the boat from the water at low tide, dragging it through mud that came up to the knees, and putting the boat back onto the truck, was extremely difficult.

Nevertheless, I was grateful that I no longer had to swim with crocodiles!

On the bank around a campfire, engulfed in smoke from cattle dung smouldering in the fire, which chased the mosquitoes away, we were protected from being bitten.

In the boat, we did not have the same protection, so we crawled inside a sack bag, while waiting for low tide to retrieve the nets from a creek.

Even doing that, did not stop the constant dive-bombing of the mosquitoes, invading in swarms from the lagoons and swampland nearby, almost carrying us off.

On the upside, rowing the boat was good and developed my shoulders, making me fitter and stronger than all siblings, and mostly everyone at school.

During a holiday he spent on the farm, I went fishing with my older brother in the boat, and we sought warmth around a campfire at night when it got cold.

In our younger days, he took great delight in punching me in the belly to make me cry.

When I woke to find him sitting on my chest, thumping my back into the ground, I was about to swing a left cross, when I realized the coat that I was wearing had caught fire, and that my brother was trying to put it out.

Fortunately, he had learnt that I could be talking in my sleep, which was correct, and he reacted instinctively, otherwise I would have suffered burns to the back.

I was extremely tired and got too close to the campfire, which was not the first incident of this kind, as I had previously put a foot in a fire during another fishing trip with others, suffering burns to the toes when the sock worn caught fire.

Not only can the smell of smoke, particularly cigarette smoke, take my breath away, and make me lightheaded, often causing me to become disorientated, but also it can result in me going into a very deep sleep.

That is obviously what happened on those two occasions, as those around me smoked cigarettes, with my older brother starting at 12 years.

I have not smoked and never will!

Yes, I have tried, but I did not actually inhale, and I did not like the taste of a thousand camels sleeping in my mouth, when I woke in the morning.

After the success achieved at the Sarina and District All School Sports, at which time I was the school captain, my parents removed me from school before I turned 14 years.

This was despite the Head Teacher, Howard Foster, driving out to the farm to convince my parents that I should at least complete the Scholarship Examination for Grade 8.

Any aspiration that I had of becoming a pilot in the RAAF, made known to Howard Foster, went flying out the window on the back of that decision!

The catalyst was a decision made by the Plane Creek Sugar Mill to relocate our sugarcane drop-off from Karremal Siding, close and south-east of the farm, much further in the opposite direction to Turnors Paddock, near Koumala.

Still the liftman at Karremal Siding, making it impossible for my father to cart our sugarcane to Turnors Paddock, instead of asking my old brother to come home, my parents removed me from school, and denied me an education.

So, I became a farm hand before I was 14 years, cutting, loading, and carting the harvested sugarcane to the siding at Turnors Paddock, and, in the process, continuously stopped by Constables John Harris and Pat Bruton from Sarina.

"Neil," they would plead, "after dropping the load off at the siding, go home, and don't come back out again!"

I did as John and Pat instructed, going home after dropping off the load, but I would go back out onto the road again with another load, receiving a similar warning whenever either of them came upon me.

Because of depressed sugar prices, and challenging times on sugarcane farms, other sons of farmers were doing the same, some killing themselves when either the truck or tractor they were driving rolled over.

In fact, I had an accident on our farm the year before, when I doubled the clutch and missed the gear, and instead of turning to the right onto the headland of the paddock, I acted instinctively and drove straight ahead into a creek.

Expecting the worst, I was surprised when my father praised me, saying that if I had done the turn onto the headland, the truck would have rolled over.

Despite being bogged, we towed the truck easily out of the creek, load still intact, which my father delivered that afternoon to the Karremal Siding.

Shortly after the incident, my father went on a *bender* for four days.

While I did all the work on the farm, I could not do any of my father's work as the liftman, and he lost that work at the end of the crushing season.

Not long after the *bender*, and at night when the family was about to go to bed, a fire broke out in a neighbour's paddock, adjoining our farm, which threatened to burn the unharvested sugarcane on both farms.

Going with my father, and with assistance from the neighbour, we extinguished the fire around 10 pm.

Instead of going straight home, we went to the neighbour's house where, after one glass, my father got involved in another of his drinking sessions.

Arriving home around midnight, my older sister, holding a loaded rifle and aimed in our direction, confronted us as we were about to enter at the rear of the house.

While we were away, unidentified persons terrorized the family to the extent that my sister warned them that she would shoot if any of them tried to enter the house.

Fortunately, she did not shoot us!

A mutual acquaintance later told me that it was a payback for what my father got up to while on the *bender*, the family suffering because of what he did.

Once again, although he got me to do things that I should not have done, sober he was a good man. I despised him when he was drunk, however, causing me to form an opinion at an early age that I would be a much better person to my wife and children, if I went down that path.

Without the income earned as the liftman, Bob Lamb agreed with my father, because I was too young, that my father would sign the contract, and I would cut and load Bob's 560 tons of sugarcane the following year.

Earning sometimes £32 after tax a week, which equates to

$949.57 nowadays, the money went to my father in a cheque made out to him.[19]

Not having anything decent to wear, not only around the house, but also for going out, begrudgingly, my mother bought clothing and shoes, and I began to dress again, same as how it was when I was much younger.

Apart from also buying a horse, which is the grey one in the photograph at the end of this chapter, as well as a saddle, no money earned by me, was banked in an account, and only pocket money of ten shillings was provided for me to spend, as the rest of the money went towards support of the family.

Coming home early one day from Bob Lamb's farm, I came upon my mother in the arms of my father's so-called good friend, who had separated from my maternal cousin, and who left the farm, suddenly, the following day.

When quizzed, I told my father nothing, same as I had done for his extramarital affairs.

And try though he may, the so-called friend ignored my father's approaches to meet up again, even in later life when he returned to Mackay.

Bob Lamb and Albert Carr were excellent horse riders!

Gaining my independence, I went with Bob and Albert during mustering on the Tedlands' cattle property and caught my first barramundi in the lagoon near the homestead.[20]

Having recently won the novice bullock riding event at the Flaggy Rock rodeo, under Albert's guidance, the manager of Tedlands, George Bailey, told me to select a steer that I could ride when we got back to the yards.

Somehow, it had grown taller to when I saw it last, and after six jolting bucks across the yard, I rolled off the steer's back, just as it was about to crash headlong over the gate, not seen again until the next muster.

Bending over to collect my hat, spontaneous laughter broke out behind me, followed by George telling me that I had just ridden one of the angriest steers on the property.

That was the first and not the last time they took the *mickey* out of me!

Another instance of socialization included going with Bob, Albert, and other older and experienced stockmen, known as *old-timers*, to round up the Brumbies on the properties around Karremal Siding, Mount Christian, and Turnors Paddock.

Mostly staying silent, except to ask a question to clarify something, I was enthralled by the stories told by the *old-timers* around campfires, some appearing in my first book *Voices from The Past: Law Enforcement on the Central Highlands*.

Being a former Aboriginal stockman, who served during World War One, Albert not only taught me roughriding of horses and bullocks, but he also showed me how to use a rifle and revolver.[21]

In addition to rodeos where I competed, Albert also took me fishing and camping around what is known as the Cape Palmerston National Park.

It was there that he showed me shell middens made by his ancestors, the Guwinmal people, so I believe, and he taught me how to live off the land.[22,23]

"You can eat anything," Albert would say, "that you see a bird eating!"

Then, he made me suck a pebble to produce saliva, moistening the mouth, until water was found.

At the end of 1961, without consulting the bank manager, my parents sold the farm.

Discovering what they had done, the bank manager told my parents, who were concerned that they were going backwards rather than forwards, that he would have approved a loan to buy another farm.

His reasoning was that two sons were already working, and as there were three other sons to help later, the best way forward would have been for my parents to expand and buy another farm, rather than sell.

Neither had any business sense, and what they wanted, slipped out of the hands of my parents.

In fact, Bob Lamb became the new owner of our farm during the early part of 1962, transferring the assignment from our farm to his farm, doubling what he could harvest.

With a profit from the sale, my parents paid cash for a new vehicle and put a substantial deposit on a house in Mackay where the family went to live.

By that time, treated far too long as either *backward* or *stupid*, I did not go with them to Mackay, and I started living away from the family.

Moreover, I had enough of others saying, "Neil did this," and "Neil did that," and with being accused of saying or doing what others said or did.

It surprised me when my parents agreed that I could go out on my own, but now that I know more about myself, doing so removed a burden from the family.

I did not have a place to go, so I moved into Albert's house, without asking him, and while he was away, taking him by surprise when he returned.

It was foolhardy, but it taught me what I needed to do, in life away from the family.

So, I left the family at 15 years and moved in with Albert Carr on his farm at Karremal Siding.

Soon after, during what he described as a minor operation, and after saying that he would not be away for long, Albert died in the hospital at Townsville.

With Albert gone, and despite having a verbal agreement to cut the sugarcane for Bob Lamb, I had nowhere to live, so I moved back into the family, but not for long.

While casting for bait in Baker's Creek, south from Mackay, my older brother became annoyed when each cast did not produce anything.

Blaming me for scaring the bait, once too often, I picked my brother up and threw him in the water, then held his head under the water, until I saw bubbles coming out of his mouth.

It was not my intention to hurt him, only to give my brother a fright, and to convey a message to him and others, that I had had enough.

"We are brothers, and we shouldn't fight," my brother said, gasping for air, prompting me to respond, "Well, you should have thought about that when we were younger, punching me in the guts to make me cry!"

Although four years older than me, I had grown taller and stronger, and not only did my brother get a fright, but also, I was surprised by the strength I mustered.

When my brother told our parents what happened, I moved out of the family again and went to work for another paternal uncle, Douglas (Doug) Bradford, on his sugarcane farm at Yukan, south from Sarina.

During my early days, I was taught to box with gloves by a maternal cousin's husband, Lawrie Taylor, who, allegedly, was a better boxer than his cousins, Ollie, and Wally Taylor, of Empire Games' fame.[24]

Apart from riding in competitions with the pony club at Sarina, and at the various rodeos in the Mackay district, I began playing rugby league at Mackay, as well as I sparred with the amateur boxers at Sarina.

At the end of this chapter, there are photographs of me, one when I went to work and live in 1962 at Yukan, and another of me taking part in competition with the Sarina Pony Club.

Trying to impress a girlfriend, and being in the same weight division, I got into the ring with her brother, just before he was about to compete in the Golden Gloves at Brisbane.

After leading with a right, followed by a left cross, often landing a flurry of punches to the head and body, a frown soon appeared on the face of my opponent, resulting in his trainer stopping the session early.

My girlfriend's brother, who fought with an orthodox stance, had never competed against a southpaw, sending a shiver through the training camp.

He did not, however, face a southpaw and brought home the title for his division of the Golden Gloves.

Suffice to say, if it had been a contest when we sparred that night, I would have easily outpointed my girlfriend's brother to win the fight.

Surprisingly, it turned out that the girlfriend and brother were third cousins, ending that relationship, upon intervention of my mother, before it had time to flourish.

Despite the relationship ending abruptly, it was the beginning of interaction with others, and a life different to what it was like during those adolescent years in the family.

**Author riding on the farm at Karremal
in 1959**
(Private Source)

**Author about to go mustering on Tedlands
in 1961**
(Private Source)

Crocodile that killed Mary and Thelma Tuckett in 1933
(Courtesy of *The Mackay Daily Mercury*, ID 172925885)

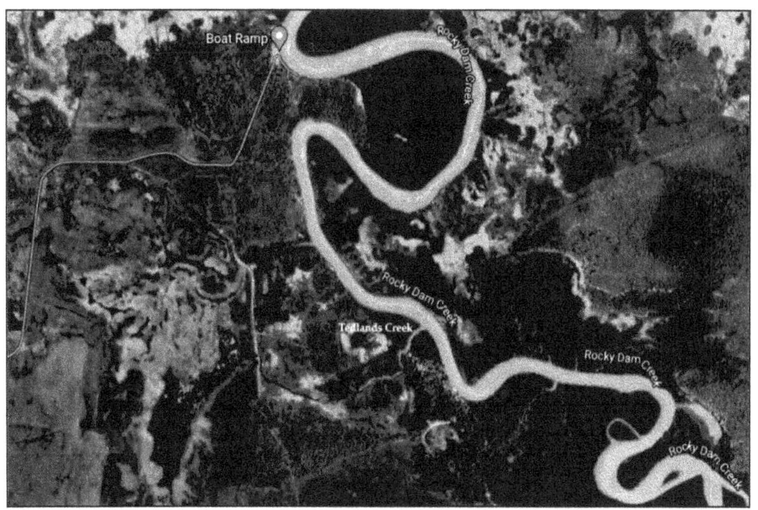

Tributary of Tedlands Creek in Rocky Dam Creek
(Courtesy of © OpenStreetMap contributors)

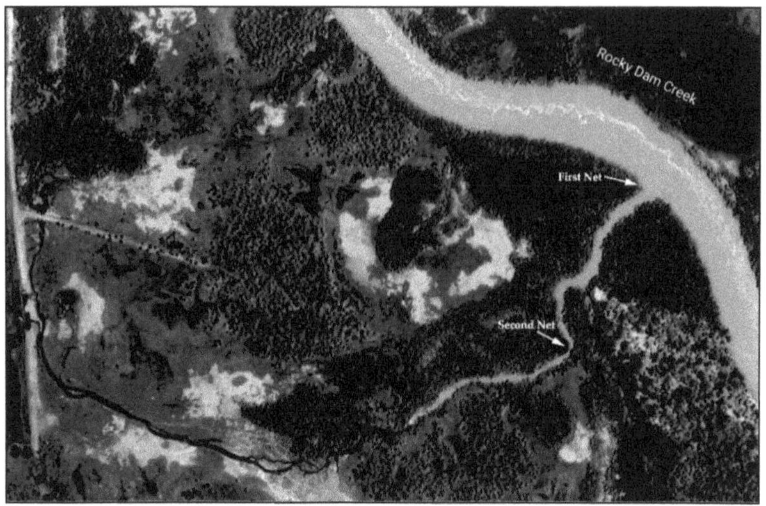

Locations where the author swam fishing nets across Tedlands Creek
(Courtesy of © OpenStreetMap contributors)

Author's certificate for the 100 yards in 1959
(Courtesy of Sarina and District All School Sports Association)

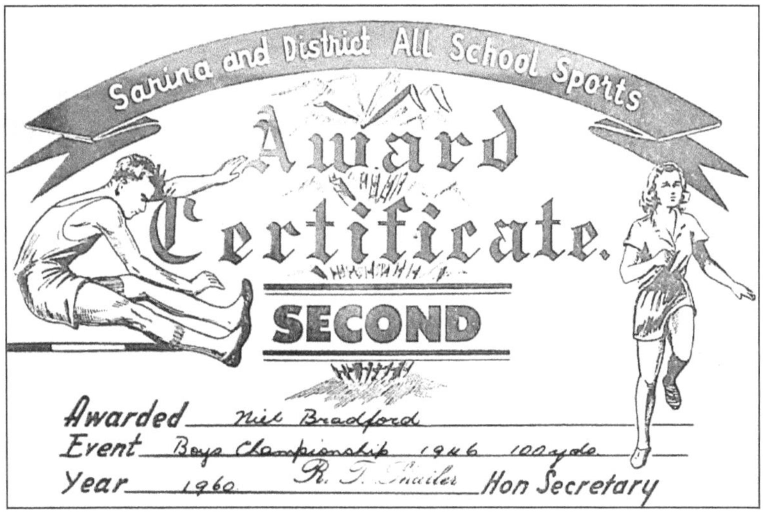

Author's certificate for the 100 yards in 1960
(Courtesy of Sarina and District All School Sports Association)

Author's certificate for the Open Hurdle in 1960
(Courtesy of Sarina and District All School Sports Association)

Author's certificate for the Senior High Jump in 1960
(Courtesy of Sarina and District All School Sports Association)

Author's certificate for the Senior Broad Jump in 1960
(Courtesy of Sarina and District All School Sports Association)

**Author (right) and a cousin on Anzac
Day at Sarina in 1962**
(Private Source)

**Author competing with the Sarina
Pony Club during 1962/63**
(Private Source)

3

NEW BEGINNING

Going to live with Uncle Doug at Yukan, I expected to be treated the same as my older brother, who lived in the house with Uncle Slim at Shinfield. Astonishingly, at the age of 15 years, my place of abode was the barracks for a sugarcane cutter, set on low blocks, one bedroom in which there was a kerosene lamp and an old stretcher with sagging wire and mattress, no other furniture or floor coverings, a kitchen with a wood stove and kerosene refrigerator, corrugated iron roof and walls, not lined underneath the roof or on the inside of the walls, a veranda, doused in sump oil, and resident rats and snakes.

Apart from having to use the family's outdoor toilet, often referred to as a *dunny*, the bathing facilities consisted of a timber and corrugated iron structure, enclosed on three sides, no roof or light, and a shower bucket suspended from a piece of timber.

Having a shower, after heating the water on the wood stove, I put the hot water into the bucket, then pull the rope attached to a lever to operate the shower.

Believing one night that it was the rope, I pulled and down on top of me came a yellow-bellied black tree snake, making me retreat hastily, stark naked, resulting in me going thereafter to the shower with a lit candle.

There also were incidents inside the barracks with snakes of all types, and it became necessary for me, while sleeping in the stretcher at night, to cover myself with a mosquito net, tucked in at the side, to avoid snake bites.

Not only did I have to pay for all meals and washing of my clothes, towels, and bed linen, but I also had to pay rent for the substandard accommodation. I had lived in worse before, however, with my family, and after buying a wardrobe and cupboard, the barracks became my main place of abode for the next four years.

Having sold the grey horse, seen in a photograph at the end of Chapter 2, when I was able do so, I bought the other horse for the pony club and competition at rodeos.

Then, if I wanted to get around locally, the horse became my main transport, and to go into Sarina, I had to rely on a seat in Uncle Doug's vehicle or catch a train at the Yukan Railway Station.

Farm life agreed with me, and weighing up the good with the bad, I soon became content with my new surroundings and secured an agreement with Uncle Doug to cut his sugarcane crop of about 1100 tons during 1963.

Unbeknown to Uncle Doug and his wife, Evelyn, I did not have a bank account, and I was still handing over the bulk of my money to my parents for support of the family.

That all came to a head when my parents and siblings, still at home, arrived unexpectedly one night at Uncle Doug's house, and my mother demand that I give her money.

Incensed by what she saw, Aunt Evelyn lunged at my mother, and soon both were slapping, scratching, hissing, and rolling around on the floor.

Absolutely embarrassed by the spectacle, after saying that the family could no longer expect any money from me, I went to the barracks, followed by Uncle Doug, who apologized for what Aunt Evelyn had done.

That night, Aunt Evelyn did me a favour, as her physical confrontation with my mother brought an end to money being handed over to my parents.

This was around my seventeenth birthday, and when Uncle Doug discovered that I did not have a bank account or any money saved, he gave me an advance as the deposit, even went guarantor for me, to buy a vehicle of my own.

Unlike me, from the money saved in a bank account, my older brother paid cash for his first vehicle.

Finally, I had broken loose from the shackles, restraining me during those adolescent years, and despite living in sub-standard conditions, I began to enjoy the peace and quiet away from the constant arguments between my parents.

In 1963, not long after I started cutting the sugarcane crop of about 1100 tons for Uncle Doug, an obnoxious person coming into the paddock, said to me, "Stop cutting. I want to talk to you!"

"No, I'm too busy," I responded, "so go away!"

"Do you have a ticket to cut the cane?"

Believing that he was a crazy person, who somehow found his way onto the farm, "I don't need a ticket," I responded, "so bugger off, and let me do my work!"

"If you don't have a ticket, I will stop harvesting on this farm, do you understand?"

The sugarcane knife raised at the top of a swing, "Bugger off," I said, as I looked in his direction.

"You're threatening me," he screamed, as he ran towards the farmhouse.

Over the lunch, Uncle Doug said to me, "Did you have a visitor in the paddock this morning?"

"Yes," I replied, "when he told me that I needed a ticket to cut the cane, I thought he was mad, so I told him to bugger off."

"That was the AWU Representative from Mackay," said Uncle Doug. "I gave him a cheque for your ticket, and the money will be deducted from your next pay."

Yes, it was the representative from Mackay for the Australian Workers' Union (AWU), who visited farms throughout the district to ensure that all cutters had the compulsory ticket.

And, no, I did not threaten him with the knife, as it was at the top of the swing, and appeared that way to the representative, who made something out of nothing.

During the holidays of 1963, I was left to mind the farm while Uncle Doug, and his family, spent Christmas and New Year at his beach shack.

Suffering from severe cramps in the middle of my stomach, I drove into Mackay and spoke to my mother.

"You're bound up," said my mother, "so have a double dose of Eno, and you will be right!"

After the double dose of Eno, I drove back to the farm, and went to bed.

Suddenly, I was vomiting violently, so severe it was like my stomach was coming out through my mouth, causing me to collapse to the floor, trembling, and sweating profusely.

Unable to walk, I crawled over to the farmhouse and telephoned a neighbour, who took me to a doctor in Sarina.

After telling him not to do so, when he inserted a finger in my rectum to do a test, I sat upright abruptly and vomited all over the doctor.

Recovering, "I told you that would happen," I said, "but you didn't listen to me!"

Looking at me with *dagger eyes*, the doctor muttered something, and then made a telephone call.

Soon thereafter, I was in an ambulance, speeding with lights flashing and siren whaling.

I had a ruptured appendix, with the onset of peritonitis!

Because the surgery was complicated, the ambulance took me to the Lister Private Hospital where the family's doctor by this time, Duncan Robertson, was waiting.

After the surgery, I was unconscious for four days, and due to fever and elevated temperature, it was necessary for nine changes of pyjamas on one of those days.

I was in the hospital for twelve weeks and had reactions to everything injected or ingested, and when Doctor Robertson stopped prescribing medication, I recovered.

When well enough, "We were told you would not live longer than two hours after the operation," my mother said, which surprised me.

Diagnosed with an acute form of PCT, thirty-five years later, I am no longer surprised!

Upon my release from hospital, and with a huge bill waiting

for me, I was disappointed when Uncle Doug told me that he had no work for me until the planting season.

A maternal uncle, Cecil William Joseph (Bill) Bedford, however, gave me employment with Rocla Pipes at Paget, Mackay, where I manufactured concrete pipes.

The work was very physical, shovelling and combining sand, gravel, and cement in a large mixer, spread evenly inside a mould spun around by a mechanical wheel.

Using an endless chain and rollers on a rail, I pushed the mould from the shed to a location in the sun, and when the concrete had set, I removed the pipe from the mould.

Satisfying Uncle Bill that I could do the work, he offered me permanent work at Rocla Pipes, only for Uncle Doug to contact me to start planting at once, also saying that I had the contract to cut his sugarcane.

Torn between loyalty to uncles from both sides of the family, whom I respected, I chose work that I liked the most, and that was with Uncle Doug on the farm at Yukan.

Unfortunately, I left Uncle Bill short of a worker, and he barred me from working again at Rocla Pipes.

While working for Rocla Pipes at Paget, I had consultations with Doctor Robertson, where he worked at the practice of Doctor Paul Hopkins, for the surgery at the Lister Private Hospital.

During the consultation, Doctor Hopkins came into the room, and he and Doctor Robertson discussed the reactions that I had with prescribed medication, touching on when I was a patient at the Lister Private Hospital, sixteen years earlier, and they made a connection, which I did not pursue.

If my parents had told me more, I would have pursued the doctors' discussion that day, and I am certain that I would have discover then that I was *autistic*.

In my parents' defence, it is my belief that stigmatization might have been behind their decision not to say anything, as others would have looked down on the family, if it had been common knowledge that one child had *autism*.

But I did not pursue anything during the consultation, as I was normal, as far as I was concerned, and others were not!

Doctor Hopkins died the following year, and all that would have remained, about the diagnosis in 1948 at the Lister Private Hospital, would have been his records.

When I enquired, staff at the practice told me that my records with Doctor Hopkins are no longer available, as I had not been a patient of the practice since 1963.

Returning to Uncle Doug's farm, I helped in the planting of his crop for the next season and cutting of the 1100 tons of sugarcane during 1964.

At the end of this chapter, there are photographs of me, beefed up from the strenuous work at Rocla Pipes, cutting and loading the sugarcane during that year.

Uncle Doug was a good influence for me, as he served in the Australian Army during World War Two, and he encouraged me to join the Citizens Military Forces (CMF).[1,2]

June 2, 1964 – I joined the 42nd Battalion, Royal Queensland Regiment (RQR) and served in the mortar platoon at Sarina.[3,4]

Part of my training included a Signaller's course that enabled me to use various radios, such as a portable Very High Frequency (VHF) radio, during bivouacs and camps.

At the end of this chapter, there is a record of my service in the army, and an acknowledgement from the police force that I was competent in the use of radios in the CMF.[1,3,5]

I also attended and passed a Map Reading course that enabled me to use a compass and map with the 42nd, 31st, and 51st Battalions, RQR, on exercises conducted in the dense rainforest and scrub at Mount Blackwood, High Range, and Seaview Range in the Mackay, Townsville, and Ingham districts.[6,7]

Therefore, I had vast Radio and Map Reading experience from that training, spanning the period from 1964 to 1969, putting me in good stead for the future challenges in 1970 on Bell Peak North.[4]

Apart from involvement with the CMF, I competed also in competitions at rodeos, and I played rugby league for the Magpies Under-19 team.

That socialization made acquaintances, but I never allowed any to become long-time friends.

There were other girlfriends, apart from the third cousin, but none appear compatible, and those relationships were over, before they had time to begin.

A mate from the CMF, however, arranged a *blind date* for me on a Saturday night in Sarina, coinciding with the day Uncle Doug asked if I would make up the numbers of his social cricket team for the final game played at Koumala.

Not only did I snare a *hat trick* with the ball, Uncle Doug taking a spectacular catch in the slips from a ball I bowled, but I also hit the winning runs, resulting in the opponents crying *foul play* over my last-minute inclusion.

Despite not really having consumed alcohol and being under the legal drinking age of 21 years, they took me to the Koumala Hotel where they bought *schooner* after *schooner* of beer for me, even after I pleaded, "No more, please!"

Back at the barracks on Uncle Doug's farm, I decided that I had too much to drink, so I crawled into bed, effectively cancelling the *blind date*.

The mate, and others from the CMF, had other ideas, and they drove to Uncle Doug's farm, threw me under the shower, cold as charity, helped me dress, and then drove me to Sarina for the *blind date* at Cecil and Joyce Kay's picture theatre.

My *blind date* was Patricia Frances Pannell, daughter of Walter Joseph Alfred (Wally) Pannell and Madeline Grace (Madge) Pannell, formerly Porter, of Sarina.

Having been on dates before, I found it difficult to look into the eyes of those females. However, probably because I was still *under-the-weather*, but I would like to think otherwise, as soon as I looked into Patricia's eyes, I was smitten.

Arriving for a second date, after announcing that I was there to take Patty Pannell to the picture theatre, I was turned away when Madge Pannell said, "Oh, she has already gone!"

Walking away with drooped shoulders, "No, come back," urged Madge, "she is changing a light bulb in the laundry!"

What started out as a *blind date*, quickly became a relationship that I have never regretted.

Not a tall person, Madge had my respect, and taking me to task one day, "Neil," said Madge, "you are not listening to me!"

"Of course, I am, Madge," I responded. "If you want, I can tell you what I am reading in the newspaper, what is on the television, and what you have said."

Not only do I have *eidetic memory*, but I also have *photographic memory*, and I recalled everything in print, said on the television, and Madge's conversation, word-for-word.[8]

By then, Madge had not come to terms with me not looking at her, while she was speaking, however, she never doubted me after that sorting out.

In the Dedication, there is a photograph of Wally and Madge Pannell.

At the end of the crushing season, I worked for McDonnell Constructions, as a rigger's offsider, on the new bridge built to replace the old swinging bridge over Sandy Creek, south from Mackay.

Foundations for the piers supporting the new bridge were inside cofferdams constructed in Sandy Creek.

The job with the rigger was with a crane and setting up of pulleys, cables, ropes, and other equipment during the building of the cofferdams, and afterwards the piers.

Experience gained in how to couple and uncouple heavy equipment with the crane, and training thereafter with an army helicopter in the Seaview Range, near Ingham, prepared me for what I would do, five years later, on Bell Peak North.

One day, while others wasted valuable time, wondering how

to get a rope across Sandy Creek, I dove into the water and swam with the rope to the other side, same as what I had done with the fishing nets in *Tedlands*.

Others were pleased that I resolved the issue quickly, earning me a reprimanded, as management believed a crocodile or shark could have taken me.

From experience, the noise made during the construction of the bridge would have chased away any threat, so I took the risk and swam the rope across Sandy Creek.

Management hoped that I would stay and go with the company to another project in Western Australia, but I left in 1965 when Uncle Doug said that he was ready to start planting, again cutting and loading his crop of 1100 tons that year.

At the end of this chapter, there are photographs of me cutting sugarcane, and of me partnering Patricia when she made her debut that year.

There is also another photograph of the 1965 Magpies Under-19 Premiership Team.

Despite playing five-eighth for the entire season, because I did not attend training regularly, the club did not advise as to when and where to go for the photograph.

So, there is an insert of me in the top left corner of the photograph to show that I was part of the winning team.

The coach was my cousin, Les Bradford, aided by his brother, Ivan, who, from the left, are standing in the second row, third and fourth, respectively.

Together with another brother, Ernie, they played with the Magpies A Grade team, the trio being the bulk of the forward pack in the Foley Shield team for Mackay.

Going with Patricia to the pictures, after scoring five tries during a game, Cecil Kay, a selector, stopped me and said that I would be the five-eight for the Mackay Under-19 team.

When he put my name forward, my cousin, Les, vetoed the selection on the basis that I did not attend training regularly, ending my aspiration of being in the Mackay team.

That is how others, even my cousins, have treated me!

Suffering an injury playing rugby league during the crushing season, which did not require time off work, I had a disagreement with Uncle Doug over playing rugby league and commitments with the CMF.

I respected my uncle, but he asked me to quit playing rugby league, and for me to give up being a soldier in the CMF, even stop competing in rodeos.

Uncle Doug's main concern was that I could suffer an injury during one of those activities, requiring time off work, leaving him to find someone else to harvest his sugar cane.

I did not give up the CMF, and I kept competing at rodeos, but I stopped going to rugby league training in Mackay, as explained to my cousin, Les, who took the opposite view to Uncle Doug.

So, I even found it difficult to please relatives, other than my family. They were right, and I was always wrong, and when I protested, I was arguing!

In hindsight, I involved myself in too many activities whereby I could not fully commit to training, and I now accept the blame for what happened.

After what I went through during my adolescence and early teens, the world was my oyster, and I was hellbent on pursuing any opportunity that came along.

However, I should have slowed down and, now and again, and smelt the roses!

Socializing became easier through the CMF, playing rugby league, and other sports, but what I found difficult then, and still do, is knowing what I should or should not do to please the expectations of others.

I think and behave differently to others, but they judge me by their standards, mostly impossible to change, as not everyone accepts that another might be *different*.

When others persist with that view, I walk away, causing others to believe I consider myself to be *better* than them, or that I am up to something.

Uncle Doug made it clear that he was going with a mechanical harvester to cut his crop the following year. This meant that I would have to find employment elsewhere, as his son and my cousin, would take over the work that I did on the farm.

Discovering we were compatible and would like to spend the rest of our lives together, Patricia and I were engaged during the crushing season.

This was after Madge Pannell stipulated that we could not marry until I had *permanent* employment, as cutting sugarcane by hand or farm work was *seasonal*.

After playing rugby league on a Sunday, while walking past the Mackay Police Station, Patricia and I saw a sign, asking those desirous of joining the police force to apply within.

Boldly walking into the police station, I was handed a form to complete.

Not having completed Grade 8, "This, is a waste of time and effort," I thought, as I struggled with answers to questions, and spelling of words.

About a month later, which surprised me, I received a letter from the Commissioner of Police, advising when and where I was to present myself for a written test.

Late on a Friday afternoon, full of bravado and confidence, I walked into the Mackay Police Station, and met another applicant, Keith Dunster.

Our supervisor for the test was Inspector Tom Boyle.

Ushering us into his office, Tom explained the process, and then left us unsupervised.

Breaking into a cold sweat, "What the hell do they mean by that question," I said to myself.

Hearing Keith moaning and groaning, I looked sideways, and I saw he was sweating profusely, and that he also was having trouble with the questions.

Mutually agreeing that two heads were better than one, we confided with each other, but the answers still did not come freely to us.

Just as we were about to admit defeat, Tom walked back into the room.

Obviously sensing our predicament, "Look, I'm late for a session with my mates at the pub," said Tom. "I'll give you the answers, but don't tell anyone I helped you!"

Sorry, Tom, but after all those years of remaining silent, I am doing what you asked me not to do!

Without Tom's help, I would not have embarked on the greatest adventure of my life.

Instead of leaving Uncle Doug on good terms, a matter arose within the family, which was untruthful, but my uncle sided with his family.

Believing that it might affect the processing of my application, I took the matter to John Harris and Pat Bruton at the Sarina Police Station, and they interviewed Uncle Doug, who refused to make a complaint, or say anything about the matter.

Worthy of note, Uncle Doug was my main referee, and he had the opportunity to say something, but he did not, and after 33 years, he raised the untruth with my father on his death bed, which was despicable, to say the least.

That upheaval over, John and Pat interviewed me for allegedly telling an untruth that no one in my immediate family had a criminal conviction.

This was the time, as mentioned before, I thought my father was in the watchhouse for *drunkenness*, rather than him being there on a charge of *going armed so as to cause fear*.

After the interview, John and Pat vouched for me that I had answered the question truthfully in the application.

This delay meant that if approved, I would not commence training at the Police Depot until the second intake starting on April 12, 1966.

While waiting for confirmation, I went on a two-week training camp with the CMF at the army training area of Shoalwater Bay, near Rockhampton.[9]

Albert Carr taught me well, and the CMF found I was proficient with a ·38 calibre revolver, SLR rifle, Owen submachine gun, and M60 machine gun, and classified me as a *Rifleman*.

Throwing a hand grenade was impressive, however, taking part in a sectional shoot with the mortars was spectacular, but frightening after considering the carnage each bomb could cause!

The range was on a rise overlooking a horse-shoe bend in a saltwater creek.

Instead of exploding beyond the creek, the first round from a mortar, made us wonder as to what the shiny objects were in the sprays of water.

With nothing much to do, until the trucks arrived to take us back to camp, I went down to the water's edge and saw stunned fish being swept along on the incoming tide.

Having had enough of Vienna sausages and baked beans, not to mention the boiled bacon and powdered scrambled eggs, I stripped off, dove into the saltwater, and retrieved six large barramundis from the creek.

Arriving back at camp, for that misdemeanour, I had to appear before the Company Sergeant Major (CSM).

While my platoon enjoyed leave in Rockhampton, I was denied leave and confined to camp, as punishment for my misdemeanour, and during a hearty meal of grilled barramundi, "Thank you," the CSM whispered into my ear, "this is the best meal I have had since coming into camp!"

During that training, the Sarina Police informed me through Patricia as to when I was to report for training at the Police Depot, Petrie Terrace, Brisbane.[10]

I got off the *troop* train at Sarina, and virtually boarded another train bound for Brisbane.

Not having been in the *Big Smoke* since a child, the hustle and bustle of city life in Brisbane, was very confronting for a *Country Boy*, so much so that I almost turned around and caught another train back to Sarina.

What kept me going, as I walked from the Roma Street Railway Station to the Police Depot on Petrie Terrace, were the parting words of my mother, "You'll soon come crawling back home with your tail between your legs!"

Not only did her floggings make me strong-willed, but those parting words spurred me on!

On reflection, it is possible that my mother thought the course would be beyond my mental capabilities, and if so, she did not know anything about what was going on in my mind.

April 10, 1966 – arriving at the Police Depot on a Sunday, which was the Easter long weekend, the Duty Sergeant impolitely told me to go away and come back on the Tuesday.

Fortunately, Sergeant Tom Molloy overheard what the Duty Sergeant said and showed me to my room, overlooking the Central Business District (CBD) of Brisbane, which was an impressive sight, particularly at night.

Same as the written test, the going was tough from the beginning at the Police Depot.

I was determined, however, that I would not fail, having in mind the stipulation of Patricia's mother, Madge Pannell, that we could not marry until I had permanent employment, and then there were the parting words of my mother.

Moreover, I also had those words of encouragement and support from another, who I believe was my late great-great-grandfather, urging me on to brighter and better things.

So, day and night, weekend after weekend, while others on the course were enjoying themselves away from the classroom on the Gold Coast beaches, often becoming frustrated, my head was constantly in the law books.

While going through the books, I came across the archaic rule that a Probationary Constable could not marry within the first 12 months of service.

After hastily writing a heartfelt letter to Madge, assuring her that I would have permanent employment at the end of the course, Madge agreed that we could marry before the swearing-in parade, thereby circumventing the archaic rule.

June 4, 1966 – I was married to Patricia in St Luke's Parish Church at Sarina.

Later, at the reception held in the function room at Carlon's Hotel, "Why wasn't your older brother the best man," questioned my mother.

"He has never treated me like a brother," I responded, "so I didn't ask him!"

I am sure that others would have done differently, but I am who I am, and because of the way I *think* and *behave*, he did not deserve to be my best man.

The best man, who was then going with the bridesmaid, was not my original choice, but we played rugby league against each other, and there was mutual respect between us, so I agreed to him being my best man.

Originally, the best man was the mate from the CMF, who arranged the *blind date* for me with Patricia, and I was so looking forward to him being my best man.

However, my mate's relationship with the bridesmaid took a nosedive, and because the bridesmaid was Patricia's best friend, and the bridesmaid did not want anything further to do with my mate, I agreed to the current boyfriend being the best man.

I should have fought harder for my mate, but I was marrying Patricia to spend the rest of our lives together, which was more important, so I capitulated.

We spent that night, as spouses, in our vehicle on the highway at Marlborough, between Sarina and Rockhampton, sleeping among a herd of cattle, as I had to be back in the Police Depot by 6 am on the Monday morning.

Patricia has appreciated my spontaneity over the years, which has taken us to exciting places, but I am not certain if our first night met with her expectations!

Arriving back in Brisbane during late Sunday afternoon, I spent the night with Patricia in a furnished flat that I rented at 17 Scott Street, Red Hill, returning to the Police Depot before 6 am on the Monday morning.

Walking past the front office, the loud bellowing of "Come here that man," stopped me midstride.

Coming out of the office, "What are those things on your feet, Probationary," questioned Tom Molloy.

"Moccasins, Sergeant!"

"Bodgie boots, Probationary. You are to parade with the boots before Sub-Inspector Barlow at 9 am, and never to wear them again, do you understand?"

"Yes, Sergeant!"

I stood outside Sub-Inspector Barlow's office for about a half-hour with the Moccasins, before another sergeant came along and told me to take them back to the flat at Red Hill, and that I was not to wear them again at the Police Depot.

While training, I was assessed as having *little ability as a horseman*, going against my experience over many years of riding a horse in a pony club, for pleasure, during stock work, and in competitions at rodeos, including the riding of a bucking horse.[11]

At the end of Chapter 2, there is evidence of my riding skills in three photographs.

Other testing at the Police Depot included boat rowing for which I was assessed by the Brisbane Water Police as suitable for *ordinary dinghy work* and *flood rescue*, also putting me in good stead for the challenges that I would face the following year during the flood at Gordonvale.[12]

At the end of this chapter, there is evidence of those tests in horsemanship and ability to row a boat.

June 30, 1966 – I achieved what others believed was impossible, particularly my mother, and after taking the Oath of Office at the end of this chapter, I was sworn in as a Constable of the Queensland Police Force.[5,10,13]

Patricia had been less than a month in Brisbane, and concerned for her safety and wellbeing, walking back alone to the flat, I did not agree with her attending the swearing-in parade, something that I have regretted ever since.

I hurt Patricia's feelings on that occasion, and she cried, and ever since then, I have done my best to allow Patricia into my world, *different* to those without *autism*.

After three months' training at the Bardon Police Station in the suburbs of Brisbane, I arrived on transfer at the Roma Street Police Station in the Brisbane CBD where I was rostered for beat work from 10 pm to 6 am.[10]

Armed with only a notebook, baton, and handcuffs, and without any training whatsoever, other than what I had read in the General Instructions, I was walking the required one-and-a-half miles per hour by the left when a burglar alarm, not too far away from my location, began ringing loudly.

Hand-held radios not available then, "What the hell do I do now," I thought, before walking quickly to a menswear store where the alarm was sounding.

Finding the door wide open, "How do I tell someone without leaving the store," I asked myself, when suddenly two burly detectives in an unmarked Criminal Investigation Branch (CIB) vehicle pulled up.

Brushing past me, they entered the store and came out with two suits each.

After placing the suits on the back seat, they speed off without saying anything, leaving me scratching my head, wondering what I had just seen.

Not long after, the Beat Sergeant, who also heard the alarm, joined me at the store.

Explaining what I had seen, "The suits are covered by insurance," the Sergeant cautioned. "So, if you want to stay in the force, you did not see anything, do you understand?"

No, I did not understand, however, I cautiously responded, "Yes, Sergeant!"

With that, a uniform patrol vehicle arrived and took over the investigation, allowing me to continue with my beat.

Yes, I confirmed that the store had been broken and entered, but by whom, and apart from the four suits, I did not know what else might have been stolen.

Starting out full of ambition that I would be enforcing the laws with other police officers to protect and preserve life and property in compliance with the Oath of Office taken, it became obvious to me in those early days that others were on the opposite side, working against the law.

Within a week of being at the Roma Street Police Station, "Bloody hell," I thought, "what have I got myself into!"

Compounding that dilemma, despite having experience as a receptionist and had declined a prestigious job offer in Mackay to be with me, Patricia was refused work by employers in Brisbane on the grounds that she was married to a police officer, who could be transferred.

Quitting seemed the best way out, but remembering the parting words of my mother, I took another way forward and had an interview with Sub-Inspector John O'Toole.

In his office, standing before him, "What can I do for you, Constable," said O'Toole, sternly.

"Sir, I am a *Country Boy*," I responded, nervously, "lost in the city!"

O'Toole's expression softening, "Where would you like to go, son?"

"Anywhere in the north of Queensland, will do, sir!"

Dismissed by O'Toole, I returned to my rostered duty as a reserve, sitting in the dayroom, twiddling my thumbs, until asked to do something.

Called into his office the following day, O'Toole said, "How does Gordonvale sound to you, son?"

"Can I leave, tomorrow, sir?"

"No," said O'Toole, smiling. "You need to check first to see if there is rental accommodation at Gordonvale!"

Before turning around to leave, "Thank you, sir," was my grateful response to O'Toole, who restored my confidence in the police force, adding, "I deeply appreciate what you have done for me."

Obviously beaming, as if I had won the lottery, "Why are you so happy in this dump of a place," queried a Senior Constable who, on my first day at the Roma Street Police Station, showed me where to hide from the Commissioned Officers.

"I've been transferred to Gordonvale!"

"How did you do that," he questioned. "I've been here for years and can't get a transfer!"

"A poor attitude might be the cause," I thought, at the same time feeling the urge to enlighten him that a family member, once living opposite to O'Toole at West Chermside, was friendly with the Sub-Inspector.

At the end of this chapter, there is a photograph taken for my Identity Card, and a copy of my service during the next 31 years as a police officer.

A radio message from Cairns confirmed that a furnished house at Gordonvale, vacated by another constable and his wife, was available. I wanted to leave the next day, but I had to wait, until the Inspector in charge of the Brisbane Police District gave me permission to depart on transfer.

Author cutting sugarcane at Yukan in 1964
(Private Source)

Author with a wagon of sugarcane at Yukan in 1964
(Private Source)

Certificate of Service

Private
Neil Raymond Bradford

Served with	From	To
Citizen Military Forces	2 June 1964	8 December 1966
Citizen Military Forces	1 March 1967	19 June 1967
Citizen Military Forces	19 February 1968	7 December 1969

J.R. Moug
Colonel
for Chief of Army

5 August 2002

Author's Australian Army Service from 1964 to1969
(Courtesy of Australian Army)

FULL NAME...BLADFOLD.Neil.Raymond.............................
APPOINTED PROBATIONARY.12.5.66.......DATE AND PLACE OF BIRTH.████.Mackay
PRESENT ADDRESS..Petrie.Terrace,.Police.Barracks................
HOME ADDRESS.17.Scott.Street,.Red.Hill.(Furnished.Flat)..........
                    (Show whether residing in own home, flat,
                    or house- furnished or otherwise)
EX-SERVICEMAN (UNIT)C.M.F.42BN.STANDARD OF EDUCATION..8th.Grade.(Didn't.sit
PREVIOUS OCCUPATIONS.Labourer.................................
PREVIOUS POLICE SERVICE.....Nil..............................
LICENSED TO OPERATE A:- MOTOR CAR?.Yes.APPROVED?(std)...No..........
                                            (Auto)..No...........
                    MOTOR CYCLE?..No...APPROVED?.....No..........
                    MOTOR TRUCK?.Yes...APPROVED?....No...........
LICENSE NUMBER..████...........CLASSES..(s)(c)×(g)................
IF MARRIED, STATE DATE OF MARRIAGE..4.6..66...................
DATES OF BIRTH AND SEX OF CHILDREN..Nil......................
IF SINGLE, SHOW WHETHER ENGAGED TO BE MARRIED.................
****
REG.NO. and NUMERALS.████.........DATE SWORN IN.....30th.June,.1966....
TRADE..No...
ANY OTHER QUALIFICATIONS?....No..............................
FIRST AID CERTIFICATE.Yes..ROWING BOAT..Good..MOTOR BOAT..No.experience.
BICYCLE.Experienced.SWIMMER..Fair.(Resuscitation)..HORSEMANSHIP..Bad......
BUSH WORK.Little experience......HANDLING STOCK......Little.experience..
WIRELESS OPERATOR..C.M.F........FOOTDRILL.Fair...REVOLVER SHOOTING..Fair..
                    Some experience
CLERICAL WORK.No experience..................................
WHERE SCHOOLED.Meumala.State.School,.Glenella.State.School,.Alligator....
Creek.State.School..
SHORTHAND....Nil.........(W.P.M.)   TYPING.......14.......(W.P.M.)
LAW RESULTS:- .....69%........   TRAINING STATION.Bardon...........

REMARKS:.Suitable.for.general.duty.t.wn.or.country...Expressed.a.desire.
for.country.service.in.any.part.of.the.State.................
....
....████████████..............
..............................Sub-Inspector.................

Author's Personal Details, Qualifications, and Experience in 1966
(Courtesy of Queensland Police Service)

**Author cutting sugarcane at Yukan
in 1965**
(Private Source)

**Author with Patricia Frances Pannell
at her debut in 1965**
(Private Source)

Author's ID Photograph in 1966
Registered Number 7418
(Courtesy of Queensland Police Museum)

Magpies Under-19 Premiership Team in 1965
Author (left insert), Ivan and Les Bradford, second row, third and
fourth, respectively
(Private Source)

```
                                    Police Station,
                                    OXLEY. 13 th. April, 1966.
                                    ....................

MEMORANDUM:

                    The Inspector of Police,
                        DEPOT.


        Probationary Neil Raymond BRADFORD.
        ________________________________________

reported to Oxley Police Station to be tested in

horsemanship on the  13 th. April, 1966
                     _____________________


            Result of this test is as follows:-
                                  Bad.
(a)   MOUNTING AND SEAT.............................
                                  Fair.
(b)   GENERAL CONTROL OF HORSE.....................

(c)   CAPABILITY OF SCHOOLING CORRECTLY
      AN  UNTRAINED OR FRACTIOUS HORSE.
      (To be answered only in the case
      of outstanding ability)...................

(d)   IF CONSIDERED SUITABLE FOR:
                                  No.
      (1)  Ceremonial Parades.....................
                                  Yes.
      (2)  Bush Patrol Work.......................
                                  Bad.
(e)   GENERAL CLASSIFICATION.....................

(f)   REMARKS  This Probationary showed little ability
      as a horseman...............................
      ............................................
      ............................................
      ............................................
      ............................................
      ............................................

(Classifications for (a), (b), (c) and (e) should
 be shown as - Very Good, Good, Fair or Bad.)

                                    A.M. COYNE.
                                    Sergeant 2/c No. 4351.
```

Author Tested for Horsemanship at Oxley in 1966
(Courtesy of Queensland Police Service)

Police Depot,
Educational Section,
26th May, 1966.

MEMORANDUM:

The Inspector of Police,
DEPOT.

Probationary BRADFORD.N.R ....reported at the
Water Police Station to be tested in boat rowing on the
17th May, 1966

Result of the test is as following:-

(a) Experience in rowing: GOOD

(b) General control of boat: GOOD

(c) Outstanding efficiency: YES

(d) If considered suitable
    for flood rescue work: YES

(e) If considered suitable
    for ordinary dingy work: YES

(Classifications for (a) and (b) should
be shown as - Very Good, Good, Fair or Bad).

Sub-Inspector

Author evaluated for Boat Rowing competency in 1966
(Courtesy of Queensland Police Service)

"I, ...

swear by Almighty God that I will well and truly serve our

Sovereign Lady Queen Elizabeth the Second and Her Heirs

and Successors according to law in the office of constable or

in such other capacity as I may be hereafter appointed,

promoted, or reduced, without favour of affection, malice or

ill-will, from this date and until I am legally discharged; that

I will see and cause Her Majesty's peace to be kept and

preserved; and that I will prevent to the best of my power all

offences against the same; and that while I shall continue to

be a member of the Police Force of Queensland I will to the

best of my skill and knowledge discharge all the duties legally

imposed upon me faithfully and according to law. So help me

God."

Oath of Office taken by the Author in 1966
(Courtesy of Queensland Police Museum)

QUEENSLAND POLICE SERVICE

WORKFORCE MANAGEMENT
200 Roma Street, Brisbane 4000
Box 1440, G.P.O. Brisbane 4001

TELEPHONE (07) 3364 6748   FACSIMILE (07) 3364 6957

DETAILS OF SERVICE

Neil Raymond BRADFORD Reg.No. ███

RANK

Probationary:	12 April 1966
Constable:	30 June 1966
Constable (1st Class):	30 June 1971
Senior Constable:	30 June 1976
Sergeant (2nd Class):	7 May 1979
Sergeant (1st Class)	7 September 1981
Senior Sergeant	20 January 1986
Inspector (Grade 3)	16 October 1989
Senior Sergeant	11 February 1992

STATIONS/ESTABLISHMENTS

Police Depot:	12 April 1966
Bardon:	30 June 1966
Roma Street:	26 September 1966
Gordonvale:	13 October 1966
Moranbah:	15 January 1972
Mackay:	31 May 1973
Wallumbilla:	21 March 1975
Toowoomba:	31 January 1978
Mount Isa (Clerical Functions):	20 July 1979
Cairns (Clerical Functions):	22 February 1982
Mackay:	9 May 1986
Fortitude Valley District:	13 November 1989
North Brisbane District:	28 May 1990
State Traffic Support Group (secondment)	15 April 1993
Metropolitan North Region:	21 November 1994

RELIEVING AS INSPECTOR AT MACKAY

Acting Inspector:	28 November to 23 December 1988
Acting Inspector:	29 May to 18 June 1989
Acting Inspector:	17 July to 6 August 1989
Acting Inspector:	4 September to 15 October 1989

SEPARATION

Resigned (under Special Provisions)	15 August 1997

QUEENSLAND POLICE SERVICE

Author's Details of Service from 1966 to 1997
(Courtesy of Queensland Police Service)

4

GORDONVALE FLOOD

In the 1950s, together with her parents, Patricia visited Cairns and Gordonvale, but I had not ventured any further north from Mackay than Proserpine. Not having had the experience of visiting the Far North of Queensland, filled by a sense of adventure, scenes of tropical rainforest and crystal-clear flowing streams, occupied my nightly dreams.

Both then 20 and 18 years, respectively, and with Patricia expecting our first child, the departure date from Brisbane to Gordonvale came quickly.

With our possessions packed into the vehicle, we said goodbye to our flat owners, Vittoria, and Wanda Meneguzzo, who treated us like their children, and then set out from 17 Scott Street, Red Hill, Brisbane, on another exciting journey of our young lives, north to Gordonvale.

Our first stop was at Sarina where we stayed with Patricia's parents.

Knowing that we were short of money, Madge gave us two dollars so that we could make it to Gordonvale where, on arrival, I expected my fortnightly pay cheque would be.

October 13, 1966 – arriving at Gordonvale, I reported to Sergeant First Class William Crossley (Bill) Jenkins, relieving Officer in Charge, who was the bearer of bad tidings – the cheque had not arrived![1]

Standing before him with drooped shoulders, head bowed, and obviously him sensing my disappointment, "Will this tide you over until it arrives," said Bill, as he took a $20 note from his wallet and handed it to me.

"More than sufficient, Sergeant," I responded, graciously. "It's almost what my pay will be!"

That elation, however, turned to disappointment when shown

the furnished accommodation.

Looking back on our lives, if given a second opportunity, we would do the same again, however, we would do certain things far better than before.

Instead of being a house in the town, as advised in the radio message, the accommodation turned out to be barracks, once known as Munro's barracks, three kilometres outside of town, southern side of the Mulgrave River, on a sugarcane farm owned by Bill and Lena Boccalatte.

Patricia had never lived outside a town, and as the barracks consisting of two bedrooms, small lounge, kitchen/eating area, and a veranda, giving access to all rooms, running along the front, which only had one light, and the switch being on the veranda, I was concerned about her welfare and safety.

Other wives would have refused, there and then, but until we found something better, Patricia supported me and agreed to occupy the barracks.

Someone gave us a dog that we named *Rex*, enhancing our security.

Rex was a silly dog, but he took immense pride in guarding the barracks, quickly disposing of any *Taipan* that slithered out of the sugarcane paddock towards the barracks.

Any missed by *Rex*, I quickly dispatched with a meter-long length of 8-gauge plain wire.

Soon after arriving, I was rostered on a Friday night with the senior of four constables at Gordonvale.

Around 9.30 pm, the colleague asked me to drive north from Gordonvale to a farmhouse on Maitland Road where he got out to have a cup of tea, allegedly, with the farmer's spouse.

I am not naïve, but not wishing to create waves, I did as the colleague instructed, returning an hour later, finding him and the farmer's spouse embracing in the front yard.

After a kiss on the cheek from the farmer's spouse, obviously for being part of their infidelity, I had not driven far from the house when a speeding vehicle went past, drawing the startled response from my colleague, "Shit, that's the husband!"

The following morning, together with Patricia, we were having morning tea with the colleague and his wife at their house on the police reserve, not far from the police station.

Barging past the colleague's son at the front door, after throwing a pair of underpants on the table, "Next time you visit my wife late at night," said the husband to my colleague, "take your underwear with you!"

In disbelief that he could be so stupid to leave his underwear behind at the farmer's house, when I saw the pained expression on the face of my colleague's wife, "That's it," I thought, "I won't get involved in anything like that again!"

Having suffered enough physically and mentally with my parents, I decided that I did not desire anymore exposure to that trauma, not for that colleague, nor for anyone else.

Naturally, I explained to Patricia back at the barracks as to what was behind the incident at the colleague's house. Without her asking, I gave an assurance that I would not be involved in anything like that again.

Hearing about the incident, Alan Charles (Alan) Schwenke, one of the taxi drivers at Gordonvale, who became like an older brother to me, took me aside and gave friendly advice.

Alan was a Mason, and the first of the extended Masonic family at Gordonvale to take an interest in me.

Over time, the Masonic fraternity would invite me to join the Pyramid Highleigh Lodge at Gordonvale.

After urging to watch my back, Alan told me that the husband took part in illegal gambling and prostitution at Cairns, and allegedly carried a revolver.

Rather than say nothing, until something arose, because I am who I am, I told the colleague that I did not wish to be involved in any further infidelity.

Mainstream society will deal with things differently, but an *au-*

tistic person will be up front and open, and this is how I dealt with the issue of the colleague's infidelity.

The colleague became nasty, and I was never rostered with him again at Gordonvale, which suited me, as I had pledged my loyalty to Patricia.

That also was the end of socializing with the colleague's family, same as what happened when I withdrew from others, previously, to avoid a conflict.

Now that I know more about myself, I could have done things better, but it was a matter of *right* and *wrong*, and *right* came before *wrong*.

Soon after, Sergeant First Class William Cowan (Bill) Putt arrived on promotion and transfer as the Officer in Charge of the Gordonvale Police Station.

On advice and direction of Inspector Allan Cameron (Tubby) Gunn of Cairns, Bill questioned me about my involvement in the incident, resulting in me giving a similar assurance to Bill that I would not be involved in anything of the kind again.

While discussing his alleged possession of a revolver with an acquaintance in the Cairns CIB, the acquaintance told me that the husband participated in the corruption known as the *Joke*, and that it was him who brought my involvement in the colleague's infidelity to Tubby's notice.[2]

This was a serious moment in my policing career, which could have been over before it began, if the husband had made an official complaint.

More than likely, the Commissioner would have dismissed me!

With the year about to end, Bill asked me to go with him to find a small pine tree that he and his family would use as their Christmas tree.

Once down the Gillies Range Road, after Bill found and stuffed the tree to his liking in the boot of the police vehicle, we stopped at the Mountain View Hotel.

On entering, despite both of us being in uniform, Bill put a dollar note on the bar and asked for two beers.

"Put your money away, gents," said the publican. "The beers are on the house!"

After consuming the one beer, "Have a Merry Christmas," said Bill, as we left the hotel.

It was common at Mackay to see a police officer enter a bar in uniform.

If the cap or hat remained on the head, it meant that the police officer was on official duty, and a caution for the locals not to get involved.

However, if the police officer removed the cap or hat, it meant that he wanted a beer, putting the locals at ease, often resulting in locals divulging information of interest to him.

Unless obviously under the influence of alcohol to the extent of being incapable of driving, often a police officer would ignore those indiscretions, until the carnage became so bad that the police force had to respond.

That is how society functioned in those days!

Involvement in a colleague's infidelity was serious, but drinking in uniform whilst on duty was far worse, leaving me in a quandary of what to do, without upsetting others?

Over time, the Fitzgerald Commission of Inquiry would bring that conduct and behaviour to an end.[2]

Suffering from *light* sensitivity, the dayroom at Gordonvale, which had fluorescent lights, was unsuitable for me, and I had to wear sunglasses while typing a report.

It was said by others that I was *weird* or *stupid*, but I did not care, as my *needs* were more important!

In one of those reports, I made application for a *kaki slouch hat,* instead of a *khaki slouch hat,* exposing my lack of education. This became the bane of a joke peddled around the Cairns District by one of the Inspector's clerks, later Administration Branch, Brisbane, who climbed Bell Peak North on the third day of the mission.

To him, I say bugger off, as your comments then, and later,

were not appreciated!

And for those thinking that bugger is a swear word, it is not.

From thereon, however, the spelling of words uncertain to me came from a Concise Oxford English Dictionary!

Today, I rely on the spelling checker in word, so if anything is misspelt, I do not apologise.

Gordonvale was notorious for the high incidence of fatal and serious traffic accidents.

The man accidentally killed by my father was the first dead body that I saw, but soon after my arrival at Gordonvale, I saw others, from natural causes, murders, suicides, drownings, and sometimes three in a traffic accident.

At Gordonvale, my work as a police officer placed me in close contact with the Queensland Ambulance Transport Brigade (QATB) and Fire Brigade.

One of the QATB bearers was Robert James (Bob) Wallace, whom I came to respect immensely. The sensitivity displayed during the gruesome task of scraping up body parts from the surface of the bitumen, so that others did not see the consequences of the carnage, was impressive to my young mind.

Looking at a deceased person did not bother me, but I had to put a handkerchief doused with Patricia's scent over the nose during a post-mortem to avoid becoming nauseated and disorientated by the smells.

Observing how close Doctor Janos Brody performed the post-mortems, "Do the smells bother you," I asked.

"No," he said, "I don't have the sense of smell!"

We then had a talk about my issue, and he agreed that what I was doing, with a handkerchief doused in Patricia's scent, was the best way forward for me.

Taking command and control of situations, such as directing people and vehicles at scenes of traffic accidents, came easily to me, credited to what I had learnt during *contact engagements* while on manoeuvres in the CMF.

However, I was never one to respond as if it was a *Charge of the Light Horse Brigade*, preferring instead to become familiar with my surroundings, and what we had to do, before issuing orders and instructions.

That methodical approach was criticised by Ray Hickling, Alan Broughton, and Kevin Murgatroyd, years after the Search and Recovery mission on Bell Peak North.[3]

Those three did the opposite on the ascent of Bell Peak North on the first day of the mission, which could have ended up in searchers becoming lost in the dense rainforest, if I had not kept two groups of the party together.

Speed and alcohol combined with road conditions were the major contributing factors of traffic accidents at Gordonvale.

After intercepting the driver of a vehicle for disobeying a give way sign at a one-way bridge on the Gillies Range Road, "Sir," I asked, "could I see your driver's licence, please?"

"Certainly," the driver replied, handing over his licence.

"Sir, you disobeyed a sign and did not give way to me on the one-way bridge. Is there a lawful reason for not stopping?"

"I believed you were far enough away for me to cross the bridge."

"No, sir, it is not what happened. I had to brake suddenly to avoid a collision!"

"That is a matter of your opinion against mine."

"Sir, your opinion is contrary to what I saw, so I will issue you with a notice for the offence. Do you understand?"

"Constable, do you know who I am?"

Glancing at his driver's licence, "Certainly, Mr Pizzey," I responded, at the same time raising an eyebrow as if to ask him the question, "Should I be worried?"

Of course, I knew he was Jack Pizzey, Deputy Leader of the Country Party and Minister for Education and Police in the Queensland Parliament, which did not entitle him, in my *autistic* way of thinking, then and now, to be issued with a caution for a life-endangering offence.[4]

Others would have retreated in this confrontation, and they would not have issued a ticket, but I did not retreat, and not bowing to him, enraged Pizzey, who, physically shaking, threatened, "You will hear about this!"

"Sure, I have heard that before," I thought, prior to saying, "Good, sir, here is the ticket," snatched angrily out of my hand by Pizzey.

Back at the police station, "Neil, could I see you in my office," said Bill Putt.

In his office, "Did you give a motorist a ticket," said Bill, "for failing to give way at a one-way bridge?"

"Yes."

"Do you remember the name of the motorist?"

"Yes, Mr Pizzey."

"According to Tubby, Frank Bischof's bellowing in Brisbane could be heard all the way to Cairns, and the Commissioner has instructed that the ticket is to be cancelled, and that is what is going to happen?"

The Commissioner referred to in the conversation was Francis Erich (Frank) Bischof.

"But" I pleaded, "I could have been injured!"

"Look, Neil, it might be what happened, but Tubby would like to know what you thought you were doing, giving Jack Pizzey the ticket?"

"He is no different to anyone else, as far as I am concerned," I responded stubbornly, "so tell him that I was doing my job, and I will do it again, if I have the opportunity."

At times, a respected colleague, Robert Stevenson (Bob) Rodger, told me that I was *subtle as a train smash* during a discussion with another, often offending the feelings of others, and that is how it was on this occasion.

Upon hearing the rumour at the Police Depot, about Bischof being corrupt, I gave him the benefit of the doubt. However, what he did for Pizzey, confirmed there possibly was corruption, commonly known as the *Joke*, not only in the police force, but also within the Government.[5]

In his memoirs, when asked by Gordon Chalk, leader of the Liberals, if he could waive a speeding ticket, former Commissioner of Police, Raymond Wells (Ray) Whitrod, reflected:

> *I thought about the request and then said, "Look, I am sorry. I cannot interfere with the traffic constable's decision. He's issued a ticket. Members of the force know my policy not to interfere with any prosecution.*[6]

Yes, it was Ray Whitrod's policy, but he did nothing to amend or update the 1965 Commissioner's Memorandum for the issue of traffic offence notices in Queensland.

You might gather that this is personal to me, so I will indulge your attention and elaborate for a moment.

During and after Ray's time as the Commissioner, I served as the Officer in Charge of Clerical Functions at Toowoomba, Mount Isa, and Cairns, and the Officer in Charge of Mackay Police Station and Acting District Officer of Mackay Police District.

During that time, no Commissioner did anything to amend or updated the 1965 Commissioner's Memorandum until replaced by policy, orders, and procedures of the Queensland Police Service (QPS).[7]

Because of my wealth of administrative experience, as outlined above, the 1991 Project Team seconded me from the Metropolitan North Region to formulate new policy, orders, and procedures for the QPS. That is how I know that the statement, about no one amending or updating the 1965 memorandum until replaced after 1991, is correct.

Until then, it was *improper* under Whitrod's policy to waive a ticket issued for a life-endangering offence, such as speeding, mentioned by Whitrod, or not giving way, Pizzey being a prime example, unless there was an error, such as an incorrect date or registration number, in the ticket.

However, it was *proper* under Whitrod's policy to waive a ticket for a non-life-endangering offence, such as parking, if it was in the best interest of the public to do so.

Responding to unlawfulness in the Fortitude Valley Division, Whitrod formed a task force of *a Sergeant and eight hand-picked men* to work *independently of the Fortitude Valley divisional officers*, instructing that they were to *report directly to* [him] *and to take orders only from* [him].[6]

In later life, Whitrod wanted to know where he went wrong, and if alive, today, I would tell him that what he did in the Valley, is one of the instances.

Obviously, there was a managerial issue at the Fortitude Valley Police District office, located at the Fortitude Valley Police Station, and that is where Whitrod should have done something, as subordinates were champing at the bit to clean up the Valley.

Led by Vince Murphy, the task force soon became known as *Murphy's Marauders* through their overzealous enforcement of the traffic laws.[6]

When *the Fortitude Valley divisional officers* received complaints from aggrieved motorists, and because the task force was directly answerable to him, Whitrod introduced policy that it was *proper* to waive a ticket for a non-life-endangering offence, such as parking, if it was in the interest of the public to do so.[6]

Through my experience in Clerical Functions, and as an Officer in Charge, and Acting District Officer, I knew to read Whitrod's policy together with the 1965 Commissioner's Memorandum to gain an understanding of what to do, and what not to do.

Others without that experience, such as the Disciplinary Officer at my later demotion, and a former senior Non-Commissioned Officer at Cairns, who provided him with advice, were ignorant of the procedure.

During an inspection of financial records at the Gordonvale Police Station, the Inspector from the Auditor-General's Department was livid and made a major issue out of the improper cancellation of the notice, done on Bischof's instructions, inferring that he would have my *guts for garters*.

After making that threat, the Inspector had a discussion with his superior in Brisbane, resulting in another capitulation, same as what happened with me, and the Inspector certified that everything was in order.

It was not in order, as all copies of the notice, except for the one issued to Pizzey, instead of distribution to the various parties, such as the Clerk of the Court at Gordonvale, remained in the book, and with the destruction of the book, there would be no record of the ticket having been issued to Pizzey.

February of 1967 – the Mulgrave River, winding its way from the catchments at Goldsborough and Little Mulgrave through the countryside around Gordonvale to the ocean, began to flood, sometimes over the railway bridge, but never over the traffic bridge on the Bruce Highway.

Living through major flooding at Mackay, I asked how safe it was where we lived, and no one said anything about the barracks being on the floodplain of the Mulgrave River.

March 11, 1967 – which was a Friday, acting on instructions from Bill, I moved on two homeless men, taking shelter from the rain in the tennis court sheds in Norman Park.

After ceasing duty at 4 pm, I dove home and saw that the floodwater in the Mulgrave River was under the railway bridge, same as what I had seen before.

This did not concern me, and as I pulled up at the barracks, I saw that the two homeless men, after I spoke to them, had made their way from the tennis court sheds to the railway shed on the opposite side of the line to the barracks.

At the end of this chapter, there are photographs of the traffic and railway bridges, and the Mulgrave River in flood.

Going to bed that night, the rain was falling heavily, and had for hours, same as experienced before, which did not unduly concern me.

Around midnight, however, I woke to a bumping noise that I

thought might be rats from a nearby sugarcane paddock, running along the bearers underneath the lowset building.

Walking out onto the veranda, I was shocked and dismayed by the comical sight of a bandicoot riding a 44-gallon drum, bobbing along like a cork in floodwater.

Instead of it being rats responsible for the noise under the building, it was floodwater lapping underneath the floorboards that woke me from my sleep!

When a *Taipan* slithered from the water onto the veranda, I broke its back with the 8-gauge plain wire, kept handy for that purpose, and its life ended quickly, so that it was no longer a danger to anyone at the barracks.

Killing anything, just because I could do so, is something that I learnt not to do in my teens, unless it was necessary.

The *Taipan*, obviously concerned in the floodwater, was too deadly to have around, as one strike from the snake, meant that the life of the person bitten would be over soon.

Instinctively, I knew that our vehicle at the rear of the barracks would be under water, so I woke Patricia and our niece, Tracey Hansen, with us at the time.

After telling them not to ask questions, we changed quickly from pyjamas into more suitable clothing.

Leaving *Rex* behind to fend for himself, which was heart wrenching, to say the least, we tried walking to safe ground, only for our progress coming to a halt in deep water at a hollow on Moss Road, just before the railway crossing.

At the end of this chapter, there are photographs of Walshs Pyramid, opposite side of the Bruce Highway to the barracks, and another, looking at the barracks from the Gillies Range.

After the water from Little Mulgrave and Goldsborough joined in the Mulgrave River, a wall of water breached the bank near Walshs Pyramid and flowed across the floodplain, barracks in its path, to the other side of the horseshoe bend.

Same as the floodwater flowing through Toowoomba during

2011, that is what I saw coming towards the barracks when I walked out onto the veranda.

Both unable to swim, I carried Tracey on my shoulders, and I held firmly onto Patricia, who was seven months' pregnant with our first son, Mark, as we slowly and cautiously made our way through the floodwater.

Unable to gain a firm footing in the raging floodwater, I realised that what I was trying to do, was too dangerous, so I returned to the barracks.

By that time, the floodwater had risen above the floorboards, so I took Patricia, Tracey, and *Rex* into the kitchen and got them to stand on the table.

Drawing a line on the wall, I proved that the floodwater rose thirty centimetres in fifteen minutes, and again over the same time, it was lapping the top of the kitchen table, seventy-six centimetres above the floorboards.

It was time to make our way to the roof, so I lifted Tracey and *Rex*, out through the kitchen window, onto the roof, but I was unable to do the same with Patricia.

Not expecting help from the homeless men, I moved on during the afternoon from the tennis court sheds, I was extremely grateful when one of the men made his way through the floodwater to help with my predicament.

With help from the homeless man, who held no grudge against me for moving him on from shelter at the tennis court sheds, we soon had Patricia on the roof.

He then swam back to the railway shed where he and the other homeless man took refuge on the roof.

Drenched from head-to-toes, it did not take long for us to shiver from the chilly rain.

So, with only blankets wrapped around us, as protection from the elements, we huddle together on the roof, *Rex* worming his way into the middle.

Slithering onto the roof towards us, I killed another *Taipan* with the 8-gauge plain wire.

When another tried to do the same, I found that I could not kill it in the water. The blows, however, made the snake retreat, and it swam away in search of somewhere else to shelter.

Settling down, a sizzling noise over the side of the building made me investigate.

It was the power box, partially in water, and at every attempt that I made to turn the electricity off, I received a shock, compelling me to stop.

While debatable, an electrician from the local board told me later that if I had turned the power off at the box, more than likely, I would have electrocuted everyone.[8,9]

The floodwater kept rising, and soon the water was lapping the guttering around the roof.

Believing the entire roof could go under, the plan was to drift with the flow of the floodwater to large mango trees, just east of the barracks, keeping both Patricia and Tracey afloat.

It was an impossible task, but I would do my best!

Gary Stroud coming to have a look at the floodwater near Walshs Pyramid was our saviour. He saw me flashing the torch, and after calling out something, he disappeared, giving the impression that he was going for help.

Afterwards, Gary revealed to me that he telephoned the police station and spoke to the colleague involved in the infidelity with the farmer's spouse.

Gary and others became incensed when the colleague told them that it was our choice to live there, and that the police would not do anything until the morning.

It was not the lack of action but what the colleague said to inspire the *Northerner* at Cairns into publishing a sketch of two police officers in a boat, rowing away from two adults, a child, and dog on the barracks' roof.

Considering Ray Whitrod's comments in his memoirs that some police officers sought *revenge for others' refusal to be "yes men,"* there is no doubt in my mind that what the colleague said, and did not do, was *revenge* for refusing to be a *yes man*![6]

When told of the circumstances, because I am who I am, I did what I usually do, and that was to say nothing and distance myself completely from any further discussion.

In other words, I turned myself off, shutting out any further discussion from entering my mind, which others often interpreted as a sign of guilt!

So, despite pleading my innocence, the colleague and others accused me of being the one responsible for the sketch appearing in the *Northerner*!

In fact, I was extremely embarrassed as it was something that I did not do or would ever do!

Displeased with what the colleague said to him, Gary telephoned Stan Baulch, who lived on a sugarcane farm, not too far from the Stroud family.

Shortly after, with an old bond-wood rowboat loaned by another neighbour, Gary and Stan mounted a rescue mission from where the floodwater was on Anderson Road, at the intersection with Moss Road, now known as Pyramid Siding Road.

At the end of this chapter, there is an overhead map, outlining the boat launching location.

What Gary and Stan did that night was extremely courageous and dangerous.

From the roof, it soon became clear that Gary and Stan were not experienced rowers, and my heart sank, each time the boat almost capsized.

When they arrived, the floodwater was over the guttering, covering all but the tip of the roof by the time the flood peaked on the Sunday.

Assuring Gary and Stan that I was an experienced boat rower, assessed by the Brisbane Water Police as *suitable for flood rescue*, found at the end of Chapter 3, they readily handed the oars over to me, and I became the rower.

Rowing the boat to Anderson Road, I kept on the western side of the telephone lines, running parallel to the railway line, just in case the boat capsized.

Without life jackets, I thought that if someone could grab hold of a wire, they might be able to pull themselves along to the safety of a pole.

After seeing Patricia, Tracey, and *Rex* safely on high ground, I accepted responsibility for the two homeless men being on the roof of the railway shed.

When I informed the others that I was going back to rescue them, Stan volunteered to go with me, even though I urged him and the others not to do so.

After rescuing the homeless men, while lifting the boat onto a truck, eaten by termites, a side came away, making the rescue by Gary and Stan more significant and courageous.

Neither Gary nor Stan received any official recognition for their heroic deeds!

Draining two catchments, one at Goldsborough and the other at Little Mulgrave, the Mulgrave River flows south to where it joins with the Russell River at Mutchero Inlet, flowing from there through Russell Heads to the sea.[10,11]

Officially, the records of the Bureau of Meteorology (BOM) show that a total of 578 millimetres of rain fell at Gordonvale for a period of 48 hours to 9 am on Sunday March 13, 1967, with the majority falling over 24 hours to 9 am on Saturday March 12, 1967.[12]

Unofficially, for a period of more than 22 hours from Friday to Saturday morning, Albert Gordon (Gordon) Cotterill of Aloomba emptied a total of 762 millimetres of rainwater from the gauge on his sugarcane farm on Bennett Road, located six kilometres from the barracks.[13]

March 13, 1967 – the floodwater peaked at 17.5 metres, which is the highest on record for the Mulgrave River.[11]

At the end of this chapter, there are two records from the Bureau of Meteorology, confirming that the 1967 flood is the largest ever recorded.

When the floodwater receded, we returned to the barracks and found that our possessions had been either washed away or soiled by the floodwater, leaving us with little to salvage.

After castigating the colleague for what he said to Gary Stroud, Bill Putt arranged flood relief for us, and through him practicing at Gordonvale, the Mason family rallied around and provided us with accommodation in the township.

Others, such as Tom and Jean Simons, became pseudo parents, and the friendship that flourished with their daughter, Adrian, is longstanding.

It was not a good start to our married life, but after accepting alternative accommodation from Thomas (Tom) Bryce, Merchant, of Gordonvale, and with money from the Flood Relief, we paid for our medical needs, bought food and essential clothing, and re-established ourselves once again as a family at Gordonvale.

At the end of this chapter, there is a photograph, taken soon after the flood, of me in uniform.

May 4, 1967 – Mark was born at the Gordonvale Memorial Hospital, mother and son doing well, considering what both went through during the flood.

At the end of this chapter, there is a photograph of Patricia and Mark.

July 30, 1967 – Bill Putt, the sole occupant, died in a single-vehicle traffic accident near Innisfail, leaving behind a widow and three young children.

Even today, his sudden and unexpected demise was extremely hard to understand, as a good man, even though I disagreed with him over the Pizzey matter, departed from this life, far too soon.

Proving how popular he had been, not only as a person, but also as a police officer, residents lined the streets of Townsville when the cortege made its way to the cemetery.

While others carried Bill's coffin from the hearse to the grave, a large contingent of police, particularly from the North and Far

North Queensland, in which I took part, formed an honour guard.

At the graveside, I saw the Masonic fraternity, one by one, throwing red poppies into the grave.

At the end of this chapter, there is a photograph of Bill Putt's funeral at Townsville.

Vale, Bill, it was an honour to know you, albeit only briefly!

Floodwater under the bridge over the Mulgrave River in 1967
(Private Source)

Floodwater lapping the railway bridge in 1967
(Private Source)

Walshs Pyramid
(Private Source)

Barracks on the floodplain of the Mulgrave River
(Private Source)

Rescued by boat from the rooftop of the barracks
(Courtesy of © OpenStreetMap contributors)

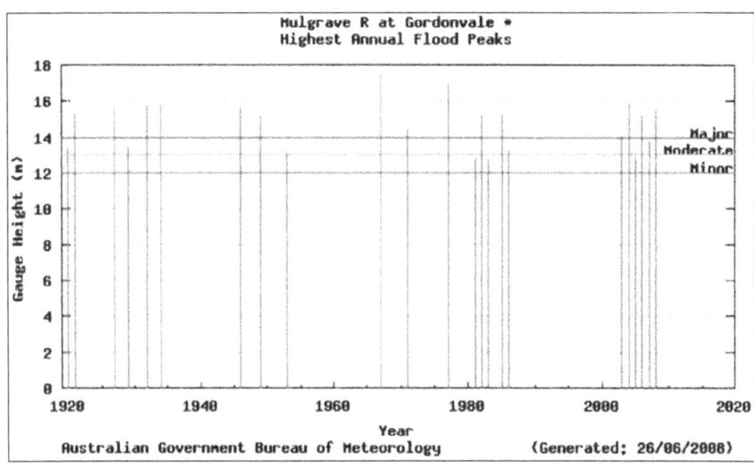

Flood peaks for the Mulgrave River from 1920 to 2008
(Courtesy of Australian Government Bureau of Meteorology)

```
                        Bureau of Meteorology


                        PEAK FLOOD HEIGHTS
                       (Chronological Listing)

Station :  GORDONVALE ALERT                          CBM No : 531051
Stream  :  MULGRAVE RIVER                            AWRC No : 111800
Flood Classifications:  MINOR  12.0  MODERATE  13.0  MAJOR  14.0

Date            Time     Gauge     Site   Data            Data         Obs
                         Height           Source          Type         Site
                         (metres)

21/04/1920      0900     13.44 *    A     DNRM            MANUAL OBS    A
25/03/1921      1100     15.27 *    A     DNRM            MANUAL OBS    A
09/02/1927      0900     15.57 *    A     DNRM            MANUAL OBS    A
25/02/1929      1700     13.44 *    A     DNRM            MANUAL OBS    A
19/01/1932      0600     15.73 *    A     DNRM            MANUAL OBS    A
13/03/1934      0830     15.74 *    A     DNRM            MANUAL OBS    A
02/03/1946      1000     15.70 *    A     DNRM            MANUAL OBS    A
30/03/1949      1615     15.22 *    A     DNRM            MANUAL OBS    A
30/01/1953      1300     13.19 *    A     DNRM            MANUAL OBS    A
   03/1967              17.50       A     OTHER           FLOOD MARK    A
11/03/1971      0900     14.42 *    A     DNRM            MANUAL OBS    A
14/02/1977              17.00       A     OTHER           FLOOD MARK    A
09/01/1981      2030     12.69 *    A     DNRM            MANUAL OBS    A
26/02/1981      1330     12.70 *    A     DNRM            MANUAL OBS    A
26/02/1981      2100     12.84 *    A     DNRM            MANUAL OBS    A
14/04/1982      1800     12.24 *    A     DNRM            MANUAL OBS    A
15/04/1982      0730     15.22 *    A     DNRM            MANUAL OBS    A
15/04/1982      1800     14.64 *    A     LOG SHEET       MANUAL OBS    A
10/03/1983      0930     12.75 *    A     DNRM            MANUAL OBS    A
07/02/1985      0323     12.48 *    A     DNRM            MANUAL OBS    A
07/02/1985      0621     12.69 *    A     DNRM            MANUAL OBS    A
22/03/1985      1737     14.51 *    A     DNRM            MANUAL OBS    A
22/03/1985      1900     15.19 *    A     DNRM            MANUAL OBS    A
22/03/1985      2213     15.24 *    A     DNRM            MANUAL OBS    A
01/02/1986      2150     13.23 *    A     DNRM            MANUAL OBS    A
26/01/2003      1633     14.04       A     LOG SHEET       INSTRUMENT    A
05/02/2004      1250     12.24       A     LOG SHEET       INSTRUMENT    A
06/02/2004      1550     13.14       A     LOG SHEET       INSTRUMENT    A
06/02/2004      1600     13.14       A     LOG SHEET       INSTRUMENT    A
11/02/2004      1410     12.59       A     LOG SHEET       INSTRUMENT    A
15/03/2004      1900     12.44       A     LOG SHEET       INSTRUMENT    A
18/03/2004      1410     13.49       A     LOG SHEET       INSTRUMENT    A
19/03/2004      2235     15.84       A     LOG SHEET       INSTRUMENT    A
19/03/2004      0711     14.49       A     LOG SHEET       INSTRUMENT    A
19/03/2004      0711     14.49       A     LOG SHEET       INSTRUMENT    A
12/03/2005      1521     12.89       A     LOG SHEET       INSTRUMENT    A
20/03/2006      1426     15.19       A     LOG SHEET       INSTRUMENT    A
30/03/2006      2224     12.24       A     LOG SHEET       INSTRUMENT    A
13/04/2006      0930     11.59       A     LOG SHEET       INSTRUMENT    A
05/02/2007      1520     13.79       A     LOG SHEET       INSTRUMENT    A
```

Peak Flood Heights of the Mulgrave River from 1920 to 2007

(Courtesy of Australian Government Bureau of Meteorology)

Author at Gordonvale in 1967
(Private Source)

Patricia and Mark in 1967
(Private Source)

Bill Putt's funeral at Townsville in 1967
Author is at the head of the second row
(Courtesy of Queensland Police Union of Employees)

5

WALL OF SILENCE

Bill Putt's replacement was Sergeant First Class Ronald George (Ron) Morrisson. After 26 years' experience in the CIB, it appears that Frank Bischof transferred Ron back to general duties for arresting one of Bischof's mates, which sounded credible to me. A devout Catholic, Ron despised the Masonic fraternity, as not only was Bischof a Mason, but his replacement, Norwin William (Norm) Bauer, also belong to the fraternity. That hatred for the Masonic Lodge had an impact on my service at Gordonvale.

Ron arrived at Gordonvale with no knowledge of General Duties and Administration. However, the experience Ron passed on to subordinates in Criminal Investigations, brought about a remarkable improvement in the clear-up rate for crime, which the community appreciated.

I certainly appreciated Ron passing on that experience to me, as the thought of becoming a criminal investigator had entered my mind, which was due to the Cairns CIB, before Ron's arrival, taking credit for criminal offence arrests at Gordonvale.

For instance, together with another constable, possibly Barry Joseph Vincent (Barry) Downs, we saw a stranger with a suitcase, leaving a house on the outskirts of Gordonvale.

Stopping the stranger as he walked along the Bruce Highway, dragging the suitcase behind him, he supplied unsatisfactory answers to questions, and when asked to open the suitcase, admitted the property did not belong to him.

It was a straightforward offence of breaking, entering, and stealing, but we had to request the attendance of the Cairns CIB, who took over, and we gained no experience, other than how to detect offences.

Soon, Ron had everyone at Gordonvale taking Records of Interview and charging offenders with most criminal offences that angered the Cairns CIB.

In early 1968, I took a bold step and began correspondence and open-learning studies to educate myself to *Senior level*, completed a course in *Fundamentals of Information Processing*, and eventually awarded a *Certificate in Police Studies*, and *Batchelor of Community Welfare* degree by 1995.[1,2]

When asked if he would make up the crew, Ron rostered himself off on a weekday to go fishing, leaving me alone to deal with counter inquiries and duty away from the police station.

Everything was flowing smoothly, until the sounding of the siren at the QATB centre, followed by another at the Fire Brigade, alerted me that something serious had happened.

It turned out to be a horrific traffic accident at the intersection of the Bruce Highway and Gillies Range Road!

Arriving at the scene, I found that a large semi-trailer, driven in a northerly direction on the Bruce Highway towards Cairns, had crashed into and was on top of a utility, heading in a westerly direction along the Gillies Range Road.

At first, a column of burning fuel, snaking its way from the semi-trailer towards the fuel pumps of a nearby service station, was the focus of my attention.

The Fire Brigade was attending to that threat, so I went to the other side of the semi-trailer and saw that those in attendance had removed a severely injured male passenger from the burning utility, mostly under the semi-trailer.

While trying to free the male driver, bursts of burning fuel forced everyone, repeatedly, to retreat to safety, and eventually it was impossible to go near the cabin, until the Fire Brigade was able to extinguish the fire.

Later, a reassurance to me, but of little comfort to those who knew the driver, the post-mortem revealed that he died instantly in the collision.

On his way home from fishing, "What have you done, Neil," were the first words uttered by Ron, prompting me to think, "Not a bloody thing, except the best that I could."

About this time, as requested by me, two members from the traffic branch at Cairns took over traffic control, freeing me up to begin the investigation.

Returning to the scene, Ron and I took statements from witnesses and the semi-trail driver, employed by a large transport company in Brisbane.

Weighing up the evidence, Ron charged the semi-trailer driver with dangerous driving causing death, and I was the corroborating officer.

Frank Bischof, however, instructed that police were to offer no evidence when the charge came before the court, and the charge was withdrawn.

Incensed by this, Magistrate Cedric Smith said from the Bench, in the presence of the solicitor acting for the semi-trailer driver, that he would commit the driver for trial at the inquest.

The legal team defending the driver were much smarter and arranged for the inquest to open in Brisbane, which is where the driver appeared and declined to give evidence.

The magistrate, therefore, could not compel the driver to attend the hearing adjourned to Gordonvale, waylaying the openly stated intentions, as the magistrate had no authority to commit without the driver being present.

Blame of seventy-five per cent was apportioned to the driver of the semi-trailer at a civil hearing for damages brought on by the passenger in the utility.

Ron's nemesis had another win, typical of what it was like during the *Joke*!

When scrutinised, Bischof *took leave suddenly on 13 February 1969* and was later *boarded out of the force on medical grounds*.[3]

Another son, Christopher, was born at the Gordonvale Memorial Hospital.

When the former house of the Officer in Charge became available for a constable to occupy, reluctantly, Ron recommended that I should occupy the house.

Ron's choice was the Constable replacing the colleague involved in the extramarital affair, who lost respect and transferred out of Gordonvale.

At the end of this chapter, there is a photograph of the residence in the yard adjoining the joint police station, courthouse, and clerk of the court building.

Unsuitable for a large family, Ron exchanged the house for a residence with more rooms, occupied previously by the Constable involved in the extramarital affair.

Already a loner in the policing family at Gordonvale, studies undertaken to improve my education, distanced me further from my colleagues, and away from work, I was committed to the CMF, playing rugby league for Souths, and raising two young sons with Patricia.

As much as possible, I spent time away from Gordonvale with my young family, touring the Atherton Tablelands, or swimming at the magnificent beaches north of Cairns.

At the end of this chapter, there is a photograph of me with Mark and Christopher, enjoying a family outing on a beach.

Exploring the Atherton Tablelands thereafter, I got the urge and began driving towards Croydon, around five hundred kilometres by road from Gordonvale.[4]

"It is not far to Croydon," a female voice said, but I knew that it was, as the drive to and from the town was too much to do in one day, so I turned around halfway at Mount Surprise, and went back to Gordonvale.

It so happened that a maternal great-great-grandmother, Maria Clements, formerly Warr, went missing in 1877 from the family at Mackay, soon after the birth of her ninth child, and had no further contact with the family.

"Hey, Uncle Neil, could this be our ancestor," queried and excited niece, one hundred and thirty-eight years later.

And, sure enough, it was!

Adding an 'n' to her given name, Maria became Marian, a small town, west from Mackay, and using her maiden surname, spelt Ward sometimes back in England, my great-great-grandmother became known as Marian Ward.[5]

This was the name provided by Charles James Noland, who was much younger than Maria, of their alleged marriage in 1877 at Bathurst in New South Wales.[6]

It is difficult to understand, but easier to be judgemental, as to how my great-great-grandmother could leave the children behind at Mackay, never to see them again!

That being so, I will confine what one needs to say, to what happened.

After leaving Mackay, the couple went to Bathurst in New South Wales where allegedly they were married, but there is no record, to that effect.[5,6]

From Bathurst, they made their way back into Queensland to the goldfields of Croydon where Marian became a laundress, and Charles worked as a carrier.[5,6]

Also known as Marion Parker Noland in the Electoral Roll, I assume that my great-great-grandmother missed her family and left clues for someone to discover what became of her.[7]

December 19, 1909 – Marian Noland passed away at Croydon, and the names of her parents were provided in the death record as Robert Ward and Mary Ann Parker, which was correct, except that Ward should have been Warr.[5]

February 13, 1912 – Charles James Noland passed away at Croydon.[6]

Once lost but now found, knowledge of which has passed on to others, I would like to believe that it was Marian, urging me to come to Croydon!

Extrasensory perception (ESP), which is *a claimed paranormal ability pertaining to reception of information not gained through the recognized physical senses, but sensed with the mind*, is common in the family.[8]

Obviously, the ability to *sense with the mind* that I have is, in fact, heightened by *autism*.[9]

Allowed to do so by Magistrate Cedric Smith, "What colour is my car," questioned the defendant, issued with a notice for driving with a defective muffler.

"Look out the door," said the voice, comforting me at the Police Depot, "and there it is!"

"Red," I responded, and after looking to the Heavens, and throwing his arms into the air, an exasperated defendant resumed his seat.

When I intercepted the defendant's vehicle, it was at night on the Bruce Highway at a location where there were no lights, and neither was there a moon.

I had forgotten the colour, but I knew the make and type, and when I saw the red-coloured vehicle parked at the front of the courtroom, I knew it belonged to the defendant.

"What did I tell you about watching your back," the voice said sternly, which was after I arrested a driver for unlawful use of a motor vehicle on the Bruce Highway at Deeral.

Responding to information from Babinda police, who could not keep up with the speeding vehicle, I intercepted it at Deeral, and took the driver into custody.

Others were in the stolen vehicle, and while putting the driver into the rear seat of the police vehicle, they came at me, and when I looked in their direction, the driver sized the opportunity and punched the back of my head.

Arriving around this time, the Babinda police quickly took the others into custody.

From there on, I heeded the advice to watch my back, particularly when I worked alone.

When other wives saw us returning from those trips over the Atherton Tablelands, or swimming on the northern beaches of Cairns, colleagues accused me of intentionally making things difficult for them with their wives.

Rather than say anything, I withdrew further away from those colleagues, gravitating instead to others, such as Alan Schwenke, whom I helped restore a 17-foot bond-wood boat, which I named later as the *Yellow Submarine*.[10]

Apart from Gordon Cotterill, another acquaintance was Raymond Frederick (Ray) Morris, sugarcane farmer of Dalton Road, Aloomba, who allowed me, same as Gordon, to enhance my experience as a farm worker, albeit unpaid, just in case I decided the police force was not a long-term direction in life that I should follow.

I looked upon Alan as an older brother, but Gordon and Ray were like fathers to me.

After Alan and I sanded back the bond-wood boat, we fibre-glassed the bottom, painting it and the sides white, and yellow for the half-cabin.

Proud of our achievement, we took our families and launched the boat in the Trinity Inlet at Cairns.

Suddenly, the boat became lopsided when it started filling up with water.

Quickly realizing we had not inserted the bung, Alan gunned the motor, and soon the boat was planing on the surface, water draining out through the bung hole.

When Alan cut the motor, I reached over the side at the rear and inserted the bung.

Those in the boat never forgot that outing!

On our first trip to Michaelmas Reef off Cairns, after spending more time under rather than riding over the waves, I named the boat the *Yellow Submarine*, based on a song of the same name sung by *The Beatles*.[10]

Under Ron Morrisson's supervision, apart from discovering that I had a flair for clerical work, keeping records, and doing returns, I confidently investigated crime, so much so that I started applying for plain clothes' positions in the CIB.

Just before Christmas of 1968, I was on patrol at night when instructed by the radio operator at Cairns that Ron wanted to see me at the police station.

After instructing that I was to take him to the Mountain View Hotel, "I will show you how things are done in the Branch," Ron declared, as if to make a point about something with me.

Walking into the public bar, "What'll it be, gents," asked the publican.

"Nothing for me," I responded, "I'm driving!"

In fact, I was never a drinker, as I discovered early that my mind and body had to be right for a drinking session, as one day everything might be all right, and the next, I could become violently ill after one glass.

A beer with Hops rather than Chemicals is what I preferred, but even then, everything had to be right in mind and body to have a drinking session.

The Meneguzzo family at Red Hill introduced me to red wine, and that is my preferred choice, but no more than one or two glasses at a time.

After asking for the keys, Ron pushed them towards the publican, "We have looked after you all year," said Ron, "so put a couple of cartons in the boot!"

Speaking quietly, while the publican was away, "Don't include me in that," was my response. "I don't want any part in what you are doing!"

Returning to the public bar, the publican placed the keys on the bar in front of me.

Back at the police station, I refused to have anything to do with the cartons of beer, allegedly in the boot, nor did I see anything removed, or distributed to others.

Later, when I asked if anything had been said about the applications furnished for positions in the CIB, "I don't believe you will cope with the rigours of the drinking and other things that go on in the Branch, so I wouldn't hold my breath waiting," Ron said, bringing the discussion to an end.

I was disappointed, naturally, and rather than it being improper conduct and behaviour that I saw at the Mountain View Hotel, it appears to have been a test, quite possibly set up with the publican, that I failed.

And that is how it was in those times of the corruption known as the *Joke*, colleagues encouraging you to be involved, and others evaluating you.

When it got so bad, mostly everyone carried a micro-cassette tape recorder to record conversations had with others just in case something came out of those discussions.

Success of Ron's mentoring in criminal investigations, resulted in Bischof's replacement, Commissioner Norm Bauer, commended Barry Downs for his *alertness, initiative, and devotion to duty* on June 3, 1969, for clearing up, if my memory serves me correct, something like forty-six criminal offences.[11]

Around this time, for reasons not then clear, my relationship with Ron and other colleagues at Gordonvale became very strained, and they barely spoke to me.

When told for the umpteenth time by Ron that I had to decide whether I wanted to be a police officer or soldier, I resigned from the CMF on December 7, 1969.[12]

Before resigning, however, I attended an alternative two-week training camp with the 31st Battalion in the Seaview Range, near Ingham.[12,13]

This was after Ron refused to recommend leave to attend a camp with my infantry platoon in the 51st Battalion at Wondecla on the Atherton Tablelands.[12,14,15]

Arriving at the camp, the Commanding Officer (CO) selected me as the enemy during a four-day war-games exercise and provided me with training of how to mount and repel from a helicopter into a small opening in the canopy of the rainforest on Seaview Range.

Dressed in black pyjamas, Coolie hat, and carrying a sugarbag of supplies, weapons loaded with blanks, along with three others acting as the enemy, I boarded the helicopter.

At the end of this chapter, there is a photograph of the same helicopter used by soldiers from 7th Battalion, Royal Australian Regiment (7 RAR).

Skimming across the canopy, with the landing gear brushing the rainforest, producing a large, long-bladed knife, "This will be used to cut your rope, if you get hung up," said the pilot, his offsider nodding in agreement.

Having returned recently from a tour of duty in Vietnam, the warning of the veterans was serious and necessary.

The warning evermore in our minds, the four of us made our way down the rope from the landing skids, through the opening in the canopy, safely to the ground.

After giving the thumbs up, the pilot returned to the camp and came back with three others acting as the enemy, as well as an umpire, safely seeing them also to the ground.

Over the next three days, I used a compass and map, as well as I backed up as the radio operator, when the seven-make-believe enemy, watched over by an umpire, made their way through the dense rainforest.

After ambushing the pursuers during the day, and attacking the weary soldiers at night, the umpire on the fourth day ordered us to lay down our arms and be captured.

Shortly after the camp, while on a day shift back at the police station, "Come out onto the veranda, Neil," said Ron. "There is someone I want you to meet!"

Out on the veranda, Ron introduced me to a representative from the AWU at Cairns, who said, words to the effect, "A complaint has been made about you working on farms at Aloomba, which has to stop, is that clear?"

Looking at Ron, it became clear that he had something to do with the complaint, so I questioned, "Can you tell me who made the complaint?"

"I am not at liberty to say," replied the representative.

"Are you aware that I am not being paid for the work?"

"That does not matter. What I am concerned about, is that you are doing someone out of a job, which must cease?"

Suspecting a setup arranged by Ron, I gave an assurance that I would follow the request, never to work again on any farm at Gordonvale.

Before I had time to say anything to Gordon, word had filtered out to him, ending what I enjoyed doing in my spare time, but our friendship continued.

What happened, was malicious, as a colleague, Neil Healey, who was the brother-in-law of Ray Hickling, often worked on the Hickling's farm, not much further along Bennett Road from the Cotterill's farm, and another colleague from Gordonvale took over from me on Gordon's farm!

That is when the *wall-of-silence* began, involving all colleagues at Gordonvale.[16]

At night, from Monday to Thursday, as well as a day shift on Sunday, I worked alone, and when I was rostered a shift with colleagues, either a Friday or Saturday night, if they did not wish to talk, other than during some official duty, so be it, was the stance that I adopted.

I did consult my good friend, Alan Schwenke, who heard about the *wall-of-silence* rumour, through his work as a taxi driver, and Alan persuaded me not to resign.[16]

When they heard, Gordon Cotterill and Ray Morris also offered similar advice, eventually inviting me to join the Masonic Pyramid Highleigh Lodge No. 161 at Gordonvale.[17]

William Bryce (Bill) and June Winfield also gave Patricia employment at their Electrical store in Gordonvale.

That backing and support from the community enabled us to weather the storm, whipped up by Ron Morrisson, same as what he claimed Bischof had done to him.

Over time, however, a more serious reason for the *wall-of-silence* would appear, resulting in colleagues calling me a *dog*, identified during the later *Fitzgerald Inquiry* as a slang word used by police officers for a colleague who *dobbed* on others, bringing my time at Gordonvale to an end.[16,18,19]

During 1969, the printed Volumes 1 and 2 of the Queensland Policeman's Manual were provided to police officers. I became conversant with the contents of those manuals.[20]

How to conduct a coronial investigation into a plane accident, which I read intently for everyday duties and an examination to qualify for the next rank, prepared me for what happen the following year on Bell Peak North.[20]

Three years earlier, Sergeant Second Class Colin Ward and Constable Colin Tapsall of the Radio Maintenance Section, Cairns Police Station, installed the first police owned Ultra High Frequency (UHF) radio linking system from Saddle Mountain, near Kuranda, to the Cairns Regional Airport.[20]

Before then, the QPF relied on the Department of Civil Aviation (DCA) at the Cairns Regional Airport.

When I arrived in 1966 at Gordonvale, the DCA were spitefully carrying on with a vendetta over QPF installing its own UHF radio linking system on Saddle Mountain, which was still raging, four years later.

Author's police residence at Gordonvale in 1970
(Private Source)

Author, Christopher, and Mark at Cairns in 1969
(Private Source)

The 7 RAR mounting a US Bell UH-1 Iroquois helicopter in 1967
(Courtesy of Australian War Memorial, ID EKT/67/0036/VN)

6

FATAL FLIGHT

January 28, 1970 – a twin-engine Cessna 402 plane piloted by Patrick John Hill and his passenger, Stewart Rutherford Drummond, lost their lives when the plane crashed into Bell Peak North on the Malbon Thompson Range, extending along the coastline from Yarrabah, near Cairns, south of Aloomba to Russell Heads.[1]

Stepping back into time, Patrick Hill served as a pilot in No. 43 (Fighter) Squadron of the Royal Air Force (RAF) in England.[2]

On March 1, 1963, No. 43 (Fighter) Squadron moved from the RAF base at Nicosia, Cyprus, to Khormaksar, Aden, as part of the Middle East Command (MEC).[2]

At Aden, Nancy McArthur, who is in the photograph at the end of this chapter, met and became friendly with Patrick Hill.[2,3]

Moreover, thanks to Nancy's daughter, Joanne Thomson, who sent me the photograph and gave permission for publishing of the photograph in this book, I was able to recognize, so many years later, which of the remains found at the crash site on Bell Peak North was that of Patrick Hill.[3]

Having *eidetic memory* capabilities, the image of Patrick Hill in the photograph is consistent with the remains that I saw near the main fuselage of the aircraft, and I can confirm that he died instantly and peacefully.

After leaving the RAF, like so many others, Patrick Hill came to Australia, hoping to secure a position with Qantas Airways, or another airline, and was close to achieving that goal.[2]

At the time, Patrick Hill, 29 years of age, was living at 51 Douglas Haig Street, Oatley, Sydney, New South Wales, while Stewart Drummond lived at 6 Wakeford Road, Strathfield, Sydney.[1,4]

The plane flown by Hill was a twin-engine Cessna 402 bearing registration number VH-RIZ of which there is a photograph of a similar aircraft at the end of this chapter.[1]

Hawker De Havilland (Australia) Pty Ltd of Sydney owned the aircraft, class of operation being private, which was on a delivery flight to Cairns.[1]

Evidence, to that effect, appeared in a report published by *The Cairns Post*, as follows:

The plane is a Cessna 402 believed to be owned by Hawker de Havilland Company in Sydney. Two company representatives were flying the plane to Cairns for a customer's inspection.[5]

Patrick Hill held a current Senior Commercial Pilot Licence, endorsed for the Cessna 402 plane, and was the holder of a Class One Instrument Rating, valid for multi-engine planes, renewed after a test flight on January 22, 1970.[1]

Hill's flying experience amounted to 2325 hours of which twenty-one was in a Cessna 402 aircraft, as well as he had 130 hours of instrument and 63 hours of night flying, confirming that Hill was, in fact, an experienced pilot.[1]

The flying of the plane was under a certificate of airworthiness, suspended before the flight under the terms of Air Navigation Regulation 34(1).[1]

Certain mandatory inspections, modifications, and overhaul of components not being in the plane maintenance records were behind the reason for the suspension.[1]

According to the DCA, the irregularities in the Maintenance Release did not in any way contribute to the accident.[1]

The DCA also concluded that the gross weight of the plane, and the position of the centre of gravity, were within the specified limits throughout the flight.[1]

It was abundantly clear that Patrick Hill was an experienced pilot, more than capable of flying the twin-engine Cessna 402 at night.

Under the applicable Instrument Flight Rules, the aircraft departed in the early afternoon from Bankstown, a south-western suburb of Sydney, proceeding north to Brisbane and then on to Mackay.[1]

At Mackay, Patrick Hill supplied a further flight plan for the sector, from Mackay to Cairns, indicating that he would continue operating to the Instrument Flight Rules, cruising at an altitude of ten thousand feet.[1]

Hill received approval for the flight to follow the normal route over Townsville and Dunk Island, and he entered the lowest safe altitude for each leg on the flight plan.[1]

Apart from the necessary radio communication frequencies for the route, in addition to the endorsement of his Instrument Rating, the navigation aids Hill nominated included the Automatic Direction Finder (ADF), VHF Omni Range, and Instrument Landing System installed in the plane.[1]

Hill, however, did not nominate the Distance Measuring Equipment (DME) fitted in the plane, which is radio navigation technology that measures the slant range (distance) between a plane and a ground station, as his Instrument Rating for the DME was not valid.[1,6]

7.49 pm – after leaving Mackay, the plane went on to Cairns under the flight plan supplied by Hill.[1]

9.18 pm – Hill made first contact with the Control Tower at the Cairns Regional Airport, reporting that the plane was over Dunk Island at ten thousand feet altitude.[1]

At the end of this chapter, there is an overhead image of Dunk Island to Cairns, and a line drawn between the two locations, which no one should interpret as the exact route taken by the plane.

Expecting to arrive around 9.43 pm at Cairns, Hill requested permission to begin his descent from ten thousand feet at 9.25 pm, at which time he anticipated that the aircraft would be approximately fifty miles from Cairns.[1]

At the time, one Air Traffic Controller working alone looked after the separate functions of area control, approach control, and aerodrome control at the Cairns Regional Airport.[1]

At the end of this chapter, there is a photograph of the Control Tower in 1970 at the airport.

The Cairns controller, after instructing Hill to make a visual approach starting at 9.25 pm, passed on the altimeter setting of 1009 millibars and requested Hill to contact the Control Tower when thirty miles from Cairns.[1]

The weather near Bell Peak North, and at Cairns, fifteen miles to the north-west of the peak, *was fine with 2/8 of cloud at 2500 feet and 2/8 of cloud at 4000 feet*, and the wind *was calm and the observed visibility at Cairns was 26 miles*.[1]

9.23 pm – despite his Instrument Rating not being valid for the DME, Hill called Cairns and asked if the DME was working, and the Cairns controller told Hill that it was.[1,6]

9.25 pm – Hill responded to the request of the Cairns controller and said that the plane was leaving ten thousand feet, asking also for the weather conditions at the airpot.[1]

The controller responded, "Two eighths of cloud, base two, five, zero, zero, and two eighths at four thousand, the wind calm, QNH one, zero, zero, nine," which was acknowledged by Hill.[1]

9.35 pm – when Hill did not respond at thirty miles from the Cairns Airport, the controller called the plane and requested its present position.[1]

Responding to the controller, Hill said the plane was seventeen miles south of the Cairns airport, and he was descending through the three thousand and five hundred feet level.[1]

Subsequently, the DCA found that by *clearing the* [plane] *to commence a visual approach while it was still at a distance in excess of* [thirty miles] *from the destination aerodrome, the Air Traffic Controller did not comply with the prescribed operating instructions*.[1]

In fact, the plane was not far off and was descending from the south on a collision course with Bell Peak North, which is the highest point at three thousand, three hundred and sixty-six feet on the Malbon Thompson Range.[7]

At the end of this chapter, there is a photograph showing the location of Gordon Cotterill's farm to Bell Peak North.

After instructing Hill to report at ten miles from the Cairns airport, the controller told Hill to expect the use of Runway 15 upon his arrival.[1]

Hill apologised for not calling at thirty miles, which was the last transmission heard from the plane.[1]

9.35 pm – just after the Cairns controller last heard from Hill, father and son, Norman Charles (Norman) Hickling and Raymond Charles (Ray) Hickling, sugarcane farmers on Bennett Road at Aloomba, heard what sounded like a plane's engine and crashing timber on the Malbon Thompson Range.[4]

The Hickling's farm was further along Bennet Road towards Bell Peak North than Gordon Cotterill's farm.

Agreeing that they heard a plane's engine followed by the sound of crashing timber and then silence, Norman and Ray estimated the sound came from Bell Peak North.[4]

9.37 pm – I was at the Gordonvale Police Station when Ray Hickling, puffing loudly, reported that he and his father heard a plane crashing into the rainforest near Bell Peak North on the Malbon Thompson Range.

It was a chance happening, Norman and Ray being in the right place at the right time, something that I experienced often during my policing career.

9.39 pm – I telephoned and told the Cairns controller that a resident of Aloomba heard a plane crashing into the rainforest near Bell Peak North on the Malbon Thompson Range.[1,4]

Cessna 402 VH-RIZ being the only plane in his area at the time, the Cairns controller repeatedly called the plane and received no response.[1]

When the Cairns controller told me that no response was received, I agreed with the Cairns controller that the plane, more than likely, had crashed near Bell Peak North on the Malbon Thompson Range.[1]

Worthy of note, the QPF, and not the DCA or a member of the community, then or now, has the authority to instigate a Search and Recovery mission.

After contacting me, because he held a private pilot's licence and was known at the airport, Ray Hickling did what he should not have done and telephoned the Cairns controller.[8]

Ray then had a telephone conversation with Don Annat, Officer in Charge of the Cairns Regional Airport.[8]

This is where the pending Search and Recovery mission went off the rails, as Ray Hickling had no authority to circumvent what the police force was doing, assisting the coroner in what might be a fatal aircraft accident`.

Responding to my telephone call to his residence on the police reserve, Ron Morrisson came to the police station, and I provided him with a briefing.

After alerting Inspector Herb Hore at Cairns, together with Superintendent Keith Howarth of the Queensland Ambulance Transport Brigade (QATB) at Gordonvale, Ron went to Aloomba and spoke to Ray and Norman Hickling, leaving me at the police station to answer the telephone.[8]

Based on Ron's feedback, I supplied the information reported in *The Cairns Post*, as follows:

> *Police said last night that it was not known whether the plane crashed on the eastern or western side of Aloomba, but that in either case, the country was rugged and covered with heavy scrub, which would seriously hamper any night-time search.*[5]

Arriving back at the police station, I gave Ron an update from the Cairns controller that a plane approaching from the south did not see anything, such as a fire, to indicate a crash site.

This information was provided to the media and reported in *The Cairns Post*, as follows:

> *The plane evidently did not burst into flames, as searchers reported no sign of fire in the area.*[5]

It was too treacherous for a search party to enter the rainforest at night, and not knowing exactly where the plane had crashed, Herb Hore instructed that a search would not begin until first light in the morning.

Suspecting that the plane crashed near Bell Peak North, Herb Hore selected the house on Ray Morris' farm at Aloomba as the base for the Search and Recovery mission, as there was an established track up along Campbell Creek to the summit.

Everything was flowing smoothly, except for the discussion going on between Ray Hickling, Don Annat, and possibly John Cassidy from the DCA.

Despite being personally known and had worked on Ray Morris' farm, and with a wealth of bush experience, Ron Morrisson excluded me from taking part in the Search and Recovery mission, and he instructed me to remain at the police station when I started rostered duty at 8.00 am the following morning.

Nancy McArthur and Patrick Hill at Aden
(Courtesy of Joanne Fletcher)

Cessna 402 aircraft on the tarmac of Cairns Airport in 1970
(Private Source)

Dunk Island to Cairns Regional Airport
(Courtesy of © OpenStreetMap contributors)

Runway of Cairns Regional Airport in 1970
Taken from the Kuranda Range
(Private Source)

Control tower at the Cairns Regional Airport in 1970
(Private Source)

Valley between the Malbon Thompson and Bellenden Ker ranges
Taken on Gordon Cotterill's farm
(Private Source)

Bell Peak North from Cotterill's farm at Aloomba in 1969
Gordon Cotterill is standing on the engine of the tractor
(Private Source)

7

SEARCH AND RECOVERY

January 29, 1970 – which was the first day of the Search and Recovery mission, Herb Hore, Ron Morrisson, and Barry Downs went at first light to set up the base on Ray Morris' farm. At the same time, Captain Colin Sheddon of the Bush Pilots' Airways, together with a police officer acting as a *spotter* in the plane, set out from the Cairns Airport to conduct an aerial search.[1,2]

Others who assemble at the base set up on Ray Morris' farm, included:

> *Keith Howarth, Bearer Bob Wallace, Honorary Bearer Frank Steene (QATB); Keith Walker, Ted Hughes (CDO); Joan Starr (The Cairns Post), and about eight locals, mostly sugarcane farmers.*[2,3]

According to Ray Morris, the Civil Defence Organisation (CDO) was the first to orchestrate a *power struggle* with QPF over command and control of the mission.

6.30 am – Colin Sheddon told the Cairns controller that he saw the missing plane at three thousand, two hundred and seventy feet on the Aloomba side of Bell Peak North, and about one hundred feet from the summit.[1,2,3,4]

Sheddon saw wreckage strewn across a hiking track, but he did not see any sign of life to suggest that the occupants survived the crash.[1,2,3]

After the Cairns controller passed that confirmed sighting on to the Cairns Police Station, the radio operator relayed the information to Ron Morrisson, then at the base on Ray Morris' farm.

In a photograph at the end of this chapter, Ron Morrisson is examining a map, obviously looking at the route up along Campbell Creek, while others were looking at where the plane had crashed near the summit of Bell Peak North.

An experienced criminal investigator, who conducted searches, the next step for Ron would have been to organize and equip a search party of physically fit persons to scale the mountain and recover the injured or deceased persons.

If not available at the Cairns Police Station, after Herb Hore made the declaration, there is no doubt in my mind that the competent Radio Maintenance Section at Cairns Police Station would have secured suitable radios for use at the base on Ray Morris' farm and another for the search party.

Apart from myself, a trained and experienced signaller in the CMF, evidence of which is at the end of Chapter 3, there also were others at the Cairns Police Station, similarly trained, as well as the main means of communication for police throughout Queensland was then by radio.

Moreover, during the floods in the Cairns district, three years earlier, the QPF organize *boat and helicopter rescues ... for stranded families* on a much larger scale than the Search and Recovery mission on Bell Peak North.[5]

So, what was about to unfold, did not have anything to do with QPF lacking training and experience for the Search and Recovery mission.

Furthermore, when a disaster exceeded the State's resources, which happened with the floods, three years earlier, assistance came from the Federal Government, such as the deployment of Iroquois helicopters reported in the *RAAF News*, as follows:

> *An Iroquois helicopter was flown from Canberra to Cairns in a Hercules to help in flood relief in North Queensland. Another helicopter was diverted to Cairns from the Rockhampton area, while two more flew from Fairbairn to Amberley where they remained on stand-by in case the flood position worsened. The Iroquois carried out many rescue missions and ferried supplies to the flood-bound Queenslanders.*[6]

At the end of this chapter, there is a photograph of the loading of an Iroquois helicopter into the Hercules for delivery to Cairns, and of another unloading supplies for the flood-bound communities in the Far North.[6]

That cooperation was open to the State Government if the Search and Recovery mission ran into a problem, requiring assistance from the Federal Government.

So, while the QPF, under the command and control of Herb Hore from Cairns, was organizing a Search and Recovery mission for the plane accident on Bell Peak North, the DCA had a meeting with Ray Hickling at his house on the Hickling's farm, thereby changing the course of the mission.[3,7]

Ray Hickling remembered the clandestine meeting at his house with the DCA, as follows:

At first light, Don Annat and John Cassidy were at my place with a radio to communicate with the search aircraft and set up a base. Don was officer in charge at Cairns Airport. John was in charge of administration at Cairns. They were both very competent in air search procedure. Fortunately, Keith Howarth did what should have done the night before. He contacted Kevin Murgatroyd who in turn contacted Alan Broughton.[7]

There is no doubt in my mind that when it came to the actual Search and Recovery mission, Don Annat and John Cassidy were both incompetent and reckless.

Now that I know more, both Don Annat and John Cassidy continued with the vindictive spitefulness that developed in 1966 when the QPF installed its own UHF radio linking system on Saddle Mountain.[8]

Instead of provide support, the DCA, obviously with authority from Brisbane or Canberra, took over command and control of the mission from QPF.

When the DCA took over command and control of the mission from QPF, Herb Hore returned to Cairns, and Ron Morrisson took a back seat during the entire operation.

Not only did the DCA take over the mission, but the DCA also moved the base from Ray Morris' farm to Thomason's farm at Highleigh.

Ray Hickling remembered how the DCA took over the mission from the QPF, and establishing of the base on Thomason's farm, as follows:

> *Personnel from the Department of Civil Aviation, who were based at Cairns, set up a communications base at Thomason's farm. We referred to this as Highleigh Base. John Cassidy, from DCA at the Cairns Airport, was in charge at Highleigh base. John was a very capable organiser. He was confronted with unforeseen setbacks but responded promptly with an alternative plan. Also involved from DCA was Don Annat, also a very capable organiser. Their experience in search and rescue was evident. Inspector Hoare from the Cairns Police was officially in charge overall.*[3]

Therein is the evidence from Ray Hickling that the DCA took over command and control from QPF, and that the DCA relocated the base from Ray Morris' farm at Aloomba to Jim and Reta Thomason's farm at Highleigh.

At the end of this chapter, there is a map outlining the location of the Hickling, Morris, and Thomason farms, and rough routes from the Morris and Thomason farms to Bell Peak North.

Ray Hickling remembered the catalyst for relocating the base, as follows:

> *Fortunately, the then Ambulance Superintendent at Gordonvale, Keith Howarth, contacted a local bushwalker, Alan Broughton, who advised that the Campbell Creek route was extremely difficult. His advice was to climb the ridge which started at Thomason's farm.*[3]

Ray Hickling, Alan Broughton, and Kevin Murgatroyd added to that assumption, as follows:

> *Whilst Alan and Kevin were talking, Keith Howarth, the Ambulance Superintendent, drove into Kevin's place and acquainted him with the details. He was told that a party was at Ray Morris' farm and was going to the top via Campbell Creek.*

Kevin knew from personal experience (having been some distance above the falls on the creek), and from earlier discussions with another bushwalker, that this route was impenetrable.[9]

8.30 am – oblivious of the schemozzle going on away from the police station, I was surprised when the radio operator at the Cairns Police Station advised that I was to take part in the mission.

The instruction was for me to also collect the three schoolteacher bushwalkers, Alan Broughton, Peter Bell, and Kevin Murgatroyd, and convey them to the base on Thomason's farm.[3]

Going to the police residence where I lived in the adjoining yard, after packing a compass, some leftover army rations, and water in an army backpack, sufficient for one day, I said good-bye to Patricia and our sons, Mark, and Christopher, and told them I would be back later that day.

At the end of this chapter, there is a photograph of the joint building for the police station, courthouse, and clerk of the court at Gordonvale, as well as photographs of the police residence where I lived in the adjoining yard, and the Mulgrave Sugar Mill.

Putting things into perspective, from the footpath of the police station, Bell Peak North is visible behind the stack of the Mulgrave Sugar Mill.

Typical of the lack of cooperation that day with QPF, I went on a wild-goose chase, as the schoolteacher bushwalkers had already made their way to Thomason's farm.[3]

8.30 am – arriving on Thomason's farm, I was shocked and dismayed to see children and extremely unfit persons setting off with the Search and Recovery party on the climb up the ridge to the summit of Bell Peak North.

I questioned Ron Morrisson about the briefing, which should have happened before the party set out on the climb, and when Ron ignored me, I assumed that his silence was a consequence of the *wall-of-silence.*[10]

Drafted into the party at the last minute, I was completely in the dark from the beginning of the climb, as to what we were doing, as well as my role in the mission.

Then, instead of leading from the front, I saw Ron Morrisson lagging at the rear.

Ray Hickling remembered that the DCA provided him with a radio and placed him in charge of the mission, as follows:

As I had a flight radio operator's license, I was issued with a portable VHF radio ... Because I operated the two-way radio, I found myself advising the group of what we were to do next.[3]

Let me make it clear, under no circumstance did Ray Hickling, or anyone else for that matter, have any official capacity to advise the QPF of how to conduct the coronial investigation into the aircraft accident!

It was the responsibility of the QPF to search for and recover injured persons or bodies, and to secure the crash site, preventing wreckage being touched or disturbed, before investigation by the Air Safety Authority (ASA) investigators.

Consequently, the QPF was in the lead role, with the DCA in a secondary role, providing support for the QPF, and arranging the investigation of the accident by the ASA investigators.

Because of the takeover by the DCA, Ray Hickling became extremely possessive with the radio, incorrectly assuming that he was in command and control of the mission on the mountain, being answerable only to the DCA.

The track, with trees already blazed by others, was easy to follow, and the climb by the party from Thomason's farm to the summit of Bell Peak North was along a long, sawtooth, razorback ridge, quite deceptive looking from the farm, as it appeared from there to be an almost even and gentle slope.[2]

There were pools of dirty water from recent rain seen during the climb, which I would not have drunk, even if I had taken the tablets provided by the army to purify the water.

Throughout the climb, when vines, small palms, and other vegetation, blocked the track, the party used a machete or sugarcane knife to clear the track, and a tomahawk added fresh marks to the already blazed trees, showing the narrow track.[2]

Shortly into the climb, the children and those extremely unfit dropped out, leaving the others to dig deep, thighs aching with each step, as the party tackled the first step ascent.[2]

It was during this part of the climb that I saw Ron Morrisson and Keith Howarth discussing something intently, following which, Ron and Keith, and another, withdrew from the climb.

Instead of being unfit, now that I know more of what happened, I have no doubt in my mind that they became dissatisfied with the takeover by the DCA, and it was for that reason they withdrew from the climb.

Before returning to the base, Ron instructed me to conduct the police investigation, and to remain on the mountain and guard the crash site until taken over by the ASA investigators.

Astounded, I asked Ron, "When are the investigators expected at the crash site?"

"They should be here," Ron replied, "during the afternoon!"

"But will they be at the crash site by this afternoon?"

"I hope so!"

Deeply disturbed by this time, "So, it is not certain they will be," I exclaimed, adding, "Just in case I get stuck up there, can I go back and get something to see me through the night?"

"No," replied Ron.

Back at my residence, I had other army rations, useful for the mission.

The items included tablets to purify water, a small Army Hoochie tent, hexamine stove and tablets, and matches I might need, as it seemed possible to me that I could be staying overnight on the mountain.

With food and water for only one day, and none of the items described in the above paragraph, I reluctantly pushed on and rejoined the party.

When Ron Morrisson and Keith Howarth went back down to Highleigh Base, they took with them the two stretchers that were too cumbersome for the party to carry during the climb to the summit of Bell Peak North.[3]

After the sorting out at five hundred feet on the ridge, *The Cairns Post* provided the names of the eighteen remaining in the party, as follows:

The three schoolteacher bushwalkers, Alan Broughton, Peter Bell, and Kevin Murgatroyd, Gordonvale Civil Defence members, Keith Walker and Ted Hughes, farmer, Ray Hickling, who had first reported the crash Wednesday night, Gordonvale ambulance bearers, Bob Wallace and Frank Steene, cane farmers, Bob Anderson, Jack and Rodney Morris, Emelio Angelino, John Myrteza, Roy Johnston, Gordonvale police constables, Barry Downs and Neil Bradford, reporter, Joan Starr, and tracker, Buddy Waria.[4]

It was an unsuitable party to send on the Search and Recovery mission, in that Keith Walker and Ted Hughes were not young or fit men, as were the majority of the seven farmers, and Rodney Morris was too young, and Joan Starr, in her own words, *had to be aided up the ridge.*[2]

After my appointment by Ron, I made notes in my official police notebook, like a running sheet, recording everything until I came down from Bell Peak North.

Climbing up small peaks and down deep hollows, sometimes climbing about two hundred feet, and then going down eighty or more, only having to climb that distance or more again, the party pushed on with its ascent of Bell Peak North.[2]

Beyond twelve hundred feet on the ridge, the grass gave way to a spongy carpet of leaf-mould, sometimes concealing deep holes, between huge and slippery moss-covered rocks, and the rainforest became denser, and denser, as the party climbed slowly upwards and onwards to the summit.[2]

11.00 am – the party unhesitatingly stopped at nineteen hundred feet to have *smoko*, consisting of sandwiches, tea, and coffee prepared by the wives of farmers.[2]

On the hour, every hour, conserving the batteries, just in case the mission became protracted, Ray Hickling turned on the radio and contact Highleigh Base.[2]

Additionally, expecting that there could be an emergency call during the climb up the ridge, Highleigh Base checked the radio on the half-hour.[2]

After Ray Hickling gave a welfare call during *smoko*, I made it clear to Ray that I had been given the task of providing the coroner with a report, effectively placing me in command of the mission, and that I would remain to guard the crash site.[2]

Ray Hickling also was left in no doubt that I wanted him to include me in all inward and outward radio communications that he had with Highleigh Base.

That is when Ray became extremely possessive and refused my request, citing that the DCA had put him in control over the use of the radio, and that he, and no one else, would be telling the party what to do.

It was absolutely an untenable situation, which was only one of the difficulties I endured and had to deal with during the mission on Bell Peak North.

Once again, this interaction identifies clearly that the DCA were spitefully carrying on with the vendetta over QPF installing its own UHF radio linking system on Saddle Mountain.[8]

Snakes had been seen, and while Rodney Morris was sitting on a log, having *smoko*, a black snake slithered out from underneath, being disposed of quickly before it had time to sink its poisonous fangs into someone.[2]

The party had a first-aid kit, including two QATB bearers, but without antivenin, if bitten by a poisonous snake, more than likely, that person would have died on Bell Peak North.

Tiger leeches, Australian hornets, wasps, mosquitoes, bull ants, March flies, and scorpions added to the danger, compounded when individuals entangled themselves in *wait-a-while* vines hanging precariously from tall trees.[2]

Checking on the party's water supply, Highleigh Base advised that when close to the summit of Bell Peak North, a light plane would drop food in boxes and tyre tubes filled with water.[2]

How the progress of the party was watched by a circling plane, and the dropping of the supplies to the party, was reported in *The Cairns Post*, as follows:

A light aircraft flew over the area almost constantly and was in radio contact with the rescue party to whom it dropped the supplies.[4]

Joan Starr remembered how the party strung out into two groups, as follows:

The party, which had been closely grouped at the beginning of the climb, had long ago strung out and at times split into two sections, with the experienced bushwalkers leading the field.[4]

While Barry Downs kept up with the first group of Ray Hickling, Alan Broughton, Peter Bell, and Kevin Murgatroyd, I alternated between the two groups, constantly urging the second group to quicken their pace and stay in touch with the leaders.[4]

12.00 pm – Highleigh Base told Ray Hickling to stay on the radio as Colin Sheddon estimated the party was about a half-hour away from the crash site.[2,3]

12.30 pm – the circling aircraft spotted the party, just below the crash site, prompting Barry, who was the senior by service, to call the two groups together for a briefing.[2]

When the party was together, Barry instructed what the party was to do, when someone saw wreckage.[2]

Joan Starr remembered Barry giving those instructions to the party, as follows:

When we gathered together again as one party at the rest-stop at 3280 feet, Constable Barry downs of Gordonvale, who had become spokesman for the "advance" party, said anyone who was squeamish should stay back, as what we would shortly see would not be nice.[2]

Joan became aware early into the climb of my belief that she should not have been in the party, and I stopped her from taking photographs and gathering information for a story. Consequently, Joan did not mention what I did to keep the second group in touch with the *advanced* party.

Reinforcing what was said by Barry, I told the whole party to freeze when someone saw wreckage, and under no circumstance was anything to be moved or pick up, allowing the police and QATB bearers to go forward and search for survivors or bodies.

A well-trained and disciplined party would have followed those instructions, but that is not what happened!

First base established on Ray Morris' farm at Aloomba
Ron Morrisson is on the extreme right examining a map
(Courtesy of *The Cairns Post*)

**Loading of an Iroquois helicopter into a Hercules transport aircraft
at the RAAF Base, Fairbairn, for the flight to Cairns**
(Courtesy of *National Library of Australia*, ID 107031889)

Unloading supplies for the flood-bound community
(Courtesy of *National Library of Australia*, ID 28901542)

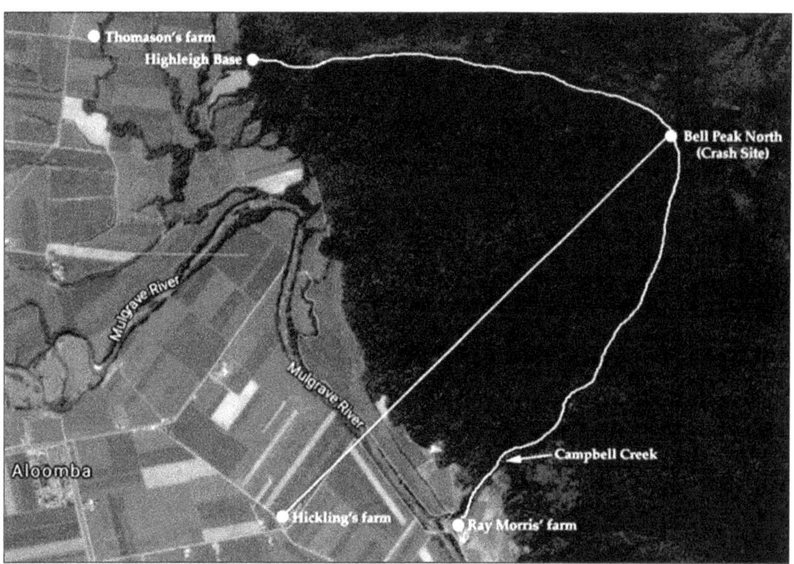

Bases established at Aloomba and Highleigh
(Courtesy of © OpenStreetMap contributors)

Gordonvale Police Station in 1970
(Private Source)

Bell Peak North behind the stack of the Mulgrave Sugar Mill
Visible from the footpath outside the Gordonvale Police Station
(Private Source)

Base established on Thomason's farm at Highleigh
Route taken to the summit of Bell Peak North
(Private Source)

Majority of the party on Bell Peak North

Front Row (L-R)   Author, Frank Steene, Barry Downs, Alan Broughton, Kevin Murgatroyd, John Myrteza, and Rob Johnston

Second Row (L-R)   Ray Hickling, Peter Bell, Ted Hughes, Emelio Angelino, Bob Wallace, Rodney Morris, and Jack Morris (obscured)

Rear   Buddy Waria

(Courtesy of Patricia Wallace)

Joan Starr posing with some of the party
(Courtesy of Patricia Wallace)

8

FORGOTTEN HEROES

Extending south along the coastline from Bessie Point on Trinity Bay to Mutchero Inlet and Russell Heads, the Malbon Thompson Range and associated foothills form more than half of the land area of Mandingalbay Yidinji Country. The highest points are May Peak (2736 feet), Grey Peaks (2113 feet), Bell Peak North (3366 feet), and Bell Peak South (3081).[1] Not only is Bell Peak North the tallest, but it also has majestic views of the Pacific Ocean and the valley encompassing the sugarcane farming districts of Aloomba and Gordonvale.

It is truly a magnificent part of Australia in which to live, and if I had not been subject to transfer in the police force, we would have happily settled down at Gordonvale, as the locals, after the flood, treated us as if we were family.

Despite making it abundantly clear the aircraft accident was a coronial investigation conducted by police, followed by the DCA investigation to establish the cause, as soon as the first person spotted wreckage from the aircraft, the ill-disciplined party, ignoring the instructions given by the police, ran forward to the crash site.

Ray Hickling remembered that he and others in the party ignored the police, as follows:

We had stumbled onto the wreckage. We followed the trail of wreckage a short distance to where the main wreckage lay. The damage to the aircraft was extensive. What remained of the fuselage was standing nose down against a tree. It had been torn open revealing the entire floor. This severe damage to the fuselage would have been compounded by the exit of an engine which was being carried as cargo. The sound of the crash, as I remember it, lasted just a fraction of a second. It seemed inconceivable to me that so much damage could occur in an instant. Fortunately, there had been no fire.[2]

"Stay where you are," I remember yelling, but everyone, except Barry, Bob Wallace, Francis James (Frank) Steene, and I, ran forward, contaminating the crash site.

Before long, those who ignored the instructions of the police, soon came stumbling and staggering back down the ridge, physically ill and vomiting as they did so.

Joan Starr also remembered that she and others in the party ignored the police, as follows:

Wreckage was strewn over an area, about 200 yards long by about 100 yards wide. Trees, palms, and vines were smashed, and pieces of the aircraft were scattered among rocks and hung from broken vines and on limbs from trees. Foam plastic padding torn from the upholstery hung like grotesque blooms from high branches. Clothes and personal effects were also widely scattered. I saw shaving gear and a toothbrush lying among rotting leaves beside a moss-covered rock. The flight manual and other papers flapped lazily in a tiny breeze here high on the mountain. A book one of the men had carried lay open. Parts of the plane which were almost unrecognisable, lay everywhere we looked. The radio was a crumpled, useless thing and the blades of the propellors were twisted pieces of metal fit for scrap. A tangled heap of insulated wiring with alligator clips looked strangely out of place beside an empty oxygen bottle. Then we found the main part of the plane's fuselage – and the bodies.[3]

At the end of this chapter, in a photograph taken by Joan Starr, Kevin Murgatroyd is holding wreckage in his hands, which should have remained untouched at the crash site.[3]

This is exactly why the police tape off a crime scene and guard it to prevent unruly people from touching or souveniring items of interest to the investigation.

The crash site was the same as a crime scene!

Therefore, neither Kevin Murgatroyd, nor anyone else for that matter, had authority or permission to touch or move anything at the crash site.

I expected better behaviour from the schoolteachers, but that did not happen on the mountain.

And blame for that happening rests with the DCA for sending an ill-disciplined party on the mission.

Upon seeing Joan Starr sifting through personal belongings, and taking photographs, such as the one with Kevin Murgatroyd, I told Joan to cease, and I instructed her to move away from the crash site, which she refused to do.

Joan Starr remembered how she ignored my instructions and sifted through the wreckage, as follows:

A clock picked up by a member of the rescue party had stopped at 9.45. A compass had jammed in position and was picked up, too, for later checking by DCA.[3]

Further confirmation of Joan and others sifting through the wreckage appeared in *The Cairns Post*, as follows:

Among items recovered by the rescue team yesterday were the flight manual and other papers and an alarm clock which had stopped at 9.45.[4]

Being the police officer responsible for securing the crash site, I did not recover any of those items, nor were they handed over to me by Joan or others in the party.

It is my belief that the pilot and passenger did not see anything before the plane crashed into the dense rainforest and boulders on Bell Peak North, about one hundred feet down from the summit, killing both instantly.

At the end of this chapter, there are photographs, providing an insight into how the aircraft broke up on impact, wreckage strewing thereafter throughout the rainforest.

Joan Starr remembered how Bob Wallace and I prepared the bodies for the return down the ridge, as follows:

Ambulance bearers Bob Wallace and Frank Steene of Gordon-vale, with help from Barry Downs and fellow-constable Neil Bradford, wrapped the bodies in blankets and other materials, and strapped them into slings hung on single poles for carry-

ing.[3]

That is how the task began, but when I saw the party picking up remains, and I had not recorded the location, I asked Barry Downs and Frank Steene to move the party away from the crash site, leaving Bob Wallace and me alone to record and place the remains in body bags.

Using the excuse that the light plane was about to drop the supply of food and water, Barry and Frank ushered the party to the summit, away from the crash site.

Unhindered, Bob and I finished the task of placing the remains in the body bags, using *upholstery lining* from the plane's cabin to wrap around the bags.[2,3]

The bags were then place in tarpaulins, which were securely bound with rope and strapped to poles, ready for the journey back down the mountain.[2,3]

While completing the task, and without any warning from Ray Hickling, the light plane dropped cartons of food and water-filled tubes, which crashed to the ground around Bob and me, forcing us to take cover behind boulders.

Fortunately, none of what the plane dropped, hit Bob or me, otherwise we would have suffered an injury that could have been life-threatening!

Moreover, Bob served in the Australian Army during the Second World War, and he thought for a moment that it was an air attack by the Japanese, instead of a food drop.

Ray Hickling remembered how the plane dropped food and water to the party, as follows:

Aviation Department personnel had worked out a solution to the water problem. They had car tubes filled with water and loaded them into a Cessna aircraft that had the right-hand seat and door removed. The pilot couldn't see us among the trees. I had to guide him with my radio. I used simple instructions like left, right, hold it, drop, etc. When I thought they were in the right position, and the right distance, I would say drop and his assistance would roll the tube out. We all had to take shelter behind trees. It was quite a sight to see these tubes come hurtling down towards us. It was a bit like Aerial Coits. None volunteered to be the post. The target area on the summit was quite narrow. On the first two attempts the tubes went down the steep slope. From then on, we got fairly skilled, and most were dropping almost at our feet. Some of the tubes burst on impact but we were able to save some water. However, most remained intact. The water was foul to drink. We didn't know which was worse, drinking the Dunlop water, the Goodyear water, or dying of thirst. We figured Burke and Wills would have welcomed it, so we drank it.[2]

Therein is evidence that the first two drops fell short, resulting in supplies landing near where Bob and I were reading the bodies for the journey back down the mountain.

Same as Bob, but under friendly fire, during training at High Range, near Townsville, which was the year before the camp in the Seaview Range, along with other soldiers, we were finding and marking unexploded mortars, when bombs peppered the hill in front of us.

On the way to the firing range, we passed the Australian Army cleaning their howitzers, not knowing what was about to happen, while we were at the range.

When the sound of popping came from the direction of the howitzers, "Freeze," said the officer with us, whom we had not seen before, and we did so without asking, "Why?"

After screeching overhead, the bombs thudded into the hill, exploding on impact, providing us with a front-row seat at friendly fireworks display!

And, yes, it was a planned and well-organized test conducted by the Australian Army to see how the CMF would react under live fire, which we passed.

Comparing that experience with the supply drops organized by the DCA, what the DCA did was foolhardy and dangerous, which could have resulted in the death of someone.

Joan Star also remembered how the plane dropped food and water to the party, as follows:

A bright yellow marker-tarpaulin had been spread over the top branches of a large tree, and a light plane came over to drop food and water. The first package of food landed somewhere down in a ravine half a mile away, and two of the six car tubes of water were lost over the jungle. Ray began to direct the pilot by radio. The rest of us took cover while we were "bombed." Two more tubes of water hung up in the topmost branches of trees, one was recovered from the ground nearby, and another burst on impact. A carton of apples and one of oranges were gifts from the Gods.[3]

When the returning party had their fill of food and water, the DCA instructed the party to return down the ridge to Highleigh Base with the bodies.

When they left, I was alone without a radio at the summit to guard the crash site, but I had food and water to see me through until the arrival of the ASA investigators, so I thought.

It was a daunting task, but not overly perturbing, as I had faced and overcome challenges in my earlier life, and I was confident that I would do the same again.

If I had not remained to guard the crash site, others would have looted and contaminated it further.

Ray Hickling, Alan Broughton, and Kevin Murgatroyd recalled that this almost happened, as follows:

During that afternoon the first "sightseers" arrived to have a look at the crash, two local farmers. They made the trip easier than the party had the day before – they were younger and fitter than most of the original party, and the conditions on Friday, whilst still very tropical, were much more tolerable than on the day before.[5]

If I had not been there in a police uniform to stop them and send them back down the mountain, and others after them, there is no doubt in my mind that they also would have contaminated and souvenired wreckage from the plane.

More to the point, none of those turned away had a guide, such as the three schoolteacher bushwalkers, to find their way up and down the ridge.

Any concern that I had about the DCA leaving me on the mountain by myself, quickly disappeared when the party returned to the crash site, saying that it was too dangerous to carry the bodies down the ridge.

And I agree that it was too dangerous for the unfit and ill-disciplined party to complete!

However, if the contingent of police officers, who climbed to the summit on the third day, had been in the party, there is no doubt in my mind that they would have carried the bodies down on the first day.

When Ray Hickling advised the DCA that the party had failed, the DCA asked if there was level ground at the summit for a helicopter to land and pick up the bodies.[3]

Based on my training with an Army helicopter in the Seaview Range, I advised Ray Hickling to tell the DCA that there was no suitable landing zone at the summit.

Ignoring that advice, the DCA instructed the party to clear a landing zone.

With only machetes, sugarcane knives, and tomahawks, the party tried, but soon gave up that farcical task.

The DCA, however, continued with the plan and did not cancel the services of a Bell 47 helicopter on its way from Ingham.[2,3]

At the end of this chapter, there is a photograph of a similar Bell 47 helicopter.

While others were trying to clear trees and shrubs for a landing zone, Joan Starr, disrespectfully and without my permission, took a photograph of the bodies secured in the tarpaulins, also found at the end of this chapter.

Joan Starr remembered that the DCA instructed a section of the party to make their way back down the ridge to Highleigh Base, as follows:

A hasty conference was held. It was decided that if the party intended being back down the mountain that day, they would have to leave the summit no later than 4 o'clock, or they would be caught in the dark. Night in the jungle, with a storm brewing and no means of navigation, was not to be taken lightly. In the end, nine of us made our way down the incredibly steep track, now made more hazardous by the light shower of rain which had fallen while we were on the summit. Rocks were slippery as glass and the ground was like butter under wet leaves.[3]

Those who made their way back down the ridge to Highleigh Base on Thomason's farm included Barry Downs, Frank Steene, Keith Walker, Ted Hughes, Jack Morris, Rodney Morris, Roy Johnstone, Buddy Waria, and Joan Starr.

Soon after their departure, the Bell 47 helicopter flew over the summit of Bell Peak North.

Joan Starr remembered seeing the arrival of the helicopter, as follows:

When we were a few hundred feet down the mountain, we heard the "chopper" coming in. But it did not climb over the mountain, and we heard later that the afternoon air had been so turbulent that the machine was unable to reach the peak.[3]

With the storm brewing in the west, and a gale-force wind blowing easterly inland from the ocean towards the storm, the pilot flew the helicopter up the valley on the western side of the mountain to reach the top of the summit.

It shocked me to see that crop-dusting booms, same as fitted to the helicopter in the photograph at the end of this chapter, were still in place on either side of the helicopter.

Every attempt, with the engine roaring and blades flapping, reminded me what it was like to ride a bullock at a rodeo, roaring and snorting as it twisted and turned, and bucked up and down, all over the place.

When the crop-dusting booms almost became entangled in the

tops of trees, the pilot had the good sense to say, enough was enough, and he aborted that dangerous attempt to land somewhere to remove the bodies from the mountain.

The DCA then told us that the pilot was about to run out of hours and would fly on to Cairns, returning early morning of the following day to lift the bodies off the mountain.

Asking when the ASA investigators would arrive to take over the crash site, the DCA told me that the ASA investigators would not arrive in Cairns until the next day.

So, if the party had carried the bodies down the mountain on the first day, I would have been at the crash site by myself on the first night.

That spiteful vendetta of the DCA against the QPF for installing its own UHF radio linking system on Saddle Mountain went too far on the first day of the Search and Recovery mission and could have resulted in my death.[6]

Joan Starr remembered how the returning party again split up into two groups and became lost, as follows:

Legs made weary by the upward climb, and then stiffened by the pause at the top, were like rubber for the downward journey. It was almost worse than the climb. I felt that I was slowing the whole group down, and I feared I would be an encumbrance. I had to force each leg to lift. The journey seemed endless. About two thirds of the way down, the party had again split into two sections. We heard screams from down below, "Don't come near here!" Then the dark tracker with the leading group, Buddy Waria, came back to tell us that there were wasps on the track ahead, and that Barry Downs had been stung. When we reached the other party after carefully circling the wasps, Barry was still writhing in agony, with his face and head a mass of swellings from the stings.[3]

Barry Downs was a capable leader, and he had been involved in searches before at Gordonvale, but he was not bush wise and walked into a wasp nest.

It was then that the returning party became lost, and upon hearing us chopping wood for a fire during the night, Barry and others climbed in that direction, and they safely made it back to the crash site.[3]

Ray Hickling remembered what happened when Barry and others returned to the crash site, as follows:

After about 45 minutes, the parting group returned. They had got lost and returned aided by the sound of our chopping. Alan Broughton joined them and led them safely off the mountain.[7]

Alan Broughton volunteered to guide the returning party down the mountain, leaving Bob Wallace, Ray Hickling, Peter Bell, Kevin Murgatroyd, Bob Anderson, Emelio Angelino, and John Myrteza on Bell Peak North that night with me.

Joan Starr remembered how the returning party made their way out of the rainforest, as follows:

At about 300 feet the storm struck. But we were so wet and so tired it didn't matter anymore. We staggered on. The rain merely cooled us. And then we were down, and the Land rover was on the edge of the cane field before us. I have never seen a prettier sight. It was then 6.30. We had been on the mountain for 10 hours. Jack Morris, a farmer with the party and the man who, with Roy Johnstone and another farmer, had helped me carry my equipment up the mountain, drove us to a neighbour's farm. There the Thomason's had cups of hot tea and coffee and fresh scones ready for us. Never was food and drink so welcome.[3]

Therein is a further admission from Joan Starr that the DCA should not have allowed her to take part in the Search and Recovery mission.

And when approached by me afterwards for copies of the photographs, Joan ignored every telephone call that I made to *The Cairns Post*, and I was unable to include those photographs with my report to the coroner.

It is abundantly clear that Joan's participation in the mission, therefore, was only for one purpose, and that was to gain first-hand information and photographs for a story.

With little food and water left over from the earlier supply drops by the light plane, and no suitable shelter for protection from the elements, all readily agreed that it would be a miserable night spent on Bell Peak North.

Ray Hickling remembered what it was like on that first night, as follows:

We decided to spend the night at a point about midway between the crash site and the summit. We built a modest lean-to featuring a thatched roof made of leafy branches. It was small but did offer a degree of protection. We named the structure Bell Peak Motel. The ground was sloping and damp. It was a long night. We had a storm. In contrast to the stifling heat during that day, we were now wet and cold. We managed to keep a fire alight. Obviously, we had at least one smoker amongst us who was carrying matches. We told yarns all night in an effort to pass the time.[7]

At the beginning, the party was warm and comfortable around the campfire, until a storm, with lightning strikes and claps of thunder resonating through the rainforest, drenched everything, even the bedding made with the palm fronds.

The raindrops were so large, like the marbles played with in my youth, and soon small rivers of water began to flow swiftly down the slope, through the camp, putting out the fire.

Not only did the first downpour put out the warm fire, but also the stockpile of wood was so wet, it would not burn to rekindle the fire.

Everyone that night was a *hero* for doing what we did, but the one who stood out the most, was Bob Wallace, who was a quiet and unassuming man.

Watching Bob go from one tree to another, I almost agreed with the others that Bob might have *lost the plot*, more so when Bob dragged a length of a green tree into the campsite, proudly referring to it as the *Kerosene Tree*.

Looking on intently, our concerns about Bob quickly turned to relief as the green logs caught fire!

More than likely, it was the *Diesel Tree*, officially known as *Copaifera langsdorffii*, which has honeycombed wood and *capillaries filled with oil*.[8]

After cutting wells in the wood, oil seeped out, and soon we had a campfire again, which, more than likely, saved the drenched party dying from hypothermia.[8]

At the end of this chapter, according to an estimation provided by the Bureau of Meteorology, the wind chill on Bell Peak North was about 8° Celsius.[9]

It was extremely cold, having in mind that we all wore summer clothing, and rain continuously drenched the party throughout the night.

Despite having a fire burning through the night, the party agreed that we should stay awake, telling jokes that were nonsensical to me, but it kept us alive.

A quiet and unassuming person, I absolutely respected and enjoyed working with Bob as a QATB bearer.

In recent times, I discovered that Bob was formerly a Lance Sergeant during World War Two in the 31st/51st Infantry Battalion of the Australia Army, which *undertook garrison duties in Dutch New Guinea in 1943-44 before taking part in the Bougainville Campaign in 1944-45*.[10,11]

Bob joined the 31st/51st Infantry Battalion on August 17, 1940, and discharged on April 1, 1946, which was before I was born at Mackay.[10]

There is no doubt in my mind that Bob learnt the survival skills displayed that night on Bell Peak North during the *Bougainville Campaign in 1944-45*.[11]

None of the others in the party had skills and experience like Bob Wallace!

At the end of Chapter 7, Bob is in the group photograph, holding on to the stick that he used to climb up and down the ridge on Bell Peak North, which no doubt is the way he traversed the hills and mountains of Bougainville.

In fact, on the climb up the ridge, Bob brought back memories of how soldiers of the Australian Army made their way along the *Kokoda Track* during World War Two.[12]

Observing Bob, who was 50 years at the time we climbed the ridge, I saw that he was fitter and stronger than others in the party, such as Ray Hickling and Kevin Murgatroyd, and that he was better suited for the task at hand.

If there had been more like Bob on the climb, I have no doubt in my mind that the party would have carried the bodies down on the first day, as Bob had the dedication and commitment for what the party had to do.

All in the party expressed their deep gratification to Bob for saving their lives, but others, who believed they were the *principles* on the mission, soon forgot Bob's heroic efforts, done for the good of the party.[13]

Vale, Bob, it was a pleasure knowing you, and I thank you for what you did on the mission!

Kevin Murgatroyd with part of the aircraft
(Courtesy of Patricia Wallace)

Part of the fuselage that disintegrated on impact
(Courtesy of Ray Hickling)

Part of the tail section bearing VH-RIZ
(Courtesy of Ray Hickling)

Crop-dusting Bell 47 helicopter
(Courtesy of *PPRuNe.Org*)

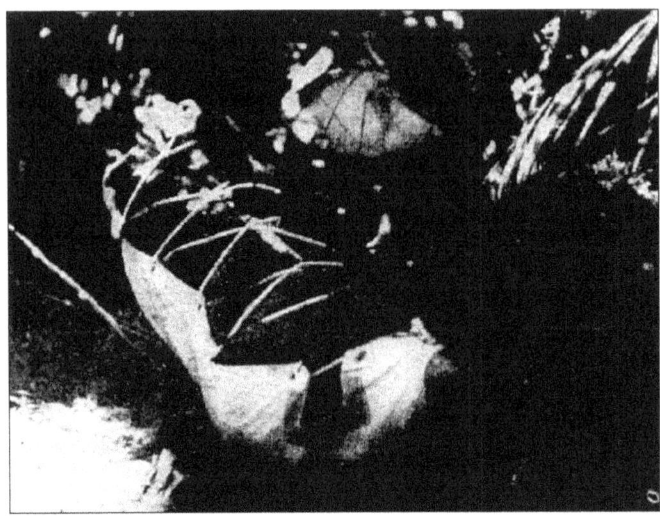

How the remains were wrapped up in tarpaulins
(Courtesy of Patricia Wallace)

Section 3: Estimation of conditions at Bell Peak North

The following section presents an indication of conditions at Bell Peak North, based on the data shown above at Townsville and Cairns in section 1, in conjunction with an estimation of apparent temperature based on wind chill from the Steadman Apparent Temperature table in section 2

The above upper air data at Townsville for 8am on the 30th January 1979 shows that at 900hPa (3149 6 ft), the air temperature was 19.3 °C. At 850hPa (4757 2 ft), the air temperature was 17.3 °C. Therefore, assuming a linear trend between these altitudes, it can be estimated that the air temperature was around 19.0 °C at 3400 ft. By comparing the temperature values between 9am on the 29th January and 8am on the 30th January, it can be seen that there is only a difference of 0.1 °C. Air temperature has less variation with time and space than most other weather elements

It must be noted that temperature generally increases as you approach the equator. This is observed in the surface temperatures of Townsville and Cairns. At 9am on the 30th January the temperature at Townsville was 27.0 °C, while at the same time further north in Cairns, the temperature was 28 2 °C. Bell Peak North is located approximately 27km from Cairns Aero and 257 km from Townville Aero. Therefore using the temperatures based on the upper air data from Townsville may be cooler than what was experienced at Bell Peak North.

In terms of wind conditions, at 8am on the 30th January at Townsville Aero, at 900 hPa the winds were measured as 28.8 km/hr. They were significantly less than this at 850hPa (14.4 km/hr).

Other wind measurements taken over the evening at 900hPa, were 54 km/hr at 20:00 (local time) on the 29th and 61.2 km/hr at 02:00 on the 30th.

Considering a worst case scenario, based on the observations available, we can estimate an apparent air temperature as follows:

Air temperature: 19 0 °C
Wind speed: 61.2 km/hr
Apparent air temperature from "Steadman Apparent Temperature as a Wind Chill": 8 °C

Estimation of conditions at Bell Peak North on January 29/30, 1979
(Courtesy of Australian Government Bureau of Bureau of Meteorology)

9

MISSION IMPOSSIBLE

January 30, 1970 – early morning of the second day, while I had to remain and guard the bodies and crash site, the others requested permission from the DCA to make their way back down the mountain. The DCA gave that approval, but when I asked Ray Hickling to hand over the radio, the DCA refused my request, leaving me without means of communicating with Highleigh Base.

That is how ludicrous and untenable the situation became, but I insisted the radio should remain, even outlined my Army training and experience in the use of the portable VHF radio, but the DCA refused again, citing that the radio could not be handed over to a police officer.

What happened confused me, as I was conversant with the instructions in the Queensland Policeman's Manual of conducting a coronial investigation into a plane accident, and what unfolded during the mission on Bell Peak North was out of kilter with those instructions.[1]

Now that I know more, everything has fallen into place, and what happened is now clear.

Once again, Sergeant Second Class Colin Ward and Constable Colin Tapsall of the Radio Maintenance Section, Cairns Police Station, installed the first police owned UHF radio linking system from Saddle Mountain, near Kuranda, to the Cairns Regional Airport.[1]

It was difficult to understand at the time of the mission, as to why I could not use the VHF radio to communicate with a police officer, such as Ron Morrisson.

During my writings, however, I remembered how the DCA carried on after installation of the UHF radio linking system on Saddle Mountain, and upon locating evidence of that being done, there is no doubt in my mind that what happened on Bell Peak North, had everything to do with the spiteful vendetta the DCA conducted thereafter against the QPF.

I also do not doubt that it was a Commonwealth versus State dispute that resulted in the DCA exerting pressure over the QPF to take command and control of the mission!

Breaking the stalemate, Ray Hickling, and Kevin Murgatroyd, who did little during the mission, agreed to remain with me on Bell Peak North.

So, during the morning of the second day, Bob Wallace, Peter Bell, Bob Anderson, Emelio Angelino, and John Myrteza went back down the mountain to the Highleigh Base.[2]

It would not have concerned me, if the DCA had left me alone on the mountain, so long as the DCA provided me with further supplies and camping equipment, as I worked better by myself, but without a radio, I was pleased that Ray, as well as Kevin, remained at the summit with me.

However, it soon became clear that I did not have anything in common with Ray and Kevin, as they were older, and both avoided speaking to me.

That did not bother me, as I was there to do a job, and that was to evacuate the bodies from the mountain and hand the crash site over to the ASA investigators.

What the DCA asked us to do next, was reported in *The Cairns Post*, as follows:

> *Three of the original party of 18 remained on the top, trying to clear an area for the helicopter to hover.*[2]

Ray Hickling remembered how the small helicopter delivered further supplies to the summit, as follows:

> *In time we were advised that the helicopter was on its way to the summit. Ideally, a helicopter needs to maintain forward speed while ascending. We watched it head south down the valley then make a 180-degree turn, then track straight back towards us. We lit a small smoke fire to indicate to the pilot the wind direction and speed. The pilot and his assistant dropped water in plastic bottles as well as food. Some of the plastic bot-*

tles broke. The quality was a welcome change from the Dunlop and Goodyear water delivered the previous day. They also lowered a chainsaw on a rope. The pilot was not prepared to come too low given the borderline performance of this aircraft.[3]

Firstly, there was an abundance of fuel on the mountain in the rainforest and at the summit, and being concerned about starting a bushfire, I objected, and a *small smoke fire* was not lit.[3]

Secondly, an article in *The Cairns Post* incorrectly reported that the small helicopter delivered a chainsaw to the summit, but that did not happen.[3,4]

Thirdly, Ray Hickling alluded to the stupidity of the DCA in moving the base from Ray Morris' farm to Thomason's farm when he described that *we watched* [the small helicopter] *head south down the valley then make a 180-degree turn, then track straight back towards us*, which was up along the valley from Ray Morris' farmhouse.[3]

Finding the ascent too steep from Thomason's farm, the pilot flew the small helicopter out into the valley between the Malbon Thompson and Bellenden Ker ranges, turned left near Ray Morris' farm, and then made a gradual ascent up along the Campbell Creek valley to the summit.

Every blunder of the DCA left me shaking my head!

If the small helicopter had delivered a chainsaw, I would have cleared the landing zone much faster than what I did with a *chopping axe*.

So, when the small helicopter returned on the second day, at which time the five were making their way down the mountain to Highleigh Base, hovering over the summit, the pilot released the rope, and the two *chopping axes* fell to the ground.[3]

The reader needs only to look at the first photograph at the end of Chapter 10 to see the handles with the equipment in front of Ray Hickling, and look at how the saplings were cut down, to confirm that a *chopping axe* was used.

Ray Hickling was unaware of that photographic evidence until he saw it for the first time in 2010, and before then, when he provided his version to the *Mulgrave Shire Historical Society*, he left out how I, alone, cleared the area at the summit with a *chopping axe*.

It was one of the blatant untruths told by others!

The plan of the DCA was for the small helicopter to land at the summit, and for us, using the rope that came with the axes, to tie the bodies to the landing skids on either side of the helicopter.

Once secured, the helicopter would take the bodies to the police and undertaker waiting at the Highleigh Base, and then on to the mortuary at Cairns.

Before then, we had to clear trees for the landing zone, and it was then Ray and Kevin admitted they had never used a *chopping axe*, extremely dangerous in the hands of the inexperienced.

Instead of Ray or Kevin suffering an injury, I alone cleared the suggested area, as if cutting down a paddock of sugarcane, and I chopped the trees off, well aboveground, as boulders surrounding the trees restricted my backswings.

With a chainsaw, I would have cut the trees down faster, and lower down the trunk near the ground.

When the pilot came back to the summit and inspected what I had done, he confirmed what I already knew, that there was no level ground for a landing zone.

On a request by the DCA, the pilot tried hovering steadily over the summit, only to experienced turbulence like the first day and was told to abort.

The small helicopter had no quick-release hook, but it did have a hook from which a wire rope suspended underneath could be attached to a cargo net containing the bodies.

After the failure of the small helicopter, the DCA requested the services of a larger helicopter.

The unsuitability of the small helicopter was reported in *The Cairns Post*, as follows:

> *… it proved unsuitable for the airlift and DCA officials were later seeking a larger machine equipped with a winch to first lower a chainsaw to the party and then raise the bodies.*[4]

Firstly, this article confirmed that the small helicopter did not deliver a chainsaw to the summit.

Instead, the pilot delivered two *chopping axes*, one of which I used to make a clearing at the summit for the small helicopter, and which, as I mentioned before, the pilot found to be unsuitable for a landing zone.

Ray Hickling erroneously mishandled the truth of what happened!

Secondly, after aborting the valiant but foolhardy attempt by the small helicopter, the DCA said that a much larger helicopter, with a winch, was on its way from Sydney, and that we could expected the helicopter to arrive during the afternoon.

The large helicopter's arrival was reported in *The Cairns Post*, as follows:

> *The helicopter was unable to fly to the area late yesterday afternoon because of turbulent winds near the peak. There were also storm clouds in the area.*[2]

Contrary to the report, the helicopter did come to the summit during the afternoon of the second day and delivered food, water, mosquito nets, sleeping bags, blankets, lanterns, torches, matches, shovel, a large heavy-duty tarpaulin, and personal items in a cargo net to the summit.

Erroneously, Ray Hickling told the *Mulgrave Shire Historical Society* that the small helicopter did the delivery, which was another blatant untruth, as it could not hover steadily over the summit, whereas the larger helicopter did so!

Having secured wagons of sugarcane, and experienced as a rigger's offsider, as well as trained in mounting and repelling from an army helicopter, I went forward and uncoupled the cargo net attached to the wire rope suspended from the quick-release hook underneath the helicopter.

I did this while the helicopter was hovering, and not until the pilot said that it was safe to move forward and do so.

Furthermore, while training with the army helicopter, I saw the hand signals used by ground crew for the pilot to move upwards, move downwards, move ahead, and all clear, provided at the end of Chapter 11.

After uncoupling the U-bolt on the wire rope, leaving the cargo net holding the supplies at the summit, I move backwards and *raised the right arm at the elbow with the thumb erect* and signal *all clear* to the pilot.[5]

The large helicopter, however, did not have a winch, and after the delivery, the pilot flew on to Cairns for fitting of a winch to the helicopter, and would return the following morning to winch the bodies off the mountain.

Even today, I cannot understand why the DCA did not tell us to place the bodies in the cargo net, and after that was done, have the helicopter return to extract the bodies, which is exactly what happened on the morning of the third day.

The DCA was prepared to strap the bodies to the landing skids of the small helicopter, but it beggars' belief as to why the DCA did not extract the bodies in the cargo net on the afternoon of the second day, and then deliver the equipment of the ASA investigators to the summit, after their arrival at Cairns!

After winching the bodies from the summit, it was the plan of the DCA to lower the ASA investigators onto Bell Peak North, and then winch Ray, Kevin, and I into the helicopter.

Having repelled from an army helicopter, I was looking forward to that adventure, but Ray and Kevin made it clear to the DCA that they would not be winched off the mountain.

Ray Hickling remembered the supply drop on the second day, as follows:

The food that was sent to us was prepared by local farmer's wives. As I later learned, they were Reta Thomason, the late Lou Angelino, and my wife Marion. Among the supplies we received was a carefully packed bottle of rum. It had a note, "With the complements of a local farmer." That night in camp, we shared the rum declaring to a man, that the farmer who sent it was indeed a gentleman among gentlemen. I later learned that my wife Marion had sent it. It was my bottle of rum.[3]

It was not rum, another blatant untruth, but a bottle of whiskey, and when Ray said it might be from his wife, Kevin and I helped Ray celebrated an early twelfth wedding anniversary for February 1, 1970.[3]

The food prepared by Reta Thomason, Lou Angelino, and Marion Hickling, was for a party of eight.

After commenting the five who went back down during the morning did not know what they were missing, we filled ourselves on food that one became accustomed to from farmers' wives during or after a disaster.

One instance being the frantic search for the young daughter of Savino and Lena Benedetti, who lived on the Mulgrave River, which was in flood at the time.[6]

In company of Barry Downs, if my memory serves me correct, we found the distressed girl during a heavy downpour, wandering along the headland of a sugarcane paddock, drenched and cold, but otherwise seemingly unhurt.

Soon after we reunited the relieved girl with her extremely grateful family, a feast of good Italian food appeared out of nowhere, and they offered us a glass of wine.

It was wrong to consume alcohol in uniform and on duty, but culturally, it was extremely insulting not to do so.

Despite pleading that we were on duty and could not accept the glasses of wine, suddenly a carton of Bosca Asti Spumante, also appeared out of nowhere and put on the back seat of the police vehicle.

On the way back to the station, we wonder what to say if sprung by Ron, but that never happened!

Ray and Kevin received a change of clothing and personal items from their wives, but I did not receive anything, which was out of character for Patricia.

More to the point, it was clear that Ray and Kevin's families knew where they were, and what they were doing, so I asked if Patricia was similarly aware, and "Yes," was the response from the DCA, "She has been informed!"

That confirmation by the DCA turned out to be untruthful and completely disrespectful!

Kevin was an experienced bushwalker, and Kevin and Ray had camped out before, but neither had any experience, according to them, in conditions prevailing on Bell Peak North.

I erected the tarpaulin for shelter, same as done in the army, used the shovel to dig a latrine trench, placed the bodies away from the camp to protect our food from the flies, and constructed a fireplace to avoid starting a bushfire.

In fact, it looked like a temporary army camp, with the large tarpaulin arranged in sections for our meals, food storage, and sleeping accommodation.

Ray and Kevin thought I was acting *oddly*, same as others before them, but little did they know anything about the survival skills I had learnt. And both referred to the camp that I set up as the *Bell Peak Motel*, not to my liking, and I did not join the frivolity, as the bodies of two men laid not far away![7]

That afternoon, the DCA said that the ASA investigators had arrived and would take over the crash site the following day.

After the evening meal, washed down with *wee nips* of the whiskey, we retired inside the sleeping bags, covered with an extra blanket, safely under a mosquito net, which was different to our experience the night before.

10

SAFELY EXTRACTED

January 31, 1970 – early morning of the third day, the DCA advised it was not possible to fit a winch to the helicopter. There was another plan, and that was for the pilot to do a reconnoitring flight over the summit to see if there was a safe landing zone. If not, the helicopter would extract the bodies in a large cargo net, which, as mentioned before, is what should have happened when the helicopter arrived on the afternoon of the second day.

This plan of action of the DCA was reported in *The Cairns Post*, as follows:

> *A police officer at Gordonvale said that an attempt could be made this morning to lift the bodies out in a sling tied to the helicopter.*[1]

After reconnoitring the mountain, the pilot agreed with my assessment that there was no safe landing zone at or near the cleared area on the summit of Bell Peak North.

The DCA then went to their backup plan and brought another cargo net to the summit, larger than the one left on the summit with the supplies delivered on the afternoon of the second day, coupled to a wire rope suspended from the quick-release hook underneath the helicopter.

While the helicopter was hovering over the summit, and after the pilot said that it was safe to do so, I moved forward and uncoupled the cargo net from the wire rope.

Stepping back from underneath the helicopter, I *raised the right arm at the elbow with the thumb erect* to signal *all clear*, and the pilot flew back to Ray Morris' farm.[2]

Ray Hickling and I then carried the bodies to the cargo net, remove the poles and placed the bodies in the net, and then contact the pilot to return to the summit.

Again, while the helicopter was hovering over the summit, and after the pilot said that it was safe to do so, I moved forward and coupled the cargo net to the wire rope.

While this was going on, a contingent of six police officers were making their way up the mountain from Thomason's farm to the summit.[1]

At the end of this chapter, there is a photograph of Ray, Kevin, and I in the cleared area at the summit, taken from the helicopter, with Ray signalling *all clear*.[2]

That is when the helicopter extracted the bodies from the summit of Bell Peak North and handed the bodies over to the police and undertaker waiting at the base, relocated to Ray Morris' farm.

Having satisfied continuity, the police and undertaker took the bodies to the mortuary at Cairns for the necessary post-mortems as to the cause of death.

The photograph, received from Ted Tovell, ASA investigator, confirms that the helicopter extracted the bodies during the morning of the third day.

If it had been the afternoon, we would have been in the shadows of the rainforest, as the sun went down to the left of where we were standing in the cleared area.

Ray Hickling and Kevin Murgatroyd believe that the helicopter extracted the bodies during the afternoon, but the photograph, not seen by Ray and Kevin until 40 years later, proves that the extraction was in the morning.[3]

Moreover, Ray Hickling, in his left hand, has the rope used to strap the body bags to the poles, which we removed before placing the bodies in the cargo net.

The photograph reveals the truth of what happened!

When the pilot flew away from the summit, Ray, Kevin, and I moved forward and occupied a grandstand seat on the huge boulders at the summit, and we saw the helicopter safely remove the bodies from the mountain.

After delivering the bodies to the police and undertake, the

DCA then placed the equipment of the ASA investigators and personal belongings of Alan Broughton in the large cargo net.

On our grandstand seats at the summit, we saw the helicopter making its climb up the valley, only to see the cargo net fall from the quick-release hook, about halfway to the summit.

It is highly unlikely that someone will find the cargo net and its contents in the dense rainforest!

When this happened, after looking at each other, shaking our heads in disbelief, I said to Ray and Kevin, "That could have been the bodies!"

Throughout my policing career of 31 years, never did I see anything so poorly organised and implemented like the mission conducted by the DCA on Bell Peak North!

About an hour behind the police contingent, also making their way up the ridge to the summit, were the ASA investigators and Alan Broughton.

They did not know about their losses until told on their way up to the summit.

Recovering, the pilot flew the helicopter to Cairns for repairs to the quick-release hook.

Once repaired, the helicopter returned to Ray Morris' farm and the pilot assessed the quick-release hook with a 44-gallon drum full of water attached to the wire rope suspended underneath the helicopter.

The pilot flew the helicopter up and down the valley, between the Malbon Thompson and Bellenden Ker ranges, until he was satisfied that the hook was in proper working order.

With nothing further to do that day, the pilot flew the helicopter back to Cairns.

Around this time, Ray Morris saw a heated and animated disagreement at his farm between Sub-Inspector Mick McCarthy of Cairns and Ron Morrisson.

Assessing me as competent for traffic duties, even though I had never served in the Traffic Branch, Herb Hore asked Mick McCarthy to obtain a report from Ron Morrisson, recommending me for a Favourable Record.[4]

In that regard, the Curator of the Queensland Police Museum, Lisa Jones, advised that around the time of the mission on Bell Peak North, the Commissioner of Police did, in fact, award Favourable Records to police officers.[4]

When Ron Morrisson refused to provide the report, obviously connected to the *wall-of-silence*, Mick McCarthy stormed off back to Cairns.[5]

Ray Hickling, Alan Broughton, and Kevin Murgatroyd were surprised by the sudden addition of six police officers in the party at the summit, as follows:

> *The next event of that day had Kevin wondering about the thought processors of officialdom. A party of six police officers arrived at the top late afternoon. For what purpose no one seemed to know. Five were so out of condition that when they reached the top they collapsed and were not capable of doing anything. They were still wearing their uniforms which were not designed for tropical conditions, let alone mountain climbing. One was still wearing his motorcycle leggings. Kevin claimed that the sergeant in charge of the Cairns police station went through that station looking for "volunteers" and the only ones he caught were those too slow to get out of his way.[6]*

While Ray, Kevin, and I were having a cup of coffee, the police contingent, who made their way up the ridge to the summit without a guide, appeared from the rainforest.

Naturally, I went forward and greeted them, and it was then that they told me, out of hearing of Ray and Kevin, the reason for them being on the mountain, which was to build a landing zone for the helicopter at the summit.

Upon realising that it was all for nothing, the contingent in unison slumped to the ground. This was interpreted incorrectly by Kevin as five police officers being *so out of condition that when they reached the top they collapsed and were not capable of doing anything*, and that they were *too slow to get out of his way* when *the sergeant in charge of the Cairns police station went through that station looking for "volunteers."*[6]

One from the contingent was a motorcyclist in the Traffic Branch, who was in the CMF and took part in the same training camp the year before in the Seaview Range.

Hearing about the poisonous snakes met on the first day, he wore his leather leggings, as he knew it was common for the *Taipan* to strike at the lower legs.[6]

If those six police officers had been with Barry Downs and I on the first day, there is no doubt in my mind that the party would have carried the bodies down the mountain on that day.

With the arrival of the police contingent at the crash site, the DCA instructed that Ray, Kevin, and I were to make our way back down the mountain, and for Ray to hand the radio over to the ASA investigators making their way up the ridge to the summit with Alan Broughton.

Once again, the DCA had no authority to tell the QPF how to conduct the coronial investigation.

Arthur Lynch, who was in the police contingent, was there to take over from me, but when I told him about the contamination on the first day, and rightly so, Arthur refused to take over the crash site from me.

Reluctantly, which was not their decision to make, the DCA agreed that I should remain to brief the ASA investigators of what happened, hand over the items retrieved to them, and to show them over the crash site.

Having a twelfth wedding anniversary to attend the following day, Ray Hickling was keen to go back down the mountain, but as soon as the DCA became aware that I would not come down until the fourth day, Ray agreed to the DCA's request and remained on Bell Peak North.[7]

Everything sorted out, Ray, Arthur, and I stayed on the summit, while Kevin and the other five in the police contingent, who needed no guide up or down the mountain, made their way back down to Thomason's farm.

On the way down, Kevin and the police officers met the ASA investigators with Alan, which is when Kevin told the party that the cargo net containing their equipment and private property had fallen from the helicopter into the rainforest.

Immediately upon his arrival, Ted Tovell used the radio and arranged through Don Annat for replacement of the lost equipment of the ASA investigators.

It was later in the afternoon when I showed Ted Tovell over the crash site, referring to what I had recorded in my police notebook, and handed over the items recovered from the party, particularly instruments.

When Ted scolded me for not leaving the instruments where they ended up after the crash, I gave Ted a brief rundown of how unruly and ill-disciplined the party was at the crash site.

Ted retracted his statement, and we had no further discussion along those lines.

At the end of this chapter, there is a photograph, taken by me during early morning of the fourth day of Alan Broughton, Tom Machan, Ted Tovell, Arthur Lynch, and Ray Hickling, having a cup of coffee around the campfire.

In fact, there were seven in the camp on the third night and early morning of the fourth day.[3]

After changing into his overalls, Ted Tovell came back with the DCA Engineer, who also was in his overalls, and I took the other photograph of the six around the campfire.

After taking the last of the two photographs on the morning of the fourth day, I set off alone and made my way back down the ridge to Thomason's farm, leaving six in the party at the summit of Bell Peak North that day.

Ray Hickling remembered a request of the pilot in a change of procedures after my departure, as follows:

The pilot had briefed [me] *on using simple hand signals and Arthur Lynch on the operation of the hook. I was to guide him over the clearing.*[3]

At the end of this chapter, there are photographs of Ray using hand signals, and Arthur coupling a cargo net to the helicopter, done by Ray and Arthur while I was making my way down the mountain to Thomason's farm.

What the pilot asked Ray and Arthur to do, the reader should in conjunction with a diagram, also at the end of this chapter, of hand signals used with a helicopter, sourced from the Civil Aviation Safety Authority.[2]

I was aghast when I saw those photographs for the first time, 40 years later!

The signals used by Ray, and what Arthur did to uncoupled and coupled the cargo net underneath the helicopter, was downright dangerous and noncompliant with the universal signals.[2]

Arthur Lynch was a widely experienced police officer, and he was well-known throughout the Far North for his wood-chopping skills and abilities.

When I saw the photographs for the first time, 40 years later, it surprised me that Arthur placed himself in that danger!

Wanting to tell someone what I endured on Bell Peak North was paramount in my mind. However, during the drive from Thomason's farm to the police station, there was complete silence, when the colleague continued with the *wall-of-silence*, snapping me back to reality.

When the bodies were extracted from Bell Peak North
Author (left), Kevin Murgatroyd (rear), Ray Hickling (right)
(Courtesy of Ted Tovell)

Those to rise early having a cup of coffee around the campfire
L-R Alan Broughton, Tom Machan, Ted Tovell, Arthur Lynch, and Ray
Hickling (rear)
(Taken by the Author)

The six who remained at the summit on the fourth day

(L-R) Ted Tovell, Alan Broughton, DCA Engineer, Tom Machan, Ray Hickling, and Arthur Lynch

(Taken by the author)

Simple hand signals used by Ray Hickling, while Arthur Lynch coupled a load underneath the helicopter

(Courtesy of Ray Hickling)

Hover

Arms extended horizontally sideways.

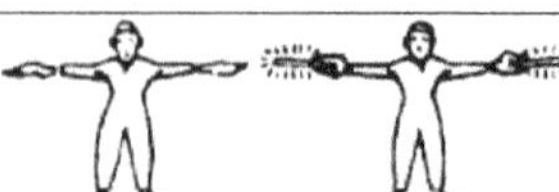

Move upwards

Arms extended horizontally to the side beckoning upwards, with palms turned up. Speed of movement indicates rate of ascent.

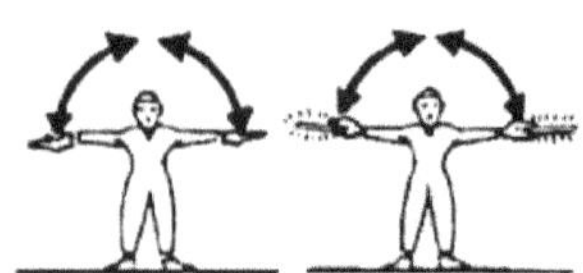

Move downwards

Arms extended horizontally to the side beckoning downwards, with palms turned down. Speed of movement indicates rate of descent.

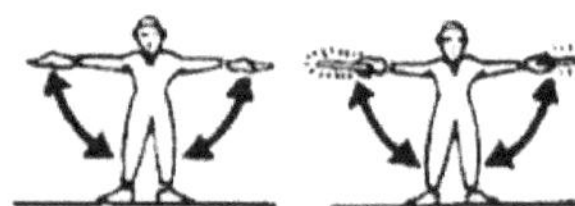

Move ahead

Arms a little aside, palms facing backward and repeatedly moved upward-backward from shoulder height.

All clear

Right arm raised at elbow with thumb erect.

Official hand signals for the operation of a helicopter
(Courtesy of CASA)

11

GREEN MAFIA

February 1, 1970 – after four days and three nights, I came down from Bell Peak North, but not entirely. Arriving home soon after, I was bitterly disappointed to discover that no colleague, not even one of the wives on the Police Reserve, had told Patricia where I was, or what I had been doing during the time away from home. Others would have made a scene, but I kept what I endured before, during, and after the mission on Bell Peak North in my mind for forty years until *The Weekend Post* published the article *Four days, three nights on Bell Peak North*.[1]

The day after *The Weekend Post* published the article, I came down from Bell Peak North!

Ron Morrisson was alive at the time, and after trying hard over the years to get him to say something to me about the plane accident, and answer questions I had about what he did or did not do during the mission, I expected that he might finally do so.

Instead, Ron's son, Graham, wrote a letter to the Editor, as follows:

The final paragraph of Neil Bradford's article on the search for the aircraft on Bell Peak (13-2-10), by inference, takes a sideway swipe at my father, Ron Morrisson, who was sergeant of police at the time. Ron, now 88 and residing in Cairns, believes Mrs Bradford was aware of Neil's part in the search. Given that most of Gordonvale was also aware of the involvement of local police and that there was local and national media coverage, it is remarkable that Mrs Bradford was unaware of Neil's whereabouts, officially or otherwise. Perhaps before his departure, it would have been prudent of Neil to have popped next door to tell her where he was going. I write this with no malice and fully acknowledge the hardship and sterling effort by all in-

volved.[2]

At 88 years of age and living at Cairns, unfortunately, Ron still did not get it!

Because media reports are invariably incorrect or distorted, it was incumbent on Ron to look after the welfare of a subordinate's family, keeping them informed, not only as to what was happening, but also when his family could expect the subordinate to return home.

That is what a good manager would do, but Ron was not a good manager, as he never left the seat of a criminal investigator to occupy the seat of the Officer in Charge at Gordonvale!

I will never forgive Ron for that failing, but if he was alive today, and knowing now what happened, I would apologise to Ron for believing what happened to me over four days and three nights on Bell Peak North was a consequence of the *wall-of-silence.*[3]

Sadly, and I mean that sincerely, Ron passed away on August 11, 2014.[4]

I hold no animosity whatsoever for the other colleagues at Gordonvale. If my story offends anyone, I do not apologise, as I needed to tell this story.

Knowing more about myself, I acknowledge that I was *different* to them, and it is my hope that they will understand as to why I was *different.*

Instead of subjecting me to a *wall-of-silence,* and encouraging the others to be involved, it was incumbent on Ron, as the supervisor of four subordinates at Gordonvale, to sail the ship evenly, rather than lopsided.

The Cairns Post published a similar remonstration from Kevin Murgatroyd, as follows:

The article concerning the Bell Peak expedition (13-2-10) omitted the names of two people who were integral to the whole operation. The Gordonvale State High then had a bushwalking program for senior students, organised by Alan Broughton, Peter Bell, and me. Keith Howarth, the local ambulance superin-

tendent, who was aware of the school's club, told me the party was assembled at Campbell Creek and intended climbing the peak via Campbell Creek Falls. I was aware jungle above the falls was impenetrable. I had never scaled Bell Peak, but Alan and Peter had, and they knew, the only way up was from Thomason's farm at the foot of the mountain at Highleigh. Alan, Peter, and I decided that they would lead a party up by that route, and the group at Campbell Creek came to Highleigh, prepared to follow Alan and Peter. After the wreck had been located, half the party decided to come down the mountain as their services were no longer required, and any camping site on the mountain was non-existent. Very soon after setting off they lost the track and returned to the top and asked for a guide. Alan volunteered to take them out, arriving at Thomason's farm in the middle of a thunderstorm, wet, bedraggled, and exhausted.[5]

Following that remonstration, Ray Hickling, Alan Broughton, and Kevin Murgatroyd published their joint memories of the mission with *ElplorOz*.[6]

Of the other colleagues at Gordonvale, if it had been one of them and not me, there is no doubt in my mind that their spouse would have gone to the police station and enquired as to where her husband was, and when could he be expected home, but that is not in Patricia's nature to do so.

The reader needs to keep in mind what I just said about Patricia, as my colleagues also unjustly accused Patricia of involvement in my alleged improper behaviour at Gordonvale.

Decades later, an Assistant Commissioner accused Patricia of doing something like that again, which has no place in the QPS, and should be done away with, if it is still going on!

"Well," might you ask, "where is your evidence for making that statement?"

In 1970, Ray Whitrod took over from Norm Bauer as the Commissioner of Police in Queensland.

Reflecting in his memoirs on what his wife, Mavis, and he endured, which happened around the time I was subject of the *wall-of-*

silence, Ray Whitrod wrote:

> *We received anonymous telephone calls and unrequested visits at all hours by medicos and taxis. The taxi companies soon got wise and took to ringing us to confirm any request for their services. But we still had to answer the phone at unearthly hours. The heart specialist who said that he had been contacted by 'one of your sergeants' arrived on our doorstep at 3.00 am expecting to find me incapacitated by a heart attack. I told him I was fine, and he went away. Getting rid of the truckload of gravel that was dumped in our driveway was more difficult.*[3,7]

In fact, I overheard Ron Morrisson telling another that it was a load of *horse manure* and not *gravel* dumped in Ray Whitrod's driveway.

Ray Whitrod also referred to other improper behaviour in his memoirs, as follows:

> *Joh must have known that Hiley had shown almost every police officer in Queensland to be participating in a giant scam, that they were accepting their immediate supervisors' assertions that arresting illegal bookmakers was out of the question.*[7]

The Joh mentioned was Sir Johannes (Joh) Bjelke-Petersen, Premier of Queensland, and the other was Sir Thomas Alfred (Tom) Hiley, former Deputy Premier of Queensland and Leader of the Liberal Party in Queensland.[8,9]

In the Queensland Parliament on November 9, 1990, responding to the death of Tom Hiley, the Honourable Wayne Keith Goss, Premier of Queensland, said:

> *Knighted in 1966, Sir Thomas Hiley will be remembered for his service to Queensland, both as a member of the Legislative Assembly and as a Treasurer of this State. He will also be remembered for his efforts to expose and eradicate corruption in public life in Queensland. In 1982, he publicly revealed instances of corruption which he said had occurred over previous decades.*[10,11]

The Government, metaphorically, buried the Hiley Report, alluded to by Ray Whitrod, as follows:

> *I have never forgiven Joh for letting me walk blindfolded into the nest of ants that was the Queensland Police Force. Joh must have been well-aware of the real estate of the Force, but he never gave me any inkling. For example, I knew nothing of the Sir Thomas Hiley exposures until three years after I'd left Queensland.*[7]

After going with a grocer from Gordonvale to the Cannon Park Racecourse at Cairns, instead of my fifty cents each way, the grocer put $400 to win on a horse.

That was a substantial amount of money at a time when the grocer's store was struggling financially, so I took an interest in his activities, and I overheard him receiving telephone calls from the South prior to going to the racecourse.

Later, the name of the grocer's son came up at the Fitzgerald Inquiry, as being involved in the *Northern Mafia*.

Concerned that he was doing something illegal, I took what I knew to Ron Morrisson, who referred me to a Sergeant in the Cairns CIB, and nothing happened.

Soon after, the grocer said that he did not want anything further to do with me.

Yes, some in the police force took part in the *giant scam*, as alluded to by Ray Whitrod, but many did not![7]

Whitrod was an outsider, but what he brought to policing in Queensland was refreshing and totally supported by me, except I did not like his *drooping-lily* handshake!

Even today, I prefer a firm handshake, and based on comments colleagues made, there is no doubt in my mind that this had a bearing on dislike for Whitrod.

Later, never judge a book by its cover, became my motto!

Already studying to improve my education, I went on and completed the course introduced by Whitrod, known by then as the Certificate in Police Studies, as well as the Crime Investigation Course at the Chelmer Police College.[12]

In his memoirs, reflecting on the absence of *an adequate filter to separate the knowledgeable from the ignorant members of the Force*, Ray Whitrod wrote:

In most police forces, this filter is provided by promotional examinations, but in Queensland the pass rate was a puzzling ninety per cent. I investigated this wonderful success rate and discovered that the exam papers were always sent out to police stations and kept there overnight before being presented to candidates the next morning.[7]

Same as what Tom Boyle did at Mackay, appreciated by me, otherwise I would not have embarked on the adventure of my lifetime, Ron Morrisson left a colleague in his office with all the books necessary to complete the answers.

When it was my turn, those responsible for the examinations delivered the papers on the morning of examinations to appointed centres throughout the State, resulting in a *pass rate drop to around fifty per cent.*[7]

I was one of the fifty per cent!

Vale, Commissioner Whitrod, I appreciated what you did to improve the police force in Queensland!

Upon arriving in Queensland, Whitrod found that *the struggle between the Irish mafia and protestant equivalent is far more intense than elsewhere.*[7]

Supplying an explanation of what he meant by the *Irish Mafia*, Whitrod wrote:

The Police Union executive was composed of Sergeants of various classifications, all of whom had some Irish association; they were known colloquially as the Green Mafia.[7]

Ron Morrisson was friendly with the *Green Mafia*, and he did whatever he could to discourage me from associating with the Masonic fraternity.

In fact, if my memory serves me correct, I was the only one of a *Protestant equivalent* at the Gordonvale Police Station.

My mother tried to stop me from seeing a Catholic girl, just like her parents stopped her from seeing a Catholic boy, but I took no notice of her, and the relationship ended when both of us agreed that we were not compatible.

That is the divide existing in those times, and it was present at the Gordonvale Police Station.

Ray Hickling remembered when everyone on the fourth day came down from Bell Peak North, as follows:

On the fourth day I helped the investigation team find components which may have been helpful in their investigation. When they had assembled all, that they required, we radioed the pilot to bring the cargo net. We repeated the previous day's procedure. It went off smoothly. After the components were safely off the mountain, my job and Arthur's was finished. We bid farewell to Alan Broughton and the investigation team and headed off down the mountain together. At the base, the ever-reliable John Cassidy was waiting with a vehicle to pick us up. I must have smelt terrible. Four days in the summer heat and no shower except for the storm rain on the first night.[6]

When I arrived earlier, there was no longer a base on Thomason's farm. However, I do not doubt that Ray Hickling and Arthur Lynch did meet up with John Cassidy where Highleigh Base was before the base was moved back to Ray Morris' farm.

Yes, there was a debriefing conducted by the DCA in the function room of the Aloomba Hotel, but I did not get an invite, and I only became aware of the debriefing through casual conversation with Gordon Cotterill.

Over beers at the Gordonvale Hotel, upon saying that he would like to see the crash site, I readily agreed to take Gordon to the summit of Bell Peak North.[13]

Respecting what was said by Ray Morris, Gordon and I agreed that we would go from Ray's farm up along Campbell Creek to the summit.

Neither of us having been that way before, at 44 years of age,

Gordon was extremely fit and agile, unlike the other farmers in the Search and Recovery party on the first day.

At 7.00 am, we left Ray Morris' farm and found the track up along Campbell Creek easy to follow, and we did not meet anything considered *impenetrable*.[5]

Unlike the first day of the mission, which took the best part of the day to complete, it did not take long for Gordon and me to arrive at the crash site.

Once there, sitting on a boulder where I had cut down the trees at the summit, looking at the valley below, I reflected on what I had seen and achieved over the four days and three nights on Bell Peak North.

In the serenity of the moment, images of the bodies I had re-covered, combined with the foolhardy bombing with food and water by the DCA, and the days and nights spent waiting for extraction of the remains, filled a tormented mind.

All I wanted to do was discuss this with colleagues, but that never happened!

Apart from going back up to show Gordon the crash site, I also searched for an heirloom ring on the finger of a hand that neither Bob nor I could find.[13]

Gordon and I searched thoroughly, but I did not find the hand or ring.[13]

There are wild dogs on the mountain, and it is possible that one might have taken the hand.

After recovering the large and heavy tarpaulin left by the DCA at the summit, Gordon and I carried the heavy and cumbersome tar-paulin back down the mountain, receiving a reward of $20 for its return to the DCA.[13]

Gordon thought I was mad, but I wanted to prove a point, that if the party had been fit and agile, the party would have brought the bodies down on the first day.

Taking turns, Gordon and I had no difficulty carrying the heavy and cumbersome tarpaulin down the mountain, which proved that a fit and disciplined party would have completed the mission on the first day.

And the weather and condition of the ground was the same as experienced on the mountain at the time of the Search and Recovery mission!

But for the untruths and criticisms others told, particularly Ray Hickling and Kevin Murgatroyd, I would have glossed over the truth of what happened.

That is what I did for the story *Four days, three nights on Bell Peak North* published in *The Weekend Post*, alluding that Ron Morrisson was to blame for what happened.[1]

Unbeknown to me, others in the party made out that they were the *principles* and led what they perceived was a successful mission on Bell Peak North, which was far from the truth of what happened there over four days and three nights.[5]

Before 4.00 pm on the day that Gordon and I went up to look over the crash site at the summit of Bell Peak North, having in mind that we left at 7.00 am, Gordon and I were having a beer at the Aloomba Hotel.[13]

Less than nine hours is all that it took for Gordon and me to climb to the summit, look over the crash site, reflect for a while, and carry the tarpaulin down the mountain!

With the directions passed on by Ray Morris, I did not need any of the three bushwalkers to guide me up along Campbell Creek to the summit, and back down to Ray's farm.

That accomplishment made a mockery out of the contention that the three schoolteacher bushwalkers were the *principles* in the Search and Recovery mission on Bell Peak North.[5]

Only Ray Hickling received official recognition from the DCA for the time and effort he put into the mission.

It surprised me that no acknowledgement came from the QPF, but now that I know more about what happened, I understand why neither Ray nor anyone else received any official recognition from the QPF.

The DCA took over command and control of the mission from the QPF!

Fortunately, there is now a trained and disciplined organisation called the State Emergency Service (SES) to aid the QPS during a mission, like the one on Bell Peak North, as well as other areas of policing.

Having been up and down the mountain from Thomason's farm, and afterwards Ray Morris' farm, it was a matter of *chalk and cheese* when comparing both routes.

The track up along Campbell Creek to the summit was much better and faster to negotiate than the track up along the ridge from Thomason's farm.

Moreover, there was an abundance of water in Campbell Creek that the party could have used, after purifying with tablets, same as I did in the army.

Even today, I am still livid with the failure of the party to complete the mission in one day, turning it into a bigger disaster than what it was, which could have resulted in further deaths on Bell Peak North.

If command and control of the mission had remained with the QPF, and if the party failed to carry the bodies down the mountain on the first day, there is no doubt in my mind, after a declaration by Herb Hore, the Federal Government would have supplied an army Iroquois helicopter.

Trained and experienced in Vietnam with extracting soldiers in difficult locations and under extreme circumstances, there is no doubt in my mind that the RAAF pilots would have successfully extracted the bodies at the first attempt.

The pilots of the two helicopters, who came to the summit, did not display any of that training or experience.

On March 5, 2010, I was surprised to receive a letter, found at the end of this chapter, from Ian Wallace, youngest son of Bob Wallace, who had passed on by that time.[14]

Finally, the heroic actions of Bob Wallace were known and appreciated by others, particularly his family.

Even today, tears well in my eyes, when I read how fondly Bob's son spoke about his father, and the kind words of appreciate that I received from Bob's family.

In contrast, not only did Ray Hickling give speeches about the Search and Recovery mission, but while in England during 2005, he visited Patrick Hill's widow, Hillary, and daughter, Louise.[15]

The mission on Bell Peak North was a defining moment in anyone's policing career.

With a *Favourable Record* and not subjected to a *wall-of-silence* or banished in disgrace from Gordonvale, more than likely, my career would have taken a vastly different path.

Also, I would not have been called a *dog* thereafter by some colleagues?[16]

Remembering the harassment suffered by his wife and himself in Queensland, Whitrod said that he *hadn't felt safe despite being the top policeman in the state*, and that he locked his *bedroom door at night and* [kept] *a firearm with* [him].[7]

Suffering similarly, but not to the same extreme, my socializing outside of work was mostly within the community.

Taking me completely by surprise, Gordon Cotterill and Ray Morris came to the police residence and invited me to join the Masonic Lodge.

Eyes and ears were everywhere, and Gordon and Ray's visit, and the reason for them being at my house, somehow got to the ears of Ron Morrisson.

Next time I was at work, "I hear that you are going to be a goat rider," questioned Ron.

In those days, it was common for a colleague to use the term *goat rider* to describe someone involved in Freemasonry, and that is what Ron did.

"Who told you," I responded.

"A little birdie told me!"

"Is there any rule or regulation that says I cannot join the Masonic Lodge?"

"No, but it has no place at this station, while I am in charge, so I wouldn't join, if I were you!"

Same as Ray Whitrod, I was aware of the conflict between *the Irish mafia and its Protestant equivalent* in the police force, so when confronted with it firsthand by Ron Morrisson, I plunged headlong into the undesirable divide and accepted the invitation to join the Masonic Lodge.[7]

5th March 2010

Mr Neil Bradford

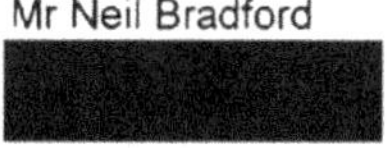

Dear Mr Bradford

I am writing to you in regards to your account of the Bells Peak Tragedy. My name is Ian Wallace, youngest son of Bob Wallace. First of all I would like to thank you for your generous recollections of my father's role in this tragedy.

To know my father as I did, he was not a man to boast of his actions and certainly did not discuss what his eyes had seen in such a situation with us at home. As we got older, small parts of the story would come out but Dad being Dad, he would refer more to parts of the plane being lodged in odd regions of the terrain you were in.

However in writing these few words, my aim is to thank you whole heartedly for your kind words of my father's role in this situation and be assured you made a family already proud of their father just that little bit more prouder. Thank you once again.

Yours faithfully

Letter from Ian Wallace
(Courtesy of Ian Wallace)

12

FALSELY ACCUSED

June 26, 1971 – a litter of red and white Pembroke Welsh Corgis was born at Abertawe Kennels on Pine Creek Road at Bessie Point, near Gordonvale. Driving past the kennels, soon after, and seeing the adult dogs bounding like rabbits across a paddock, I decided it was time the family had another dog, as *Rex* was killed by a train after the flood, four years earlier, so I turned around and select the runt of the litter, a male.

Six weeks later, catching the family completely by surprise, in the box on the back seat of the police vehicle was *Snowdon of Abertawe*, affectionally known as *Snowy*.

At the end of this chapter, there is a photograph of *Snowy* when he became part of the family.

Well do I remember seeing him scampering across the linoleum floor, concealed under a plastic motorcycle helmet, until he ran into a wall, being smashed onto his back, but getting up quickly, shaking his head, and doing it all over again, with the same result.

How such a small and affectionate puppy got me transferred in disgrace from Gordonvale, beggars' belief!

About a month later, out of the blue, and while I was working and away from the police station, the registered breeder arrived at our home to check on *Snowy's* progress.

And I say again, it was an innocent and completely *out of the blue* catching up, over a small and affectionate puppy, that was turned into something sinister!

With the breeder was a sister-in-law, who, unbeknown to Patricia and me, had made complaints against all colleagues at the Gordonvale Police Station.

Yes, I heard rumours, but I was not involved in any alleged improper conduct and behaviour, and being subjected to a *wall-of-silence*, neither Patricia nor I knew anything about the sister-in-law making those complaints.

In fact, neither of us had met the sister-in-law before, and we did not know that her husband, who worked at the Mulgrave Sugar Mill, was the breeder's brother.

Yes, I knew the complainant's husband, but only to say *G'day* to him.

If the reader knows anything about *autism*, upon hearing the rumours, and because I was not involved in any alleged improper behaviour, I turned myself off, never suspecting that this chance meeting was in any way connected with the *wall-of-silence*.

Obviously, when I turned myself off, the others took this as a sign of guilt, and that I was up to something, when all I wanted was peace and quiet, not only with my family, but also in the work that I did.

After the visit, the *wall-of-silence* became unbearable, so I asked for and was granted an interview with Inspector Max Lyndon (Max) Noakes, formerly CIB, of Cairns.

The conversation that I had with Noakes was the same as the one with the AWU representative, out on the veranda, outside the courtroom, and in the presence of Ron Morrisson.

After outlining that the sister-in-law of the breeder had lodged complaints against all colleagues for alleged improper conduct and behaviour, "I believe you have been providing her," said Noakes, "with the sensitive information!"

When Noakes confirmed that no complaint had been made against me, "Is that the reason," I responded angrily, "why no one will speak with me?"

"Yes."

"Well, it isn't me, sir!"

"If it's not you, then your wife has been providing her with the information."

"What makes you think that?"

"The complainant was seen visiting your house!"

Quickly connecting the *out of the blue* visit to our house with what Noakes said, I thought about laying the Inspector out on the floor of the veranda, but a voice cautioned me, "Don't do it, Neil. He's not worth losing your job over!"

I have no doubt in my mind that the voice was my great-great-grandfather, William James Clements, who was a Sergeant in the Native Mounted Police during the 1860s at Belyando, near Clermont, and who comforted me at the Police Depot, provided me with tuition of how to give evidence in court, and continually told me to *watch my back!*

While on patrol, as an Acting Sub-Inspector, my great-great-grandfather was speared in the back, which apparently is the reason for his resignation soon after that incident.

Relocating to Mackay, my great-great-grandfather became the first Sexton of the Mackay Cemetery, did work as a builder through his occupation as a sawyer, was a farmer, pound-man, Bailiff, and Deputy High Bailiff.

So, I firmly believe that it was my great-great-grandfather, who offered the advice during my policing career.

Gaining my composure, "If that is what everyone believes, sir," I responded, angrily, "I would like a transfer!"

More to the point, I had not been involved in any of the alleged improper conduct and behaviour, which, according to Noakes, was supplied verbatim to the complainant.

"That will be arranged," said Noakes. "We don't want this going on here at Gordonvale, or anywhere else, do you understand?"

"I understand what you are saying," I responded, "but you have got it completely wrong, as we have not provided anything to the complainant!"

Without any evidence whatsoever, other than someone, obviously a colleague, saw the complainant at our residence on the police reserve, I was transferred in disgrace to the newly established police station at Moranbah, inland from Mackay.

The transfer, however, was delayed through unavailability of rental accommodation.

Leaving Gordonvale under those circumstances was the hardest thing I have ever done in my life, as the beginnings of my married life with Patricia are deeply entrenched in the town, as both of our sons were born there, and we made friendships that withstood the test of time.

While waiting for approval to move on transfer, I gave evidence as the arresting officer for a contested drink-driving charge in the Magistrates Court at Cairns.

After finding the defendant *guilty*, "Before I close the court, Constable," said Magistrate Michael Maxwell (Max) Dwyer, "there is something I would like to say to you. I hear that you have been transferred, and during the time you have given evidence before me in this court, I have always found you to be honest, so I wish you all the best for the future."

It was uncommon to receive compliments like that from the Bench, and after collecting myself, "Thank you, sir, I deeply appreciate what you just said about me," I responded.

Up until then, sometimes when I answered a question asked by the defence, Max would clear his throat, rest his chin on the palm of his hand, face downwards, frown, and go red in the face, causing me to believe that he doubted my evidence.

What I thought turned out to be the complete opposite, and I left the courtroom with immense pride, after receiving that complement from Max Dwyer.

Thinking more about it now, it is possible that Max Dwyer knew about the allegation made against me, which was not agreeable to him, and he gave the complement.

Then, if the prosecutor did his job, those comments would have been referred to Max Noakes, possibly for my personal record to be noted, which did not happen.

Before and during my time with Max Dwyer, it was common for me to arrest a drink-driving offender in the Gordonvale Police Division, have the breathalyser test conducted at Cairns, and while returning to Gordonvale, arrest another one or two drink-drivers before getting out of the Cairns CBD.

It was said to me that I was trying to show up the Cairns Traffic Branch for not doing their job, but I am an *autistic* person, and I could not drive past what I saw.

That is the truth of what happened!

When Herb Hore assessed me as competent for traffic duties, which was uncommon for someone not working in the Cairns Traffic Branch, it came as a complete surprise to me, and it spurred on members in that traffic branch to do the same as what I was doing in the Cairns Police Division.

Unable to cope any longer with the *wall-of-silence*, despite the residence at Moranbah not being available, I was granted permission by Noakes to leave on transfer.

At the end of this chapter, there is a photograph of me, just before leaving Gordonvale.

December 24, 1971 – Cyclone Althea, with speed of wind gusts between 135 to 215 kilometres per hour, devastated Townsville on a Friday night, which was Christmas Eve, resulting in the loss of three lives.[1]

A storm surge of almost 3.66 metres was recorded just north of Townsville.[1]

The extent of damage to hundreds of homes and buildings damaged or destroyed at Townsville and on Magnetic Island was just under A$120 million.[1]

December 27, 1971 – we left Gordonvale on the Monday after Townsville was devastated by Althea.

I lived through cyclones at Mackay, but the large gum trees uprooted and lying lifeless on the ground, was and unbelievable sight, as we drove through the outskirts of Townsville.

Driving south from Townsville, we came across rivers and creeks in flood and safely negotiated sections of the Bruce Highway covered with water.

The experience, however, reminded us of what we had gone through during the 1967 Gordonvale flood, and our hearts went out to those who endured Althea.

After a day or two with Wally and Madge Pannell at Sarina, I left Patricia and the boys with them, and I went ahead on transfer to Moranbah.

January 15, 1972 – until Sergeant Second Class Kevin Nichol (Kevin) Groundwater arrived to assume his position, relieving as the Officer in Charge was Senior Constable Donald Malcolm Leslie (Don) Condie.

Inspector Arthur Gordon (AGB) Bianchi of Mackay gave an assurance that temporary accommodation would be found, but there was none, as accommodation at the Black Nugget Hotel/Motel had not been completed, and Don Condie recommended against living in a caravan park.

Moving out of a caravan park, Don parked his caravan at the rear of the police station, connected it to the electricity, and was using the toilet, kitchenette, and showers.

Without permission from anyone, I bunked in the courtroom, as Moranbah was not dedicated as a place to hold courts until after I left the town.

There was a refrigerator in the kitchenette, and counter meals were provided at the Black Nugget Hotel/Motel and doing what I had done with washing and ironing of clothes when I lived in the barracks on Uncle Doug's farm, I had temporary accommodation at Moranbah.

Soon after, I was told by Sergeant Second Class Evan Arthur (Nifty) Reason, Inspector's clerk at Mackay, that I had been moved on transfer *under a cloud of suspicion.*

This was followed by AGB saying that he would come down heavy on me if I continued with anything, like what I got up to at Gordonvale.

It was a two-man police station at Moranbah, one hundred and ninety-three kilometres from Mackay, which suited me, as I believed that working mainly by myself, and being so far from others, I would ride out the storm stirred up by Ron Morrisson.

Being police officers, I expected better, as it was necessary to establish the facts properly, before placing someone before the court to answer a charge.

But that is how it was in those times, and obviously how it still is with policing in Queensland, if the recent Royal Commission is anything to go by!

The date of completion of the Housing Commission home being constantly pushed out, and missing my family, again without any permission, I moved Patricia and the boys from Sarina to the house set aside for Kevin Groundwater.

We did it tough, and with mattresses, table, and chairs provided by someone, we lived in the house until our residence at 20 Connor Drive became available.

Subsidized weekly rent for those who worked in the coal mines was $5, while, as a police officer, I had to pay the full rent of $22 per week.

Then, miners received almost twice as much as what I was paid as a police officer.

When Kevin Groundwater arrived, I went from the frying pan into the fire!

Kevin came from Rockhampton, and if my memory serves me correct, he worked for years in the Main Roads' police, and he had little experience in General Duties, and no experience as the Officer in Charge of a police station.

He had married a widow, Betty, a lovely lady, but there was no child to that liaison.

Rumour had it that while at Rockhampton, which often was a boast of Kevin's, he used a shotgun to blow a hole in the side of a vehicle, hooning repeatedly past his residence.

It appears that Inspector Leslie James (Les) Bardwell of the Scientific Section, Brisbane, found that the shotgun had not been fired recently, and Kevin was not charged.[2]

Nevertheless, people at Moranbah heard about the rumour, and they kept their distance from Kevin.

Certainly, he made me wary of him, and while waiting one night in a darkened area for a noisy motorcycle to come past, I folded the left leg across the right, and I used the boot on the left foot to ease the gear into neutral.

When Kevin took his foot off the clutch, pressing down hard on the accelerator with the other foot, instead of the police vehicle taking off with a shower of gravel, sprayed all over the place from the rear wheels, there was only a loud roaring of the motor, and soon the motorcyclist disappeared out of sight.

There is no doubt in my mind that Kevin would have run the motorcyclist over that night, and I had no desire to be party to the offence, so I circumvented what Kevin intended doing.

Not long afterwards, but during the daytime, we came across a parked vehicle, of which the passenger's side wheels were on the footpath.

The driver offered to park correctly, but Kevin snapped, and he started punching into the driver, in full view of his two passengers, as well as those in a nearby caravan park.

Astounded by what had happened, I stepped backwards, and soon Kevin was puffing and wheezing from the flurry of blows that he swung.

When Kevin's blows became weaker and less frequent, the much smaller man retaliated, and he hit Kevin twice, which, in my opinion, was justifiable, before I separated them.

"Why didn't you help me," said Kevin.

"If he had hit you first, I would have" I replied. "But you hit him first, and I will not back you up, if you do something like that again in the future!"

Fortunately, the aggrieved party did not make a complaint, but that did not stop Kevin telling others that I did not back him up in a fight instigated by the other.

It is no wonder that I preferred working alone!

Not long after that incident, two of my former colleagues at Gordonvale, on their way to the Gemfields, called in at Moranbah, which surprised me.

Over a beer at the hotel, both apologised for falsely accusing me at Gordonvale. They admitted to me that it was a person, with whom they associated, during and outside of work, and who was a Sugarcane Inspector for the Mulgrave Sugar Mill where the complainant's husband, also was employed.

The person accused of supplying the complainant's husband with the information is in a photograph at the end of Chapter 7.

That is how the information was supplied, according to Max Noakes, verbatim to the complainant!

Being who I am, I had moved on from Gordonvale, and they accepted our offer of a bed that night, going on to the Gemfields the following morning.

During the 2010s, I saw one of those colleagues passing through the international terminal at the Brisbane Airport, where I then worked as an Aviation Protection Officer, and I told him that him that this would be included in my forthcoming book.

"Don't do that, Neil," was his response, which I have chosen to ignore, for the following reason.

At the time of their apology, I thought everyone at Gordonvale was aware, namely Ron Morrisson and the other colleague!

However, because of Ron Morrission's attitude towards me, when I went back twice to Gordonvale for the Masonic Lodge, and later in the 1980s when I visited Ron at Cairns, it is obvious to me now that they were the only two to know.

Things deteriorated when Kevin refused me time away from Moranbah to visit family at Sarina and Mackay, so Patricia went by herself with the boys.

While I was clearing up crime and attending to all work away from the police station, Kevin was more interested in earning extra money from using his private vehicle to escort mining equipment to Mackay and elsewhere.

I refused to do the same, but when Kevin said that he would ask AGB to have me transferred, I agreed and was injured on May 12, 1972, when the brakes failed on a long load that I was escorting down the Eton Range.

Suffering a whiplash injury, I got progressively worse instead of better, and it became necessary for me to be transferred to Mackay where treatment I needed was available.

On sick leave before I moved on transfer, Kevin came to my house with the relieving constable, and he invited me to fight him on the front lawn, for leaving him in the lurch.

The last image I have of Kevin Groundwater is of him shaping up to me on the front lawn!

After I moved on transfer, the number of constables at the police station increased to two, testament of how efficient and effective I was at Moranbah.

May 31, 1973 – I arrived on transfer at Mackay and began the treatment not available at Moranbah.

While in the Mackay Base Hospital for a medical procedure, I became agitated and disorientated from the medication that I was given, and in a distressed state, I booked myself out and arrived home in my pyjamas without any money to pay for the taxi.

After persuading the Medical Superintendent to allow me back into the hospital, I was given a general anaesthetic for the medical procedure and began to abuse everyone.

When the medical procedure was over, I was banned by the Medical Superintendent from ever being a patient at the hospital while he was in charge.

Fishing one day, the prescribed medication was thrown into the Pioneer River, and same as what happened when I was taken off the medication in 1964 at the Lister Private Hospital, I soon recovered sufficiently to resume operational duties at Mackay.

Having got my policing career back on track, I applied for and was selected for the position of Officer in Charge at Wallumbilla, a one-man police station, near Roma.

On my last shift at Mackay, I was directed to go to Baker's Creek, south of Mackay, where the locals were concerned that an elderly man had drowned.

Being familiar with the location, my younger partner and I arrived quickly.

With the rope attached to a wrist, the elderly man had wrapped the cast net around the same arm and was wading through neck-high saltwater to cast for bait on the other side when it appeared he had a heart attack and disappeared.

Despite the tide flowing swiftly into the creek, I knew from experience that the body would not be far from where the man was last seen, so I requested the grappling hook at the police station to be brought to my location.

While waiting, a small rowboat and oars were loaned to me for use in the search for the body.

When the grappling hook arrived, I rowed while my younger partner dragged for the body, snagging, and bringing up old crab pots and other debris to the surface.

Becoming complacent, my partner let go of the rope when the body surfaced, and the elderly man quickly sank back to the bottom, it being revealed afterwards that my partner had not been that close before to a dead body.

Composing himself, my partner found the body on the next drag, and this time, we pulled the body from the water, and then rowed back to the bank.

Unfortunately, not much was known about the man, such as did he have a vehicle, and neither did he carry anything on him to show who he was.

So, without knowing who he was, and a post-mortem being necessary, my partner and I went to log the body in the mortuary at the Mackay Base Hospital.

It was a Sunday, and being short staffed, the sister-in-charge came with the wardsman and helped remove the body to the mortuary.

While undressing the body, "That's my father," shrieked the sister, clasping her face in her hands, falling unconscious soon after to the floor.

This is something that police and other emergency personnel

try to avoid, but it happens, unexpectedly, through early difficulties in identification.

March 21, 1975 – I arrived on transfer at Wallumbilla, and on my arrival, the Inspector at Roma told me that he wanted to speak to me at the first opportunity in his office.

In his office, "Yes, sir," I questioned, "what is it that you would like to discuss?"

"Ron Morrisson has told me what you got up to at Gordonvale," said the Inspector, "and nothing like that will go on here, is that clear?"

"Yes, sir!"

Despite the two colleagues apologising to me at Moranbah, Ron Morrisson was still doing whatever he could to destroy my policing career.

January 5, 1976 – I drove to the gas pipeline south from Wallumbilla and served a summons on an itinerant worker.

Around 7.30 pm, while driving over the railway line, back into town, a speeding vehicle heading towards Roma, flashed past on the Warrego Highway.

I thought, "How dare you," as I activated the siren and flashing-blue light to give chase.

Pulling the vehicle over at Pickanjinnie, on the Roma side of Wallumbilla, I parked to the rear, and while obscured in the lights of the police vehicle on low beam, I approached the driver, who was the sole occupant.

"The speedometer in the police vehicle showed that you were speeding," I said. "Could I see your driver's licence, please?"

"Certainly," he replied, rummaging through the glove box, before adding, "here it is," and he then handed the licence to me through the opened window.

The licence produced was current and issued in New South Wales to a Bruce John Drawbridge, which was the name originally provided by the driver.

The vehicle, however, was registered in New South Wales to a

Coral Elaine Reeves of St Marys, about forty-five kilometres west from Sydney.[3]

Believing that Drawbridge was searching for something under the seat, which caused the hairs on the back of my neck to stand up, "Would you get out of the car," I urgently directed, "and stand beside it, please?"

"Certainly," said Drawbridge, aged 48 years, who got out, standing upright around 185 centimetres tall, and weighing about 115 kilograms.

In those times, a departmental-issued firearm could not be carried in a holster on the trousers belt. So, unbuttoning the shirt to show the firearm butt tucked on the inside of my belt, "Do you have permission to drive this vehicle," I questioned.

"Yes, I do. Coral is my de facto," Drawbridge responded. "She loaned it to me to come to Queensland and visit a seriously ill relative at Roma."

"Remain where you are until I check things out," I said, walking backwards slowly to the police vehicle.

Unfortunately, the location was one of the *black spots* for radio reception in the police division, and I was unable to verify the information provided by Drawbridge.

Drawbridge's explanation for use of the vehicle was plausible, and after issuing him with a speeding ticket, he was allowed to continue on his way, allegedly to Roma.

A report of what happened thereafter was published in *The Canberra Times*, as follows:

A convicted double murderer, missing from a Sydney jail, was arrested in southern Queensland today, after saying he had committed another murder at the weekend. The convict, 48, was serving a life sentence for a double murder. He had been let out of Silverwater Jail, Sydney, on a weekend pass, but failed to report back at 8 pm on Sunday. The man was detained at 4 am today at a police roadblock near Roma, after a farmer saw him throw what appeared to be blood-stained clothing from a car.

Roma police sent an urgent message to Sydney CIB when the man told them he had murdered a woman, 45, in the outer Sydney suburb of St Marys, on Sunday. A check of the car he was driving showed that it was registered in the name of the woman he claimed he had killed. Sydney police rushed to the woman's home but found no trace of her or her car. The man was charged in Roma with having unlawfully used a motorcar, and later remanded in custody. Meanwhile, 30 detectives and uniformed police today searched bushland in the St Mary's orchard hills area of Sydney for a newly dug grave. They did not find it.[3]

Missing from the report, was the fact that arriving back at the police station, I telephoned and requested the radio operator at the Roma Police Station for a licence and vehicle check with police in New South Wales.

I was contacted 20 minutes later by the Duty Sergeant at Roma who said that an urgent reply had been received from the police in New South Wales.

At 8.00 pm on January 4, 1976, Drawbridge, who was serving a life sentence for a double murder, did not return from weekend leave to the Silverwater Detention Centre.[3]

The Inspector in Charge of Roma Police District was informed, and a roadblock was set up on the Warrego Highway, just on the Wallumbilla side of Roma.

Going back out in the police vehicle, I patrolled along the Warrego Highway to the roadblock and did not find Drawbridge or the vehicle, returning thereafter to Wallumbilla.

Around 4.00 am, being suspicious of Drawbridge's behaviour, the farmer discovered that what he saw thrown from the vehicle by Drawbridge, was, in fact, bloodstained clothing.

Just as the roadblock was about to be closed, the information from the farmer was received, and Drawbridge and the vehicle were found nearby.

A search found a length of rope under the front seat of the vehicle, which no doubt would have been used to strangle me, if I had not asked Drawbridge to get out of the vehicle were I could see what he was doing.

Drawbridge's arrest at Roma was published in *The Canberra Times*, as follows:

> *Police confirmed today that a woman was missing and that they were interviewing her friends and relatives. The assistant superintendent in charge of the CIB Mr A. M. Birnie, and the man arrested at Roma had given only a vague description covering a wide area of bushland. Two detectives of the Special Crime Squad, Detective-Sergeant McCusker and Detective Senior Constable Cook left Sydney today to interview the man. Superintendent Birnie confirmed that the man they were going to question had been jailed in December 1959, for a double murder.*[3]

His arrest for the 1959 double murder appeared in *The Canberra times*, as follows:

> *The skeletons of a woman and her child were found on the veranda of a house at West Wallsend today. Detectives think both were strangled. Newcastle police tonight charged a 31-year-old man with the murder of the woman and the boy. The dead were Eva May Gallon, 24, and her son Ian, 3, of Teralba Road, West Wallsend. An 80-year-old man, Jim Blakely, has been living in the house for months not knowing a crime had been committed. Today, when he opened a door onto the veranda of the four-roomed house, he found the skeletons. The remains were removed to Royal Newcastle Hospital morgue.*[4,5]

It appears that after renewing his driver's licence, Drawbridge had permission to drive the vehicle on weekends when he stayed with the victim, which can be found in an article published in *The Canberra Times*, as follows:

> *A prisoner had admitted murdering a divorced Sydney woman on one of his "weekends off" from Long Bay Jail, Blacktown Court was told today. The prisoner, Mr Bruce John Drawbridge, 48, appeared in court charged with having murdered Mrs Coral Elaine Reeves, of St Marys, on January 4. Detective-*

Sergeant R Williams, of Penrith, told the court that when Mr Drawbridge had been arrested in Queensland two days later, he, had said he had been staying with Mrs Reeves on his weekends off from jail. Sergeant Williams said Mr Drawbridge told him he had strangled Mrs Reeves and dumped her body in bush about five miles away before driving to Queensland. Mrs Reeves' body had been found at Marsden Park with a knotted pair of Pantyhose around her neck. The hearing will resume tomorrow.[6]

The committal of Drawbridge for trial on the murder charge was published in *The Canberra Times*, as follows:

Mr Bruce John Drawbridge, 48, a Long Bay Jail prisoner, was committed for trial by Mr McKeown, SM, today on a charge of having murdered Mrs Coral Elaine Reeves in Sydney on January 4. Mr Drawbridge is alleged to have strangled Mrs Reeves while on weekend leave from jail. He pleaded not guilty to the charge o£ escaping from lawful custody at Silverwater Detention Centre on January 4.[7]

During questioning by the Roma CIB, Drawbridge admitted that he murdered Reeves and stole her car to drive through Queensland to the Northern Territory.

If I had not come across Drawbridge by chance, he would have escaped to the Northern Territory.

Moreover, if I had been at a location where use of the radio was possible, Drawbridge would have been taken into custody on the Warrego Highway at Pickanjinnie.

Same as the chance hearing of the Cessna 402 crashing into Bell Peak North, if I had not decided to pursue him for the speeding offence, it is possible that Drawbridge would have made his way into the Northern Territory.

Others received credit for the excellent work done, but I became the bane of a joke peddle around the district, that after Drawbridge admitted to me that he did not own the vehicle, I let an escaping murderer go free.

Sometimes discretion is the better part of valour, and instead of being strangled, if I had tried to take Drawbridge into custody by myself, I survived and activated the search by sending the message to police in NSW.

In that regard, the newspaper said that the message was sent after Drawbridge was taken into custody, which was incorrect, as it was sent earlier by me.

If I had not listened to my instincts and took no notice of the hairs standing up on the back of my neck, I probably would have been Drawbridge's fourth victim.

Despite not receiving any recognition for the Drawbridge apprehension, my application soon after to attend the 24th Crime Investigation Course at the Chelmer Police College in Brisbane was approved.

It was while at the course I heard of police being involved in the corruption known as the *Joke*, associated with illegal gambling and prostitution in Brisbane.

On the first weekend, I went into the CBD and was shocked to see how much the nightlife in Brisbane had changed from ten years before when I trained at the Police Depot, which made me distance myself from that activity and remained thereafter at the college on weekends off.

At the end of this chapter, there is the certificate, showing that I successfully completed the course, and a photograph of those who attended the course.

When interviewed and offered a plain clothes position in Brisbane, I respectfully declined, curtailing the aspiration I had of becoming a detective in the CIB.

Patrolling towards Yuleba, I came across Inspector Anthony (Tony) Murphy, sent by Whitrod to Longreach, broken down on the Warrego Highway.[8]

While his family were entertained by Patricia, I drove Tony into Roma where Lyle Cherry scrounged and found a replacement tyre and tube for Tony's antiquated trailer.[8]

Pondering in his memoirs, Whitrod wrote that *when Bischof died, his estate was very small, so I've no real understanding of where all the money went?*[8]

Having heard that Tony Murphy took part in the corruption known as the *Joke*, "What is happening to his money," I thought, as my family was dressed better, and his trailer looked as if it had just come out of a wrecking yard.[9]

Once the trailer was repaired, Tony and his family went on their way to Longreach.

In 1976, not long after providing that help to Tony Murphy and his family, Whitrod resigned and his replacement, Terrance Murray (Terry) Lewis, sent by Whitrod to Charleville, took over as the Commissioner.[8,10,11]

During mid-afternoon of a Sunday the following year, while mowing the lawn in the rear yard, the hair on the back of my neck stood up, warning me that danger was present.

Believing that it might be an *Inland Taipan*, the *most toxic of any snake*, even a sea snake, I search and did not find a snake in the kikuyu grass.[12]

Instincts, however, caused me to look in the direction across the rear paddock of the police station to the barracks behind the Bank of New South Wales on the Warrego Highway, and I also did not see anything of concern there.

The sensation persisted, so I turned the mower off and went inside for a cup of tea.

About an hour later, I went back out to mow the lawn, only to have the hairs on the back of my neck, stand up again, this time forcing me to turn the mower off and leave the mowing to another day.

Of the belief that something might happen, everyone in the family was told not to go out into the rear yard for the rest of that day.

Becoming friendly with the Manager of the Bank of New South Wales, John Henry (John) Truman, I thought it was a casual visit, the morning after, when he came to the police station.

Very pale and trembling, "Neil," said John, "you were fortunate not to be shot yesterday!"

"How was I almost shot, and by whom?"

"One of my clerks at the barracks had you lined up through the scope of a loaded rifle. He was about to pull the trigger when you went inside the house!"

"Who told you this?"

"The other clerk living in the barracks told me just a few minutes ago what happened yesterday."

"How did he come by the rifle?"

"He bought the ·243 rifle, scope, and ammunition from Watkins on Saturday!"

"Where is he now?"

"He's at the bank, as we speak!"

What John said coincided with the hairs standing up on the back of my neck, forcing me to stop mowing the yard.

Contacting my superior at Roma, "Have the manager go back to the bank and behave as if nothing out of the ordinary has happened. I will see him there shortly," said the Inspector.

Within 30 minutes, the Inspector, and head of the Roma CIB were at the bank.

After speaking to John and the witness, the Inspector made a telephone call to the head office of the Bank of New South Wales in Brisbane.

Soon after, John was told by his superior that the clerk was to leave at once on transfer back to Brisbane.

In events leading up to the incident, I spoke to the clerk in John's presence about complaints received for the undue noise he made around town with his vehicle.

The clerk had just recently been transferred under duress from Brisbane to Wallumbilla.

After admitting to what had been alleged, when advised that if anything like that happened again, a ticket would be issued, he agreed to behave.

Not only was he rebelling within the community, but according to John, he was chastised also for upsetting staff and customers at the bank.

Without speaking to me, the Inspector and head of the CIB went back to Roma.

Stopping at the police station on his way home from work, "My manager told me that it was a personality clash between you and my clerk," said John.

Shocked by what John said, I telephoned the Inspector, who previously made it known that he preferred not to work with me, and he refused to say anything, leaving me completely in the dark as to what was done.

Later, when I was attached to the Mount Isa Police Station, I was contacted by the Recruitment Section in Brisbane. The clerk had made application to join the police force, and he answered that he got into trouble with me at Wallumbilla.

Inquiries were made by the Recruitment Section, and it was revealed that the Inspector took no action, other than to arrange for the clerk to be transferred, and neither did the Inspector commit anything to paper.

Believing nothing further would be heard about the matter, I was shocked when the Recruitment Section contacted me afterwards at the Cairns Police Station.

The clerk answered again in a further application that he got into trouble with me at Wallumbilla.

According to John Truman, the other clerk told the Inspector and head of the CIB that he saw the colleague load and cock the rifle, line me up through the scope, and put his finger on the trigger, ready to discharge the rifle.

Again, according to John, if I had not gone inside the house, the stated intention of the clerk was to shoot me!

At the least, I expected an order would be served on the clerk, prohibiting him from owning, possessing, or using a firearm, which did not happen.

Moreover, it appears that the clerk left Wallumbilla, still in possession of the rifle.

Those were dark times in the police force, resulting in things being done by some that had no place in any police force, festering until lanced by the Fitzgerald Inquiry.

In early 1978, injuries suffered six years before in the traffic accident on the Eton Range were aggravated during the arrest of a drink-driving offender, who threatened that after doing away with me, he would get his shotgun and shoot my family.

January 31, 1978 – when the injuries did not settle down, I was transferred from Wallumbilla to Toowoomba where better treatment was available.[13]

Recovering from the injuries, I returned to operational duties and had the good fortunate to solve a spate of crime, resulting in the head of the Toowoomba CIB asking me to apply for a vacant position in the Branch.

Prior to then, I worked for Sergeant First Class Kevin John (Kevin) Gleeson in Clerical Functions.

Walking into his office one morning, "The Regional Super would like to see you in his officer," said Kevin.

"What's it about," I questioned.

Frowning and shrugging his shoulders, "I don't know," replied Kevin.

The Regional Superintendent at Toowoomba was Ernest (Ernie) Horan, formerly CIB.

Walking in his officer, "You wanted to see me, sir," I said.

"I have a complaint from the Inspector at Roma," said Ernie, sternly, "that you damaged the lock on the safe at the Wallumbilla Police Station and nothing to have it repaired!"

Beginning to mouth a defence, "Don't concern yourself, Neil," Ernie responded quickly, "I also have your report here, given to Superintendent Byles, for repairs to be done to the defective lock. I am aware of what you have been put through, and it has no place with me!"

I had been put through hell since Gordonvale, and what Ernie said restored my confidence in the administration of the Queensland Police Force.

So, when I was asked to apply for a vacancy in the Toowoomba CIB, "No, I advise you not to apply," said Ernie. "Instead, I would like you to go back into Clerical Functions and relieve Kevin Gleeson when he goes on holidays!"

Shocked by what Ernie said, I did as he asked, and I went back into Clerical Functions.

Over time, I discovered that his advice against applying for the position in the Branch was sound, as the head of the CIB was adversely mentioned during the Fitzgerald Inquiry.

Vale, Ernie, you turned me away from corruption and steered me in the direction of early promotion!

In 1979, when Premier Joh Bjelke-Petersen and his pilot, Beryl, came to Toowoomba for a function at Weis' Restaurant, I was delegated as the armed bodyguard and driver.

At the end of this chapter, there is a photograph of Joh and Beryl in the cockpit of the Government's plane.

Picking up Joh and Beryl at the restaurant, Beryl put on her seatbelt, but Joh did not, instead he looked quizzically at me, as if to ask, "Do you want me to put the seatbelt on?"

Remembering the words of Bob Rodger, about being subtle as a train smash during discussions with others, I backed off and said nothing.

Despite him being the Premier, Joh was no different to me, which is how I think and *act*, and it was not beyond the realms of possibility for me to say something, but discretion over valour was chosen on that occasion.

Everything came to a head, when a driver wearing glasses and a large hat, stopped suddenly in front of the police vehicle, and quickly reversed into a parking bay.

Braking harshly, I extended my left arm and stopped Joh from hitting his head on the windscreen.

Looking at me, "Should I put my seatbelt on," queried Joh.

"Yes, Mr Premier," I responded, "I will be pleased if you did!"

With a wry smile, Joh put on his seatbelt, and I safely delivered him and Beryl to the plane.

Already known as a *dobber*, being known as the *constable who almost put the Premier through the windscreen*, would far exceed the former, I thought!

Expecting that something would be said, I was surprised soon after when I was promoted to the rank of Sergeant Second Class and transferred to Clerical Functions at Mount Isa.

Before leaving Toowoomba on transfer, a Commissioned Officer from Brisbane gave me an assignment, telling me that the informant would name himself to me at Mount Isa.

July 20, 1979 – I arrived at Mount Isa and occupied the residence for my position on the Police Reserve, which was beside the Stipendiary Magistrate's residence. Introducing myself to the Magistrate, it came as a surprise when Kevin Peacock came forward as the informant mentioned by the Commissioned Officer from Brisbane.

Because of confidentiality, the assignment is something that I cannot divulge, however, what I uncovered, resulted in a Constable under my supervision being moved from Mount Isa to counter duties in the Brisbane CIB.

He came under my supervision again, and what he did for an acting Superintendent, was improper and resulted in my demotion from the rank of Inspector to Senior Sergeant.

It was once believed by others that a police officer working in clerical functions was just a *pencil pusher*.[14]

In the time of Commissioner William Geoffrey Cahill, it was rightly said that *the police quill-driving fraternity actually hold the thread ends of the vast web which is being daily woven by the thousand odd policemen of all ranks in the State.*[14,15]

Sixty years later, seeing a clerk doing paperwork that should be done by his superior, "Perhaps he's inspecting his stations," queried Whitrod.

"No, he's not doing that," replied Sergeant Ken Hogget. "He's just doing the rounds."

"What do you mean, the rounds?"

"In the last year of an Inspector's service," explained Ken, "he goes around and calls on all his old friends and reminds them that he will be leaving soon, and that they will be invited to his public farewell."[8]

In essence, the Inspector's clerk, before and during my time in Clerical Functions, and not the Inspector or Superintendent, was responsible for the administration of a District.

On my arrival, Inspector William John (Bill) McArthur, formerly CIB, oversaw the Mount Isa Police District.

When Bill went on annual leave, Sub-Inspector Elwynn Kenneth (Ken) Addison was appointed to the position, until Bill returned from leave.

Before taking up the position, Ken disappearing without saying anything to me, contacting me from Charleville to say that he was reporting sick.

In fact, Ken Addison was a sick man, not readily obvious, but I know this to be true, as Ken visited me at the Cairns Police Station to apologise for leaving me without warning.

Acting by the authority vested in me by Regional Superintendent Charles (Charlie) Bopf of Townsville, formerly CIB, until Bill McArthur was recalled from leave, I ran the administrative side of the district.

In 1981 – I attended a development course for Sergeants at the Chelmer Police College.

The twenty-four participants agreed and took part in testing, which I believe I am correct in saying, was associated with the Myers-Briggs Type Indicator (MBTI).[16]

When the supervisors discussed the results, it was revealed that there was a *unique* personality within the group, and I was identified as that individual.

This did not surprise me, as I had been told that I was *different* to my nine siblings, and I was basically a *loner*, with others often saying that I was a *strange* person.

Here, again, I was described by the supervisors as *different* to the other twenty-three course participants.

From the way they looked at me, and what they said, there is no doubt in my mind, based on what they would have been told by the evaluator at the University of Queensland, that the supervisors knew then that I was *autistic*!

Allegedly, the evaluation was confidential, and nothing should have been passed on to the QPF, either orally or in writing.

Split up into three groups of eight participants, after disagreeing with others during a problem-solving exercise, I moved the chair back, further each time I was asked, and had nothing to contribute, eventually not saying anything, and was sitting with arms crossed, when the supervisors entered the room.

Unbeknown to course participants, microphones and cameras were installed and in use.

After outlining what they had seen, "You disassociated from the group, Neil," said one of the supervisors. "Can you tell us why you disagreed with the others?"

Thinking for a while, "No, I can't, my mind has gone blank," I responded.

"And that is what happened," said the supervisor. "There was one in the group, who knew the answer, and the rest of you turned him off!"

For the first time in my life, I felt justified and pleased that others finally acknowledged that I was not a *strange* person, and that I had a problem-solving mind.

Suffice to say that the group I was in on that occasion, and another four years later, were the most successful when compared with the other groups.

More importantly, my tests in 1981 and 1985 returned the same result, and on both occasions, the supervisors found I had a *unique* personality, compared with all other participants.

There is no doubt in my mind that the supervisors and QPF knew from the Myers-Briggs Type Indicator evaluation that I was *autistic*, but it would have been improper for that information to be revealed to others![16,17]

Whether it had anything to do with my failure at two attempts of a Commissioner Officer's Qualifying Course is another matter that no longer can be learned.

Returning to Mount Isa, I was greeted frostily by Inspector Vincent Lloyd (Foggy) McNamara, formerly CIB, who took over just before I went on the course.

September 21, 1981 – which was soon after the course, Patricia's mother, Madge, passed away at Mackay.

I applied for seven days' short leave to attend Madge's funeral, which was rejected by *Foggy* on the grounds that Madge was not a blood relation.

Patricia went to the funeral, and I remained at Mount Isa to look after the boys.

Thereafter, while I was talking to the clerks in the Inspector's office, *Foggy* came into the room and was about to say something and stopped abruptly when he saw one of the police clerks, dialling out on a telephone with the end of a pencil.

Tapping me on the shoulder, "Could I see you in my office, Neil," said *Foggy*.

Once in his office, *Foggy* showed me marks left by the end of a pencil under the dialling mechanism of the telephone, approved for Subscriber Trunk Dialling (STD) use by the Inspector.

After work that day, *Foggy* took me to the Returned and Services League of Australia (RSL) club at Mount Isa and apologised for believing that I used his telephone to contact a certain person in the Licensing Branch at Brisbane.

What started out as a frosty relationship soon developed into mutual respect.

Vale, *Foggy*, for your friendship!

Well do I remember *Foggy* entering the police station, barking orders to those misbehaving or lolling around, and him saying in his office, "I probably shouldn't have done that?"

It might not have been done professionally, but *Foggy* earned my respect for doing something to pull misbehaving and disruptive colleagues into line at the Mount Isa Police Station.

Snowdon (Snowy) of Abertawe
(Private Source)

Author at the rear of the Gordonvale Police Station in 1971
(Private Source)

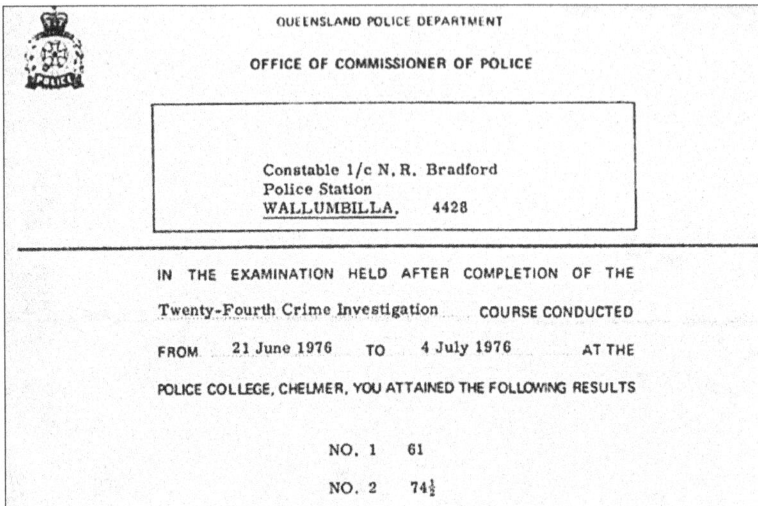

QUEENSLAND POLICE DEPARTMENT

OFFICE OF COMMISSIONER OF POLICE

Constable 1/c N. R. Bradford
Police Station
WALLUMBILLA.   4428

IN THE EXAMINATION HELD AFTER COMPLETION OF THE

Twenty-Fourth Crime Investigation   COURSE CONDUCTED

FROM   21 June 1976   TO   4 July 1976   AT THE

POLICE COLLEGE, CHELMER. YOU ATTAINED THE FOLLOWING RESULTS

NO. 1   61

NO. 2 $74\frac{1}{2}$

19 July 1976
(DATE)

(COMMISSIONER)

Author completed the 24th Crime Investigation Course
(Courtesy of Queensland Police Force)

24th Crime Investigation Course in 1976
Author is on the extreme right in the second row
(Courtesy of Queensland Police Museum)

Beryl Young and Joh Bjelke-Petersen
New Beechcraft Super King Air
(Courtesy of National Library of Australia, ID 125618949)

13

THE JOKE

September 7, 1981 – which, incidentally, was my birthday, my promotion and transfer to the rank of Sergeant First Class in Clerical Functions at the Cairns Police District Headquarters, Cairns Police Station, came into effect.[1]

Flying from Mount Isa to Cairns to buy a house, after searching and finding one that was suitable, I went to the National Australia Bank for a loan.

Sitting patiently outside the manager's office, door closed, I heard someone inside question loudly, "I need to know how you came by the five thousand dollars?"

Another in the room responded angrily, "I told you – a friend gave it to me!"

Just prior to the door opening, "I know that voice," I thought, and then before me stood Tony Murphy, red-faced and shaking, holding a briefcase.

If looks could kill, I was dead when Tony recognised and looked at me with *dagger eyes* that day!

Tony asked the manager for a loan of $150,000 to build a block of units, which he did not get. Afterwards, however, he received a smaller amount of $66,000 to construct a duplex in Carina Close at Whiterock, Cairns.[2]

February 22, 1982 – upon assuming the position for me in the Superintendent's office at Cairns, the first task was disposal of $5,000 in the safe under my control.

Out of a concern that the $5,000 in $50 notes belonged to the corruption known as the *Joke*, others were too frightened to do anything until I arrived.

So, my reputation being well-known, it fell on my shoulders to confront the *Joke*.

Between the time when I saw Tony Murphy at the bank, and before I arrived on transfer at Cairns, Tony vacated his position as the Regional Superintendent of Far North Queensland, Cairns Police Station.

One night, prior to Tony's departure, a fire broke out in the ceiling of his office, requiring the attendance of the Fire Brigade, and while putting out the fire, the Fire Brigade found the money inside a large brown paper bag in the ceiling.

And, yes, it was a large brown paper bag, same as mentioned six years later at the Fitzgerald Inquiry![3]

While at Cairns, Tony denied knowing how the money came to be in the ceiling of his office.

Messages that I left for Tony, then an Assistant Commissioner in Brisbane, went unanswered.[2]

Obviously ill-gotten gains, I could not deal with the money as lost and found, so I had the notes and paper bag fingerprinted and photographed.

I was not surprised when told that no fingerprint could be found on the money and paper bag!

Acting on advice from the Accounts Section, I banked the $5,000 into Consolidated Revenue, bringing an end to what others refused to do.

Soon after, while walking up the internal stairs of the Cairns Police Station, I looked up and saw Vincenzo (Vince) Bellino, who I knew during the 1960s and 1970s as a barber at Gordonvale, talking to Murphy's replacement at the top of the stairs.[4]

Like two rabbits caught in the crosshairs of a rifle scope, they scampered off into the Regional Superintendent's office, Tony's replacement quickly closing the door.

When Tony came out of the bank manager's office, I saw him in possession of a brown briefcase, same as the one that Vince Bellino was carrying.

Speaking soon after to the bank manager, he denied questioning Tony Murphy about the $5,000 in cash that Tony had with him in his office.

This was when allegation followed by counter-allegation was commonplace between high-ranking police officers at Cairns and Innisfail.

It was difficult to know who to trust, so I kept this information to myself.

However, when I worked later at Mackay with a Fitzgerald investigator, I passed the information on to him, but I never heard anything further about the matter.

March 21, 1984 - when Patricia's father, Wally, passed away at Mackay, without any approval from the Superintendent, after furnishing an application for short leave, I left with Patricia and attended the funeral at Mackay.

During 1985 – approval was granted for me to attend Part 1 of the Commissioned Officer's Qualifying Course at the Chelmer Police College.[5]

In his office, before leaving Cairns, "Neil, you know," said the Superintendent, "that they only let through those who they want to pass!"

This Superintendent conversed often with a very high-ranking Commissioner Officer, who arranged real-estate purchases on the Gold Coast for the Superintendent, as alluded to by Whitrod in his memoirs.[6,7]

The Superintendent had two small books, black for those he could trust, and red for those he could not trust, which he carried in the pockets of his shirt.

Leaving the books on his desk, when he went for lunch one day with a solicitor named *Mr Big* during the Fitzgerald Inquiry, my name was in the red book.[8]

Starting out around third in the course, it did not take long to slide quickly towards the bottom.

Sensing that I was going to fail, I had an interview with the Chair of the course panel.

"Does this mean that I am going to fail," I asked.

"Well, it is like this, Neil," responded the Chair, "you have to go out into the cold awhile for a past indiscretion."

"What do you mean," I retaliated. "Was it the money found in Murphy's office?"

"All I can tell you is you have to go out into the cold for a while and try again later."

"Could I see how my papers were marked?"

"No, the papers are shredded, immediately after they are marked."

Returning to Cairns after failing the course, "I told you so," said the Superintendent, gleefully.

At the end of this chapter, there is a copy of the letter saying that I was unsuccessful at the course, and a photograph of the course participants, which is a cast of a thousand.

In fact, I conveyed one of the participants, exposed during the Fitzgerald Inquiry, to the Arthur Gorrie Correctional Centre (AGCC) at Wacol.

It did not give me pleasure arresting him by warrant at his house, which no other Commissioned Officer would do, as he had been a friend of sorts, and I felt sorry for him, succumbing to the temptation of the corruption known as the *Joke*.

So, instead of arresting him upon my arrival at the house, I sat down with his family, who had gathered to say their farewells, and had morning tea with them.

Others would have made a big deal out of the moment, but he had accepted his punishment, and as my way of *behaving* and *thinking* is not the norm of mainstream society, he deserved to be treated like a human being.

When a credible witness alleged an inappropriate relationship between a senior Non-Commissioned Officer and a 15-year-old girl, the Superintendent at Cairns agreed that a Commissioned Officer should investigate the allegation.

Appearing suddenly before me, while I was sitting at my desk, "You thought you could get me into trouble and you failed," said the senior Non-Commissioned Officer, who threatened, "I will get even with you one day!"

After he left, I found that the copy of the file and letter from the informant were missing from the filing cabinet where confidential investigations were under my control, as well as the relevant page in the index book was missing.

Arriving back in his office, I confronted the Superintendent, and he denied seeing the letter from the informant, or the minute that I prepared for the investigation, and he also denied removing the page from the index book.

Only the Superintendent and I had keys to the cabinet, which meant that it was the Superintendent who removed the original and copies of the file, including the entry in the index book from the locked cabinet.

This also was at the time when allegation followed by counter-allegation was commonplace between high-ranking police officers at Cairns and Innisfail, and it was difficult to know who to trust, so I kept what happened to myself.

It was a matter of my word against the Superintendent, and I knew that the senior Non-Commissioned Officer would throw his support behind the Superintendent.

More to the point, it was a matter of me being *left up the prover-bial Creek without a paddle*!

There is no doubt in my mind the senior Non-Commissioned Officer did take his revenge by recommending later that I should revert from the rank of Inspector back to Senior Sergeant, and that it was him spoken to repeatedly by the Disciplinary Officer throughout the hearing.

Being the officer responsible for processing money paid to an informant, it surprised me when the Superintendent, out of the ordinary, asked me to hand money over to an informant, completely unknown to me.

Arriving at the agreed location where the money was to be handed over, I was about to leave when, "Under here, mate," said someone underneath a parked vehicle.

Bemused by the spectacle, I got down on my knees to look under the vehicle, "No, don't look, mate," he said. "Just hand me the money and what you want signed."

"I need to see you," I responded, "and if you don't come out from under the vehicle, I will leave without any money being handed over, do you understand?"

"Just do as you were told, and hand the money to me!"

Suspecting a setup, I went back to the Superintendent with the money and cancelled the transaction.

January 20, 1986 – my promotion to the rank of Senior Sergeant at the Mackay Police Station came into effect on this date.[1]

Before leaving Cairns, the Recruitment Section contacted me about the second application received from the bank clerk to join the police force.

As asked, a report of what happened at Wallumbilla was sent to the Recruitment Section, and after a review, the bank clerk was told again that he was unsuccessful.

Not coming as a surprise to me, the Regional Superintendent of the Far North Region, appointed after my departure, admitted to the Fitzgerald Inquiry that he took bribes at Cairns.[9]

May 9, 1986 – I assumed the position as a shift Senior Sergeant at Mackay Police Station.[1]

Just prior to the retirement of the Senior Sergeant, appointed as the Officer in Charge of Mackay Police Division, the Inspector called me into his office.

"I don't like you," declared the Inspector, "but Ben told me that you are to be the new Officer in Charge!"

Flabbergasted, and believing that another Senior Sergeant, Neil Kingdon (Neil) McNaughton, who had passed the Commissioned Officer's Qualifying Course, might be next in line, "What about Neil McNaughton, shouldn't he be the Officer in Charge?"

"Ben won't allow him to be the Officer in Charge!"

Our paths had never crossed before, so I asked, "Why don't you like me?"

"You are a *strange* person," responded the Inspector. "I don't want you as the Officer in Charge, but that decision has been taken out of my hands!"

"You're an idiot," I thought, but I left his office without uttering those words.

It was not the first time, as alluded to previously, and nor would it be the last time during my service, that a police officer would refer to me as being *strange*.

I am at peace, now that I know the way I *think* and *behave* is not the *norm* of mainstream society, and that I have a *unique* personality, which set me apart from others!

What I like to talk about, is not the conversation others want to hear, and vice versa, giving the appearance that I speak a *different* language, not understood by others.

The Ben mentioned was Benjamin Harold (Ben) Robertson, Regional Superintendent of the Central Police Region, Rockhampton Police Station.

He was another who watched over me.

Moreover, Ben did not suffer fools easily, as found in evidence given at the Fitzgerald Inquiry and published in *The Canberra Times*, as follows:

In other evidence, Superintendent Robertson said he had told Rockhampton Morning Bulletin journalist Mr Neville Brown to "drop-dead." He made the statement after the paper published a story on October 3 last year written by Mr Brown about an illegal casino. Superintendent Robertson said he had tried to "stall" the story because a police raid was planned on the casino on cither October 3 or 4. Mr Brown also gave evidence at the inquiry yesterday and said police had shunned him after the story was published. "I was actually black-banned by the police in central Queensland," Mr Brown said. He said he was also told he had cost taxpayers of Queensland $10,000 because he had "thwarted" the raid. Another witness yesterday, Sergeant Mervyn Secker, told the inquiry he was sent as an agent to the illegal casino between September 24 and October 2 *last year. He said that during his visit to the casino on October 2, he was the only gambler there and was told everyone else was "at the dogs". "In retrospect, definitely they knew who I was," Sergeant Secker said.*[10]

So, despite opposition from the Inspector, I became the Officer in Charge of the Mackay Police Division.[1]

Vale, Ben, thanks for watching over me!

When placed second last in a class of twenty-four participants at a second attempt of Part 1 of the Commissioned Officer's Qualifying Course, halfway through the course, I received approval to leave and returned to Mackay, effectively ending any aspiration that I had of becoming an Inspector.

In 1987 – when *the media reported possible police corruption involving illegal gambling and prostitution*, the Acting Queensland Premier, William Angus Manson (Bill) Gunn, ordered a *Commission of Inquiry*.[9,11]

This led to the appointment of Gerald Edward (Tony) Fitzgerald, Queen's Counsel (QC), to head the *Commission of Inquiry into Possible Illegal Activities and Associated Police Misconduct*, known as the Fitzgerald Inquiry, which began *substantive public hearings on 27 July 1987*.[9,12]

In 1988 – along with eleven other senior police officers, I accepted an invitation to attend a Special Commissioned Officer's Qualifying Course from January 11, 1988, to February 19, 1988, at the Oxley Police Academy.[13]

Accepting the invitation, close colleagues referred to me as one of the *Dirty Dozen*.

Then, being one of the five to pass the course, I became known as one of the *Filthy Five*.

At the end of this chapter, there is a copy of the letter confirming that I successfully completed the course.

Back at Mackay, I said to the then Inspector, replacing the Inspector who did not like me, "Have you heard that the Fitzgerald investigators are going through records of the banks and building societies?"

Bolting upright in his chair, "No," exclaimed the Inspector. "Where did you hear that?"

"Oh," I replied, candidly, "over a few beers with a bank manager at the Leichhardt!"

Before leaving Brisbane, a Fitzgerald investigator asked me to say something like that to a particular gathering, and I did so at a morning briefing.

It is unfortunate that others consider me a fool and treat me that way. That is how a detective at the meeting treated me, and after excusing himself, he made a telephone call that resulted in his immediate removal from Mackay.

When another Inspector took voluntary retirement, I began relieving as an Acting Inspector in the Mackay Police District.[1]

After instructing me not to hesitate and shoot to kill, I went with a Fitzgerald investigator to the memorial erected at Far Beach for the fatal aircraft accident on June 10, 1960.[14]

Best described as the standoff in the movie *The Good, the Bad, and the Ugly*, I had my right hand on the butt of my revolver tucked inside the trousers' belt, one eye on the driver of the black Mercedes sedan, eyes concealed by sunglasses, and the other on the Fitzgerald investigator while he recorded a conversation with Barrie Ronald von Snarski.[15]

Not knowing exactly what we were walking into, justification of the shoot-to-kill instructions appeared the following year in an article published by *The Canberra Times*, as follows:

> *A bribe of about $16,000 was meant to be passed to Queensland police by their NSW counterparts, a witness in a Brisbane drugs trial alleged yesterday. Barrie Ronald Von Snarski, of north Queensland, told the court he had paid the money to a Sydney man, who was to pass it to Sydney police for payment to Queensland officers to prevent prosecution for drug offences. Von Snarski, now serving a jail term for an offence not specified in court, was giving evidence during the trial of one of his al-*

*leged partners in marijuana cultivation, Mackay storekeeper
Michael Paul Falzon, 30. Falzon has pleaded not guilty to a
charge that he cultivated a 90,000-plant crop at Von Snarski's
Mount Christian property, near Mackay, in 1986. Von Snarski
told the court the Sydney man, whom he named as Kris Leach,
had successfully processed a previous bribe after Von Snarski
was charged with receiving a stolen Jaguar car. The later bribe
– one payment of $5000 and another of $ 10,000 or $ 11,000 –
was paid so a 1986 charge against Von Snarski of cultivating a
90,000-plant crop would be dropped, the court heard. Von
Snarski said it was to be paid to north Queensland police, but
when the charge against him proceeded to the Magistrates
Court, he thought Leach had "just taken me for the money".
Von Snarski also told the court he paid bribes to police in NSW,
but he refused to name the officers, claiming privilege on the
grounds that the evidence could incriminate him. Von Snarski
said he, his now deceased son Roy Von Snarski, Falzon and a
man named Mark Absolom, cultivated the crop. He alleged that
when the plants were a metre high, in about September 1986,
Falzon told him police knew about the crop and were going to
put it under surveillance. Crown Prosecutor Tony Glynn told
the court Falzon had received the tip-off, from Mackay constable Brian Anthony Marlin. The trial jury has heard that a
charge initially brought against Falzon, that he paid Marlin a
$2000 bribe for information about surveillance of the crop, has
been dropped. The trial continues.*[16]

Uncertain and dangerous times, like anything cornered, we attended the meeting with the expectation that someone might come
out swinging, hence a need to be cautious.

Moreover, while I did not know beforehand the meeting was
with Von Snarski, I knew about the allegation made by Detective
Ernest Robert (Ernie) Hockings again Detective Brian Anthony
(Brian) Marlin, which did not appear to have substance.

So, when a warrant was issued for Marlin's attendance at the
Fitzgerald Inquiry, at which time I was the Acting District Officer of

the Mackay Police District, instead of executing the warrant, the escorting officer, Sergeant First Class Malcolm John (Mal) Churchill, had it in his possession on the flight to Brisbane.

When Marlin arrived in Brisbane, upon discovering he was not under arrest, counsel aiding the Inquiry decided that Marlin's attendance was unnecessary, giving the appearance that the issue of the warrant was a grandstand act, as I suspected.

Alive after that clandestine meeting at Far Beach, I delivered the Fitzgerald investigator back to his abode, never again to have anything further to do with him or Von Snarski.

During the upheavals, life went on, and apart from being a playing member of the Mackay Golf Club, I played in the team from the Mackay Police Station that won the North Queensland Police Golf Championships (NQPGC).

At the end of this chapter, there are photographs of me with others from the winning team.

Soon after, another Inspector, then Officer in Charge of the Mackay Police District, disappeared, as if *taken by aliens*, which was a common occurrence of those times.

It was not wise to ask questions, even look sideways, and being the only Commissioned Officer still standing, albeit an Acting Inspector, I took over as the Officer in Charge of the Mackay Police District.

The age of the micro-cassette tape recorder had arrived, and soon it became commonplace to record conversations with colleagues, even when I was with the Fitzgerald investigator, as you just did not know who to trust.

For instance, there was an allegation of Fitzgerald investigators using threats, intimidation, and insults to gain evidence in *The Canberra Times*, as follows:

> *A Brisbane Supreme Court judge has ruled that Fitzgerald inquiry investigators used threats, intimidation, and insults to gain evidence of corruption from a cancer-ridden man. Justice Paul de Jersey dismissed a charge resulting from the evidence*

after he found that the man had been threatened during interviews with inquiry investigators in May last year. The man, Anthony Wallace, of Mackay, was given an indemnity from prosecution by the inquiry and testified to it on July 21 last year. He was to be the main prosecution witness in a follow-up trial involving former Mackay storekeeper Michael Paul Falzon, now of the Sunshine Coast, and Detective Constable Brian Marlin of Mackay. But Justice de Jersey, in a Supreme Court ruling made on July 19, refused to allow Wallace to testify because of threats in tape-recorded interviews made by inquiry investigators. The ruling was made public yesterday after a Supreme Court jury found Falzon not guilty on one charge of cultivating a marijuana crop valued at up to $180 million. A charge that Falzon had paid a $2000 bribe to Constable Marlin was dropped. Falzon was remanded on bail to face two further charges.[17]

Paul De Jersey became the 26th Governor of Queensland on July 29, 2014.[18]

While acting as the District Officer, I chaired a meeting of senior Non-Commissioned Officers and their wives at the White Lace Motor Inn on Nebo Road at Mackay.

After giving a presentation of the changes in the Queensland Police Force, Superintendent Brian Alan (Barney) Pitman took me aside, and in the presence of Patricia, "Neil, you are not the person described to me," said Barney. "When I get back to Brisbane, you will be promoted to Inspector!"

October 16, 1989 – Barney ignored the rumourmongers in the Administration Branch, Brisbane, and my promotion to the rank of Inspector became effective on this date.

At the end of this chapter, there is copy of certificate, together with an outline of my academic qualifications and course that led to my promotion.[1]

Worthy of note, His Excellency the Governor acting by and with the advice of the Executive Council approved my promotion to the rank of Inspector.

Until changes were made, only the Executive Council could demote me from the rank of Inspector, which had its failings, but it was a fairer process when compared with the *Kangaroo Court* of one person decided in his own mind that I was *guilty* and demoted me back to the rank of Senior Sergeant.

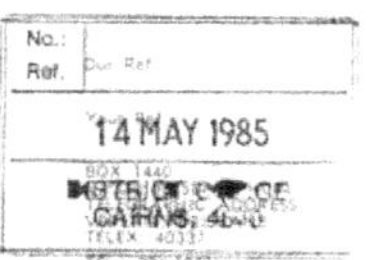

QUEENSLAND POLICE DEPARTMENT

COMMISSIONER'S OFFICE
30 MAKERSTON STREET
BRISBANE

No.:
Ref. Our Ref

14 MAY 1985

8 May 1985

Sergeant I/c N.R. Bradford
Police Station
CAIRNS

Dear Neil

It is with regret that I advise that you were unsuccessful in obtaining sufficient percentage at the 4th Commissioned Officers Qualifying Course Part I to qualify you to attend Part II of such Course.

You may, if you so wish, apply for attendance at another Commissioned Officers Qualifying Course Part I at any time after one year has elapsed from the completion of the Course just attended.

Yours sincerely

T.M. LEWIS
COMMISSIONER OF POLICE

Author's unsuccessful attempt at the 4th Commissioned Officers Qualifying Course in 1985
(Courtesy of Queensland Police Service)

4th Commissioned Officers Qualifying Course in 1985
Author is fifth from the left in the second row
(Courtesy of Queensland Police Force)

QUEENSLAND POLICE DEPARTMENT

Our Ref

Your Ref

COMMISSIONER'S OFFICE
30 MAKERSTON STREET
BRISBANE

BOX 1440.
G.P.O. BRISBANE 4001
TELEGRAPHIC ADDRESS
VEDETTE, BRISBANE
TELEX 40337
TEL. 226 6001

10 March 1988

Senior Sergeant N.R. Bradford
Police Station
MACKAY

Dear Keil

I am pleased to advise that you have successfully completed the
Special Commissioned Officers Qualifying Course held at the Police
Academy from 11 January 1988 to 5 February 1988.

As a consequence, you will be considered for promotion to Commissioned
Rank at the appropriate time.

Yours faithfully

R.J. REDMOND
ACTING COMMISSIONER OF POLICE

**Author's successful attempt at the Special Commissioned Officers
Qualifying Course in 1988**
(Courtesy of Queensland Police Service)

Victorious golfers from Mackay Police Station in 1988
Author is second from the left
(Private Source)

**Displaying trophies won at the North Queensland Police
Golf Championships in 1988**
Author is third from the left
(Private Source)

Queensland Police Department

HIS EXCELLENCY THE GOVERNOR, ACTING BY AND WITH THE ADVICE OF THE EXECUTIVE COUNCIL, AND IN PURSUANCE OF THE PROVISIONS OF THE POLICE ACT 1937 – 1989, HAS APPROVED THAT

NEIL RAYMOND BRADFORD

BE PROMOTED TO THE RANK OF

Inspector

IN THE QUEENSLAND POLICE FORCE

AS FROM

16 OCTOBER 1989

AUTHORITY: QUEENSLAND GOVERNMENT GAZETTE
21 OCTOBER 1989

Author's promotion to Inspector in 1989
(Courtesy of Queensland Police Department)

SCHEDULE

COURSES ATTENDED AND RESULTS

INSPECTOR GRADE III N.R. BRADFORD, FORTITUDE VALLEY POLICE DISTRICT

Course	Date	Results
Advanced Studies Course for Police		
Business Communications I	31.12.85	Exemption
Police Law I	31.12.85	Pass
Queensland Police Administration	1985	Exemption
Social Psychology	31.12.85	Credit
Police Law II	31.12.87	Pass
Criminology	31.12.87	Pass
Principles of Management	30.06.85	Exemption
Supervision I	30.06.85	Exemption
Special Commissioned Officers Qualifying Course Part I	11.01.88 - 19.02.88	Successful

Author's Courses Attended and Results
(Courtesy of Queensland Police Service)

14

GAME OVER

November 13, 1989 – upon my arrival in Brisbane, I assumed my assignment in the Fortitude Valley Police District at the Fortitude Valley Police Station where Superintendent Regional Brian (Lurch) Ashmore, whom I knew at Mount Isa and then Cairns, was the District Officer.[1]

"Come with me, Neil," said *Lurch*. "I want you with me at police headquarters for a meeting.

"What's the meeting about," I questioned.

"I don't know," responded *Lurch*.

That was common in those days, as meetings seldom had an agenda, and sometimes the proceedings ended abruptly, even in fisticuffs.

Driving to police headquarters in Roma Street was so different to the days in 1966 when I drove Car 54.

The Sergeant with me on the first occasion almost had a heart attack when I went through a stop sign and then drove against traffic in a one-way street.

Shortly into the shift, another Sergeant from the Roma Street Police Station took over from the nervous wreck.

So much had changed over 23 years, and it was a pleasure driving from the Fortitude Valley Police Station; no sideways gruff comment coming from *Lurch*, such as, "Watch out," or "What do you think you're doing," and we arrived calm and collected for the meeting in police headquarters, also different to when I was last in Brisbane.

One and a half hours later, not having conducted the meeting from an agenda, and with no announcement for one speaker after another, the chair said, "Well, that is it, gents! Does anyone have anything to say?"

Well, to me, that was like waving a red flag to a bull!

Seeing that others also were confused, "Sir, when I attend a meeting, I would like to know what is being discussed and who is speaking," I responded. "I have been here all the time, and I do not know who any of you are, nor do I understand what it is that has been discussed during this meeting!"

The *Country Boy* was back in the *Big Smoke*!

Others of the assembled multitude echoed my sentiments, and after a further one and a half hours, we left well-informed of the changes that would flow from the recommendations of the Fitzgerald Inquiry, prompting *Lurch* to say, "Neil, you're going to go over well in Brisbane," as we drove back to the Valley.

A Senior Constable repeatedly saying that the *dead wood* needed *bulldozing* out of the way, reminded me of the days when my father and I cleared the trees from the paddocks on the farm, but I knew that is not what he meant.

It surprised me to learn, however, that I was the *dead wood* the Senior Constable wanted to *bulldoze* aside for implementation of the Fitzgerald Inquiry reforms.

In that era of policing, I was the second earliest at 12¾ years' service to be promoted to Sergeant Second Class, and 23⅓ years' service for the rank of Inspector.

It was well known that I preferred not to work with improper conduct and behaviour and corruption in the Queensland Police Force.

As well as I embraced the new direction offered by Whitrod, and I was about to begin approved studies for a Bachelor of Community Welfare degree.

Therefore, I did not see myself as the *dead wood* that needed bulldozing out of the way.

But that is what the Senior Constable wanted to do!

And then the others would have left the room, not knowing why they had been there, if I had not come forward, and spoken up for them.

That is what sets me apart from mainstream society, who choose to snicker and speak ill behind your back, rather than to be open and honest.

Soon after, disappointingly for me, the day arrived for *Lurch* to retire, enabling him to spend more time with his wife and young daughter.

I came to miss those sideways gruff comments and wry smiles from *Lurch*!

Lurch's replacement, an Acting Superintendent, came from the Administration Branch at police headquarters. When I asked questions about what was happening with the Fitzgerald Inquiry reforms, "Neilly," he said, "you don't need to know, and I don't want to speak to you anymore, so would you please leave!"

A grown man referring to me as "Neilly," reminded me of what my family often called me, which I detested, as it was a *childish* way of referring to another.

Then, rather than judge the book by the cover, it would have been good for the Acting Superintendent to read the story before making up his mind about me.

Obviously, he believed and trusted what others said about me being a *strange* person.

At the end of this chapter, there is a photograph of me in an Inspector's uniform.

Meeting me for the first time, *Barney* soon discovered that what the *faceless* colleagues peddled around at the Administration Branch was false!

One being the former clerk in the Inspector's office at Cairns, who climbed Bell Peak North on the third day, and who, before then, made jokes about my spelling ability.

Coming a long way since then, upon approval of QPS, I began open-learning studies with the James Cook University of North Queensland at Townsville for a Bachelor of Community Welfare degree.

May 25, 1990 – the Governor, Sir Walter Campbell, after stringent vetting by the CJC, awarded me and one hundred and seventy-three other recipients with the Police Long Service and Good Conduct Medal at the Oxley Police Academy.[2]

At the end of this chapter, there is a photograph of me, circled, with the other recipients.

Having survived the corruption known as the *Joke*, and after stringent vetting by the CJC and considered a worthy recipient of the Police Long Service and Good Conduct Medal, with an aspiration of rising to a higher rank outside of Brisbane, the last thing on my mind was to do something stupid to ruin everything.

However, that is what the Disciplinary Officer believed in his own mind I did, something stupid that resulted in my demotion, never to be considered again for promotion, effectively ending my policing career.

May 28, 1990 – the Fortitude Valley Police District became defunct and replaced by the new North Brisbane Police District, resulting in relocation of staff at the Fortitude Valley Police Station to temporary accommodation at Alderley.[1]

Moving into the accommodation at Alderley, I was pleased when Superintendent Bob Rodger took over as the District Officer for North Brisbane Police District.

In the beginning, the expectation of what the Commissioned Officers in the North Brisbane Police District could or should do, was too much.

Apart from supervising five suburban police stations and overseeing internal investigations; twenty-eight complaints at the same time processed by me, I worked rotational 24/7 shifts from the North Brisbane Police District as the Regional Duty Officer (RDO) for Metropolitan North Region.

That workload was too much and took us away from our main function and duties, and that was supervising and supplying direction to suburban police stations.

This led to fellow Commissioned Officers going sick and others asking for a re-assignment to another district where it was not as stressful.

During that turmoil, the Royal Commission into Aboriginal Deaths in Custody (RCIADIC), because of his Criminal Investigation and Prosecution experience, seconded Bob Rodger from the Metropolitan North Region to work on the Commission.[3]

Bob's replacement was an Acting Superintendent, formerly CIB, who lacked administrative experience, and who did something that resulted in my demotion from the rank of Inspector.

By then, the former Acting Superintendent at the Fortitude Valley Police District had become the Assistant Commissioner for Metropolitan North Region, aided by Superintendent Barry John (John) Youngberry, formerly CIB.

Calling me into his office, "Neilly," the Assistant Commissioner said, drawing a shudder from me, "I am giving you a complaint from the nephew of the Speaker of the Legislative Assembly, and I would like to stress that there will be no political interference during your investigation. I want to make that clear – there will be no political interference, do you understand?"

"Yes, sir," I replied. "I understand what you said."

The Speaker of the Legislative Assembly of Queensland was Demetrios (Jim) Fouras.[4]

True to what the Assistant Commissioner said, there was no interference from Jim Fouras, and neither did I experience any from the Government.

Taking over from the Assistant Commissioner, "Jim's nephew is a security officer licensed to carry a firearm for his work," said John Youngberry. "After challenging a driver acting suspiciously in an industrial area at Banyo, on the second attempt of trying to run him over, the nephew drew his pistol and deflated the tyre, slowing the vehicle down. This resulted in the Nundah CIB finding the driver and charging him with a series of offences."

"Sounds like he did a good job," I replied. "So, why make a complaint?"

"The nephew alleges that the Banyo police threatened to take his license off him for shooting out the tyre. You are to investigate the complaint and supply a recommendation!"

After reading the complaint, "The nephew also complains," I queried, "that the Banyo police are overzealously enforcing parking laws at Northgate?"

"You are to narrow your investigation to what is important, Neil," said John, "and concentrate on the concern that the nephew has about losing his firearms licence, do you understand?"

"Yes," I replied, "I understand!"

Obtaining more information from the Speaker's nephew, I questioned police involved in the incident.

The Banyo police wanted an order, prohibiting the Speaker's nephew from owning, possessing, or using a firearm.

Contrary to that view, the Nundah police wanted a letter sent to the nephew, thanking him for helping police solve a series of offences in the Northgate area.

So, I found myself amid two police camps: one expecting the revocation of the nephew's firearm license, and the other demanding praise for assisting the police!

November 1, 1990 – while driving home from work along Royal Parade to where I lived at Banyo, I saw the vehicle of Patricia's employer parked about one-third forward of the parking bay at his Banyo Physiotherapy practice.

At the end of this chapter, there is a photograph of what was once the Banyo Physiotherapy and an overhead view of the location from the practice to the Banyo Police Station, as well as the Railway residence in between.

Being who I am, if the vehicle had represented a danger to any person, I would have stopped and asked Patricia's employer to park it properly, as I was still in uniform.

If Patricia's employer did not follow my request to park the vehicle properly, I would have arranged for a subordinate to issue a ticket.

That was the way in Brisbane, taught to me as a Probationary Constable at the Bardon Police Station, of attending to parking matters, before *Murphy's Marauders* invaded the Valley.

Unless a danger, break and enter offences and theft of property had priority over enforcing parking laws, best left to the local council responsible for the area.

More importantly, that is the way I *think* and *behave*!

I am not frightened by anyone or the consequences that might flow from my actions, thought out carefully, if time allows, and I will do something, there and then, rather than wait for something to happen.

Moreover, that is why I was found to be *unique* in comparison to the other twenty-three participants when evaluated in 1981 and again in 1985 by the Myers-Briggs Type Indicator.[5]

Others should not judge me by their standards because I am *different* to mainstream society!

This also was at a time when a program was in vogue with the Business Community, same as the Adopt-a-Cop program, to decrease the incidence of crime.[6]

So, when told that Patricia's employer wanted to speak to me about being issued with a $20 ticket for a parking infringement, I responded to him as a member of the Business Community in a police division that I supervised.

Furthermore, it was in the complaint of the Speaker's nephew that Banyo police, allegedly, were overzealously issuing tickets for parking infringements at Northgate, which John Youngberry told me to ignore during my investigation.

However, here was an example of what was alluded to by the Speaker's nephew!

That is why I went and spoke to Patricia's employer, admittedly, at a time when I was not rostered for duty, as overtime entitlements did not apply to Commissioned Officers, who were expected to respond to matters outside of rostered hours, and soon I would be away from the North Brisbane Police District, doing my turn as the RDO.

It was absolutely an unsatisfactory setup that a boffin at police headquarters thought up, obviously without looking at the reality of what was expected to be done!

Anyone objecting was *bulldozed* out of the way, as the Senior Constable inferred at the meeting attended with *Lurch*.

By the time I reached the practice, the vehicle was in the yard of the Railway residence, where Patricia's employer and Banyo police had permission to park.

After outlining his grievance, Patricia's employer intended taking $20 out of petty cash to pay the fine, but I suggested to him not to do so.

I explained that I already had information that the Banyo police, allegedly, were overzealously enforcing minor parking matters at Northgate.

Once again, it has never been, and never will be a major priority of police to stringently enforce parking laws, unless the parking of a vehicle is a danger, as parking matters rest with the local council responsible for the area in question.

This was a left-over of what *Murphy's Marauders* did in Fortitude Valley, which was not the path for the police force to follow, after the Fitzgerald Inquiry.

So, I told Patricia's employer that I was concerned by what happened, which I would raise with my superiors, and the ticket was handed over to me for that purpose.

And it had been established by Whitrod's policy, read in conjunction with the 1965 Commissioner's Memorandum, that a complaint could be received verbally, and not necessarily committed to writing.

The reason for doing so, is because not everyone was literate in those days!

The following day, I spoke about the matter with the Assistant Commissioner and John Youngberry.

Acting on their advice, I raised this at the morning briefing with the Acting Superintendent and other Commissioned Officers in the North Brisbane Police District.

All agreed that I was in the better position to investigate, quickly, and that I was to recommend in a report as to what I thought should be done, as payment of the ticket was within twenty-one days.

In hindsight, this is when I should have stepped away and told Patricia's employer to take $20 out of petty cash and pay the penalty in the ticket.

However, being who I am, and justice is important, I went ahead quickly with the matter, because, as mentioned before, I was about to do my turn as the RDO from the Metropolitan North Region.

So, that night, because he was away from the police station when I visited, the issuing Constable came to my residence, and I spoke to him on the footpath.

I used a micro-cassette tape recorder to record the conversation from start to finish.

"Yes, Inspector, you wanted to see me," said the constable.

"Yes," I said. "Before I say anything further, I would like you to know that my wife is the receptionist at Banyo Physiotherapy."

"I didn't know that!"

"When you were off duty, you issued a ticket to a vehicle parked at the front of the practice."

"Yes, I remember that. It was a red Alfa Romeo Sedan."

"That vehicle belongs to my wife's employer, who has permission to park in the Railway yard, where police also have permission to park."

"I didn't know that it was his."

"I saw it parked about one-third forward of the parking bay when I drove past on the way home. Can you tell me why you issued a ticket instead of looking for the owner in the practice to have it parked properly?"

"It was parked dangerously, and I had to drive over the double lines to turn left into the yard."

"Did you do anything to have it parked properly?

"No!"

"So, you thought it was parked dangerously, and you left it there?"

"Yes, I was about to start work, and there was a job we had to go to."

"You obviously went inside to get your ticket book, but you did nothing to have the vehicle parked properly. Is that correct?"

"Yes. Look Inspector, I was not aware it was your wife's employer. If you give me his copy, I will pull the ticket!"

"Being my wife's employer has nothing to do with the matter, and there will be no pulling of the ticket. I am satisfied from what I saw and what you have said that you issued the ticket to satisfy your own need and not the community. If you had the vehicle removed, then I would not be of that opinion."

"I am sorry, Inspector. I honestly did not know that it was your wife's employer."

"Again, that has nothing to do with the matter. I am investigation another matter and police overzealously issuing tickets for minor parking matters at Northgate is in that complaint."

"I'm aware that you are investigating the K…….. matter."

"After telling your Sergeant tomorrow what I am doing, I will submit a report, recommending that the ticket should be waived in the interest of improving public relations, and that report will be sent to Banyo for comment by you and your Sergeant, and then it will be sent to the Central Traffic Support Group for a decision. Do you understand?"

"Yes, Inspector, I could pull the ticket, if that is easier?"

"That belongs to the past, and there will be no pulling of tickets, do you understand?"

"Yes, Inspector!"

The next day, I advised the Sergeant at Banyo that I did not support the request for revocation of the firearm's license issued to the Speaker's nephew, which would be my recommendation to the Assistant Commissioner.

I also told the Sergeant that he and the Constable would be asked for their comments to the recommendation in my report, about waiving the ticket issued to my wife's employer in the interest of improving public relations.

Displeased with the firearm's licence decision, the Sergeant, however, agreed that the Constable should have requested my wife's employer to park properly before issuing a ticket.

The Assistant Commissioner agreed against revocation of the firearm's license.

November 6, 1990 – things went disastrously wrong with the submission of the other report on this date, about the ticket issued to my wife's employer.

At the end of this chapter, there are copies of my two-page report.

While away on RDO duties, the Acting Superintendent arranged through the former clerk at Mount Isa for retyping of the first page of my report, removing the declaration that the person issued with the ticket was my wife's employer.

November 14, 1990 – instead of my report going to the Banyo Police Station for comments from the Sergeant and Constable, a different minute to the one prepared by me, sent the report to the Central Traffic Support Group where the District Superintendent of Traffic waived the ticket without conducting a proper inquiry.

This might confuse the reader, as it did the Disciplinary Officer, who was an interloper, so I will elaborate and explain the actions that should have happened in compliance with the minute I prepared, as follows:

1. *A copy of the report should have been sent to the Clerk of the Court, Brisbane, saying that the ticket was under review, and to stop payment, until the outcome was known.*

2. *A copy of the report should have been sent to the Department of Transport, and the driver's licence record noted, despite no loss of points being involved, that the ticket was under review.*

3. *The original of the report should have been sent back to the*

> *Banyo Police Station for comments from the Sergeant and Constable.*

4. *Upon receiving those reports from the Sergeant and Constable, it was then up to the Acting Superintendent to decide if he supported the recommendation that the ticket should be waived in the interest of improving public relations.*

5. *If the Acting Superintendent agreed, he would recommend to the District Superintendent of Traffic at the Central Traffic Support Group to waive the ticket.*

6. *The District Superintendent of Traffic at Central Traffic Support Group would tell the Clerk of the Court, Brisbane, and the Department of Transport that the ticket had been waived.*

7. *If the Acting Superintendent did not agree, a letter would be sent to my wife's employer, telling him to either pay the penalty or contest the matter in court.*

8. *The Acting Superintendent would send the report to the Sergeant, Constable, and me, for noting of his decision.*

Outside of Brisbane, where I worked in charge of Clerical Functions, a District Superintendent of Traffic would not have waived the ticket without the comments of the Sergeant and Constable.

That is what was happening in Whitrod's time, and what was still happening at the Central Traffic Support Group after the Fitzgerald Inquiry.[7]

Moreover, I am not alleging that what the Acting Superintendent did was malicious. He was stuck in the *old* ways, and from what I was told, he thought I was overreacting, so he circumvented the process and recommended straight to the District Superintendent of Traffic, Central Traffic Support Group, to waive the ticket.

It was a harsh lesson to learn about the politics of policing in Brisbane!

Moreover, I was the only one investigated, despite others doing what they should not have done.

May 14, 1991 – Premier Wayne Goss opened the North Brisbane District Police Headquarters at Boondall.

Shortly thereafter, searching for an elderly woman, allegedly lost in the Boondall Wetlands, later found at Ipswich after boarding a train at Banyo, I suffered bites from mosquitoes.

The following year, I was diagnosed with having contracted Ross River Fever during the search.

July 30, 1991 – after sick leave for eight weeks following the search, and still suffering from the effects of the Ross River Virus, I attended an interview with CJC investigators.

Bob Rodger by this time had returned to the North Brisbane Police District Headquarters.

The CJC interview was for submission of the report about the ticket issued to Patricia's employer.

With Bob's help, we searched and could not find a copy of the report.

When asked by the CJC if it was my report, I responded that it was my signature on the second page, and that it looked like my report.

The interview should have ended when I saw on the first page of the report that the declaration about the ticket being issued to my wife's employer was missing.

Because the Detective Inspector conducting the interview was junior to me, it was necessary for a Commissioned Officer, senior to me, to be present during the interview.

This was done by a Detective Superintendent who was on the 1985 course panel that shredded the papers soon after marking of examination papers at the Chelmer Police College for Part 1 of the Commissioned Officer's Qualifying Course.

Why he and the others on the course panel, still serving, were not stood down, beggars' belief!

Moreover, he was part of the improper process that failed me at the course, and then he did nothing to have the matter investigated when I raised the issue about the declaration not being on the first page of my report.

While at the CJC, I saw others with tainted pasts working at the

CJC, based on discussions overheard while in Clerical Functions, but nothing was committed to paper, or could be proved, making a mockery out of what Fitzgerald intended.

Afterwards, I provided recorded evidence of conversations with the Assistant Commissioner, John Youngberry, Speaker's nephew, the Acting Superintendent, and the Sergeant and Constable at Banyo, to the CJC investigators.

Those taped conversations showed that I acted with propriety throughout the entire process.

The only thing missing was the declaration in my report that the person issued with the ticket was my wife's employer.

Returning to the officer, Bob and I searched again, but we did not find a copy of the report in the District Office records.

The year after the CJC interview, the Assistance Commissioner of Metropolitan North Region called me to Honda House.

"Neilly," he said, "there is a recommendation coming from up town about you that I do not agree with, and I will not be doing anything when it arrives. The trouble with you, Neilly, is you are too honest for your own good!"

Cringing, "What is the recommendation about," I questioned.

"I don't want to talk to you anymore, Neilly," said the Assistant Commissioner, "so please leave!"

After that confusing conversation, because of my wealth of experience as an Officer in Charge of Police Stations and Clerical Functions, I was seconded from the Metropolitan North Region to work with the Project Team formulating new policy, orders, and procedures for the Queensland Police Service.

Shortly thereafter, the Assistant Commissioner left Metropolitan North Region and went to another region.

February 11, 1992 – back in the Metropolitan North Region, I attended a Disciplinary Hearing arranged by the incoming Assistant Commissioner.

It was for submission of the report about the ticket issued to Patricia's employer.

Despite asking for a copy, the Assistant Commissioner refused to let me see the report until I was before him at the hearing.

The charges preferred were for giving preferential treatment to my wife's employer and not supplying details in writing to my Executive Officer, contrary to Section 6.1.3 of the Police Service Code of Conduct.

Cutting to the chase, I argued that it was not my report as the declaration that I had therein was missing from the first paragraph on page one.

Instead of adjourning the hearing to investigate, the Assistant Commissioner went out of the room, repeatedly, asking questions of the senior Non-Commissioned Officer from Cairns, who threated that he would get even with me.

Because of my sensory capabilities over a fair distance, there was no doubt in my mind, who it was speaking from the Roma Street Police Headquarters to the Disciplinary Officer at Honda House, and I heard what was said between them.

So, every time the Disciplinary Officer came back into the room, and he tried a different tack to catch me out, I was prepared from what I overheard, and I came back at him with responses that he did not understand.

On the last occasion, I heard the senior Non-Commissioned Officer from Cairns say to the Disciplinary Officer, "Don't listen anymore to what he has to say – just demote him!"

Extremely frustrated, after throwing the papers before him into the air, "I don't care what you say," said the Assistant Commissioner, "as there is no doubt in my mind that you did it, to impress your wife's employer, and as from midnight tonight, you will revert back to the rank of Senior Sergeant."

Storming out of the room, the Assistant Commissioner came quickly back into the room and served me with the form, which, according to a trusted clerk, had been prepared beforehand, requiring only his signature.

If he had done his job properly, the Assistant Commissioner would have investigated, what was alluded to on pages 267 and 268, to prove if what I said was correct, and then decide if I had done something wrong.

So, years of standing *toe-to-toe* with the unscrupulous, ended because a buffoon believed that an *autistic* person thought similarly to his sadistic and depraved mind.

There is no other way to describe what happened, as the hearing was over before I entered the room!

The QPS Document Examination Section was quick to find irregularities, as follows:

1.   *The letter 'g' in the fourth line of the last paragraph on page one is different to the 'g' in the fourth line of the first paragraph on page two.*

2.   *The number '4' for the time of 4.13 pm in the first line on page one is different to the '4' for the date of 14.11.90 of the minute on the left side of the same page.*

What that means is a manual typewriter, different to the one used for the original report, re-typed the first page to remove the declaration from the first paragraph. That is why the letter 'g' is different on both pages.

Then, the '4' in the date of the minute is different to the '4' for the time of 4.13 pm in the first line, both page one, means the typewriter that prepared the original report, was re-used to prepare the minute on the left side of page one.

I only used the Head Typist in the Superintendent's office for my correspondence. She confirmed that her typewriter prepared the second page and the minute, but that the typewrite did not prepare the body of the report on page one.

There was a Typing Pool, separate to the Superintendent's office, and that is where the former clerk from Mount Isa had the first page re-typed to remove the declaration.

Once re-typed, the Head Typist prepared the minute on the left side of page, and after signing by the Acting superintendent, the report went straight to the District Superintendent of Traffic at the Central Traffic Support Group.

Preferring to remain anonymous, the Head Typist named the typist responsible for re-typing the first page of my report, who became a supervisor of civilian staff, and the former police clerk at Mount Isa became a Sergeant.

Bob Rodger was present at Cairns when the former senior Non-Commissioned Officer made the threat.

The Assistant Commissioner, when he became aware of the incident, apologised through Bob, but the damage done by him, was irreversible.

Both competing in a charity golf day, and alone in toilets at the Oxley Golf Club, I thought hard but stopped myself from laying the Assistant Commissioner out on the floor!

Typical of the man, even on that occasion, he did not have the guts to apologise to me in person.

After serving me with the form, "What happens to me from here on," I queried.

"You will report to Bob Rodger at 8 am tomorrow," said the Assistant Commissioner, "and he will find something meaningful for you to do!"

Consuming a bottle of Henschke's *Hill of Grace*, thoughts of having been transportation back in time to an Iron Curtain country, entered my mind!

When morning came, being *autistic*, I became unstable, requiring sick leave.

Reporting for work at the North Brisbane Police District, I was re-located from my office as an Inspector to a small internal room used as a temporary storeroom, which had no telephone, windows, and only a desk and chair.

Despite requests if there was work that I could do, I sat for days on end, twiddling my thumbs, with colleagues treating me as if I was a leper.

Responding to complaints that my presence was a bad influence on others, I was re-located to the defunct Zillmere Police Station, which had a telephone, no floor coverings, and neither any work coming my way.

During the months there alone, because I was not on a roster, and as no one came to check on my welfare and well-being, I played golf to relieve the boredom, never asked as to what I was doing, or where I had been.

The mind-games of the QPS administration of those times, was un-Australian!

In late 1992 – I underwent endoscopic sinus surgery at Turrawan Private Hospital, Clayfield.

The morning after, "You told me that you were not allergic to any medication," said the anaesthetist.

"I had a test back in the 1980s," I replied, "and I was told that I wasn't allergic to anything!"

"Well, you died during the surgery, and I had to bring you back!"

"What happened?"

"You had a reaction to the anaesthetic I used, and you suffered a cardiac arrest."

"I was evaluated, and it came back negative, but I will consult my doctor when I see him again."

Evidence was mounting, since the appendix operation in the Lister Private Hospital to the cardiac arrest, making it obvious that prescribed drugs could be dangerous for me to take, but it took another six years for the medical condition to be named.

March 15, 1993 – the Assistant Commissioner seconded me to the Transport Registration and Integrated Licensing System (TRAILS) project at Queensland Transport (QT) in Spring Hill, Brisbane.[1,8]

Comprising ninety-two Australian and International technology experts and others experienced in specialist fields or areas of interest, the project rolled-up twenty-six standalone databases into one whole-of-government database.

Exploring modern global technology to improve efficiency and effectiveness of enforcement activities, I also closed loopholes to prevent corrupt and illegal behaviour of police officers and others using the database.

This resulted in police forces and relevant agencies in Australia having to change their business practices to avoid exposure of their undercover agents.

A vision that I followed, culminated in technology now being available and used by operational police, either carried or in a police vehicle.

This would not have come about if Bill Jordan, Director of Corporate, Queensland Transport, after two weeks of deliberation, had not listened to me.

"I know what Neil wants for QPS," declared Bill Jordan. "If we don't do something now, it will cost us millions later to include what is needed for police to carry out their duties, more efficiently and effectively!"

Using Information Engineering Facility (IEF) software provided by Texas Instruments, the decision to include what I requested on behalf of QPS, delayed the project by four weeks, but the outcome is pleasing to see.

Answerable to Superintendent Mick Hannigan of the State Traffic Support Group, Roma Street Police Headquarters, I was the sole QPS member on the project.

There was another, briefly, but after saying that I was a *strange* person, he went back to Auto Theft.

January 17, 1994 – while the Assistant Commissioner made me an Acting Inspector on the project, I remained *surplus* to the needs of QPS!

Having read a *white paper* on the issue, promotion back to the rank of Inspector was not possible, and I would remain *surplus* to the needs of QPS, until I resigned or retired.

Concluding the Business Development phase, I declined an offer from the Assistant Commissioner to remain as an Acting Inspector for the Design and Construction phase.

At the end of this chapter, there is a reference from Bill Jordon,

Director of Corporate Projects, Queensland Transport, who made comments, as follows:

> *I have found Neil to be very approachable and positive in his outlook to new opportunities and challenges.*[8]

November 21, 1994 – returning to Metropolitan North Region as a Senior Sergeant, still *surplus* to the needs of QPS, I went from pillar to post over the next three years.[1]

November 4, 1995 – approval for me to relieve until December 1, 1995, as an Acting Inspector in the Regional Duty Office, ended just after two shifts.[1]

This came about when colleagues referred to me as a *strange* person, and when they refused to work with me, I was delegated problem-solving tasks Commissioned Officers lacked the nous to complete.

Queenslanders were reluctant to take me on, but an interloper, who had his eyes on the top job, did their bidding and removed my armour.

August 15, 1997 – giving up hope of promotion, even removed from *surplus*, I separated from QPS under Special Provisions, bringing the curtain down on the most rewarding and exciting episode of my life.[1]

July 25, 1998 – my father passed away at Mackay, and during that visit to attend the funeral, a younger sister revealed she had been evaluated as positive for PCT.

September 10, 1998 – I also was evaluated as positive for PCT, as was my older sister at Mackay.[9,10]

Both sisters and I suffered blistering to the back of our hands and forearms, described as dermatitis, before we reached thirty years, which is when PCT usually manifests.[11]

The three of us have had reactions to most prescribed drugs, suggesting that our PCT is not only hereditary, but also it is an acute form.[11]

Any prescribed medication that I now take must be on the Safe list!

April 17, 1999 – less than two years after I separated from QPS, Bob Rodger passed away.

Vale, Bob, I listened to your words of wisdom, and I appreciated you being a confidant!

In 2022, it was disappointing to read the findings of a review into the QPS that there is *clear evidence of a culture where attitudes of misogyny, sexism, and racism are allowed to be expressed, and at times acted upon, largely unchecked.*[12]

Sadly, nothing has changed with policing in Queensland since I joined the QPF in 1966, and it will continue that way until there is a strong person at the top, who will say, "Not on my watch," and rid those disruptive persons from what is one of the most rewarding experiences of anyone's life!

Author at Brisbane in 1990
(Private Source)

Street view of Banyo Physiotherapy to Banyo Police Station
(Private Source)

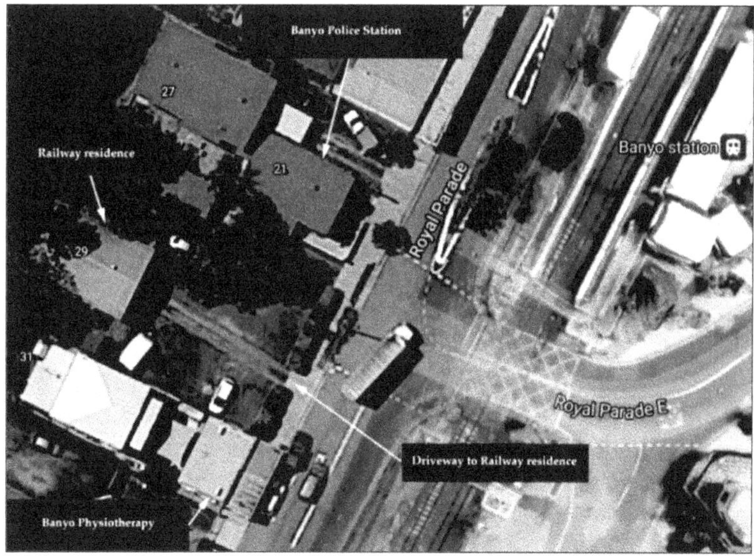

Aerial view of Banyo Physiotherapy to Banyo Police Station
(Courtesy of © OpenStreetMap contributors)

**Author (circled) and others receiving the Police Long Service
& Good Conduct Medal in 1990**
(Courtesy Queensland Police Force)

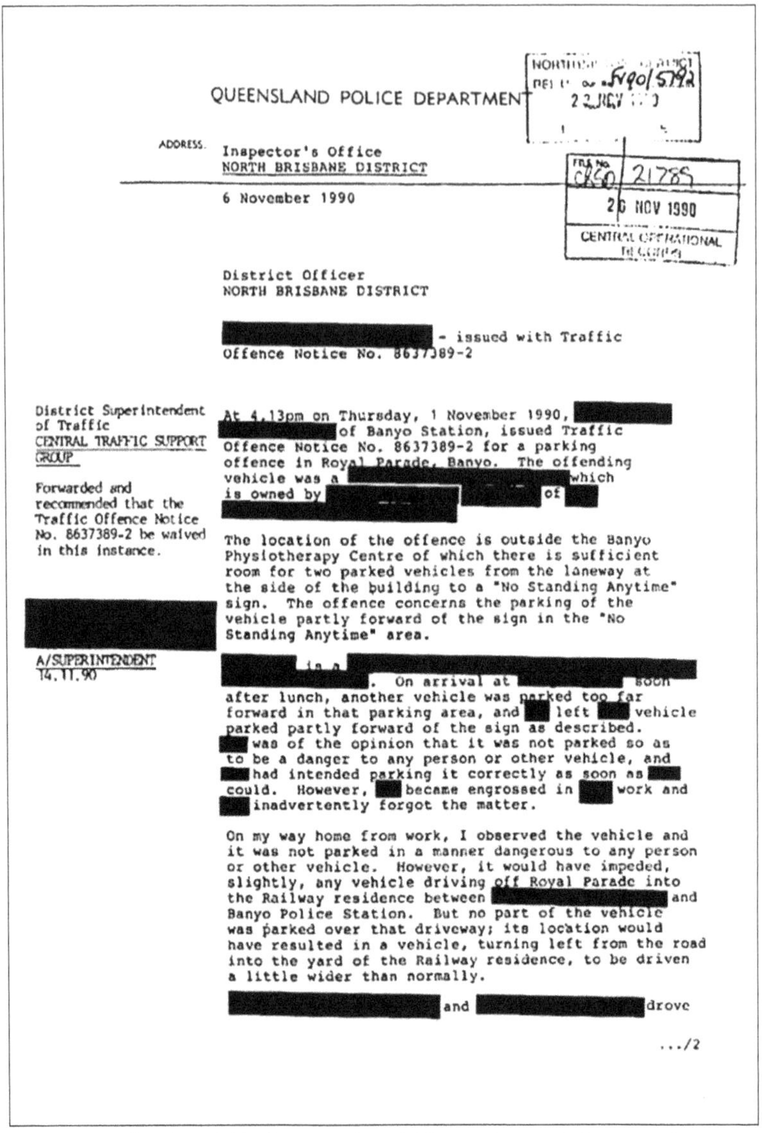

QUEENSLAND POLICE DEPARTMENT

ADDRESS. Inspector's Office
NORTH BRISBANE DISTRICT

6 November 1990

District Officer
NORTH BRISBANE DISTRICT

████████████████████ - issued with Traffic
Offence Notice No. 8637389-2

District Superintendent
of Traffic
CENTRAL TRAFFIC SUPPORT
GROUP

Forwarded and
recommended that the
Traffic Offence Notice
No. 8637389-2 be waived
in this instance.

██████████████

A/SUPERINTENDENT
14.11.90

At 4.13pm on Thursday, 1 November 1990, ████████
████████ of Banyo Station, issued Traffic
Offence Notice No. 8637389-2 for a parking
offence in Royal Parade, Banyo. The offending
vehicle was a ████████████ which
is owned by ████████ ██ of ██

The location of the offence is outside the Banyo
Physiotherapy Centre of which there is sufficient
room for two parked vehicles from the laneway at
the side of the building to a "No Standing Anytime"
sign. The offence concerns the parking of the
vehicle partly forward of the sign in the "No
Standing Anytime" area.

████████████ is a ████. On arrival at ████████ soon
after lunch, another vehicle was parked too far
forward in that parking area, and ██ left ██ vehicle
parked partly forward of the sign as described.
██ was of the opinion that it was not parked so as
to be a danger to any person or other vehicle, and
██ had intended parking it correctly as soon as ██
could. However, ██ became engrossed in ██ work and
██ inadvertently forgot the matter.

On my way home from work, I observed the vehicle and
it was not parked in a manner dangerous to any person
or other vehicle. However, it would have impeded,
slightly, any vehicle driving off Royal Parade into
the Railway residence between ████████████████ and
Banyo Police Station. But no part of the vehicle
was parked over that driveway; its location would
have resulted in a vehicle, turning left from the road
into the yard of the Railway residence, to be driven
a little wider than normally.

████████████ and ████████████ drove

...../2

Author's *falsified* report dated November 6, 1990, page 1
(Courtesy of Crime and Corruption Commission)

- Page 2 -

into the yard of the Railway residence, prior to the
time of the offence, and the Constables felt that the
parked vehicle impeded their turn off the road, and in
▆▆▆▆▆▆ words to me on the night of
2 November 1990, "it was just about obstructing the
driveway there", but under no circumstances was it
parked dangerously.

▆▆▆▆▆▆ was dismayed by being issued with a notice, but
▆▆▆ intended paying the fine. However, as I have told
▆▆▆▆▆▆ I consider that as the vehicle
has been parked there correctly for the past five
months, a fact of ownership which should have been known
by the Constables, it would have been sound public
relations to request that it be parked correctly rather
than to issue a ticket in the first instance.

I have advised the Constables and ▆▆▆▆▆▆▆▆
Officer in Charge, Banyo, that I would furnish a report
requesting that the notice be waived, in the interest
of improving public relations, and I respectfully
request that favourable consideration be given to my
request.

N.R. BRADFORD
INSPECTOR

AUTHOR'S NOTE

The QPS Document Examination Section was quick to find
irregularities, as follows:

1. *The letter 'g' in the fourth line of the last paragraph on page
   one is different to the 'g' in the fourth line of the first
   paragraph on page two.*

2. *The number '4' for the time of 4.13 pm in the first line on page
   one is different to the '4' for the date of 14.11.90 of the minute
   on the left side of the same page.*

What that means is a manual typewriter, different to the one
used for the original report, re-typed the first page to remove the
declaration from the first paragraph. That is why the letter 'g' is
different on both pages.

Then, the '4' in the date of the minute is different to the '4' for
the time of 4.13 pm in the first line, both page one, means the
typewriter that prepared the original report, was re-used to prepare
the minute on the left side of page one.

Author's *falsified* report dated November 6, 1990, page 2
(Courtesy of Crime and Corruption Commission)

QUEENSLAND TRANSPORT

Queensland Department of Transport

Corporate Projects Unit
Floor 7
477 Boundary Street
Spring Hill Q 4000

Enquiries: Bill Jordan
Telephone: 834 2298
Facsimile: 834 2200
Our Ref: BILL\REF-NB
Your Ref:

17 November 1994

To Whom it May Concern

Reference - INSPECTOR NEIL BRADFORD

Inspector Neil Bradford was assigned to the Transport Registration and Integrated Licensing System (TRAILS) Project in late 1993.

Over the past twelve months Neil has undertaken the role of Project Co-ordinator (Queensland Police Service). As a member of the TRAILS Project Management Team, the position has required Neil to provide leadership and directions in ensuring that the needs of the Queensland Police Service will be satisfied by TRAILS.

Neil has demonstrated a high commitment to the achievement of the project objectives and has ensured that relevant issues have been identified and appropriately addressed. This has included the exploration of new technology aimed at the improved efficiency and effectiveness of enforcement activities undertaken by Police Officers.

I have found Neil to be very approachable and positive in his outlook to new opportunities and challenges. I would be happy to address any specific enquiry that you may care to direct to me.

Yours sincerely

(C.W. Jordan)
DIRECTOR (CORPORATE PROJECTS)

**Author's reference from the Director (Corporate Projects),
Queensland Transport**

(Courtesy Queensland Transport)

CONCLUSION

Becoming a Security Officer after separating from QPS, seventeen years were as an Aviation Protection Officer at the International and Domestic terminals at the Brisbane Airport. "Do your handlers know that you have a knife strapped to the inside of your left ankle," I asked an agent, as I was clearing him to enter the secured area of the domestic terminal.

Before the agent had time to answer, two QPS detectives rushed forward, took the agent by the arms, and escorted him away from the screening point.

Fitted with a metal device so that his handlers could hear his conversation with another, and because he would alarm when going through the Walk-Through Metal Detector (WTMD), the relevant authority sanction secondary screening, which I conducted on instructions of my manager, also a former police officer.

The agent was there for the detectives to make a drug buy inside the secured area of the domestic terminal from a Sydney seller, who had just arrived.

"Don't ever ask me to do that again," I said, when I next spoke to my manager.

"Sorry, Neil," he responded. "They just told me what happened, and they have apologised for not patting him down!"

Fortunately, I did my work professionally, preventing what could have been a nasty incident inside the secured area of the domestic terminal.

Sadly, while working on a *fly-in* and *fly-out* basis as a highly qualified electrical fitter and mechanic for Santos at Ballera, south-western Queensland, Mark Stephen Bradford ended his life at Highfields, near Toowoomba, Queensland.

There is no doubt in my mind that if others did not think of me as a *strange* person, my eldest son would be alive today!

During 1999 – Mark estranged himself from his parents, but there were telephone calls, without the caller saying anything, except sobbing.

Getting back together again on the birth of his first child, three years later, while driving him to the Brisbane Airport, "What can I do to prevent this from happening again," I asked Mark.

"Just be yourself, dad," replied Mark.

"That's not easy, son," I thought to myself.

Suspecting he was the unidentified caller, "Did you call several times and not speak to me?"

"Yes!"

"Promise me that you will never do that again?"

"No, dad, I won't do that again!"

August 19, 2008 – at a time when Patricia and I were going through another period of estrangement with Mark, the telephone rang, and I accidentally dropped the handset.

After picking the handset up from the floor, I heard people talking in the background, but the caller did not speak.

Unfortunately, because of *crank calls* received from another party at the time, I suspected it might be him again, so I disconnected the call by hanging up the handset.

After that call, and unknown to Patricia and me, as to what he was going through, Mark had a doctor's appointment for depression, which he did not keep.

It is my belief that after making the call, probably from a public telephone, Mark decided not to go to the doctor, and he went home and end his life.

Not being there for Mark in his time of need will haunt me until it is also my time to sleep!

At the end of this Conclusion, there is a photograph of Mark in the 1984 Cairns Under-17 Rugby League Premiership Team.

While waiting for the clock to tick over past midnight on December 31, 2022, I found and completed an online *autism* test provided by Clinical Partners in England.[1]

The revelation following the online test that *your score suggests you experience many or all of the most common traits experienced by autistic people*, and that *you have a strong likelihood of being autistic*, did not surprise to me![1]

Despite being *autistic*, not only did I excel in sport, work, education, or any other endeavour, served as a soldier and police officer, but I also was awarded several medals, as follows:

- Police Long Service and Good Conduct Medal.
- National Police Service Medal.
- Queensland Police Service Medal.
- Australian Defence Medal.[2,3,4,5]

At the end of this Conclusion, there is a photograph of Patricia and me, and another of me with other recipients of the Australia Defence Medal.

Just because you are *different* to mainstream society, does not mean that you cannot follow your dreams, and that is exactly what I did, even though told that I would fail.

Author with Patricia in 1998
(Private Source)

1984 Cairns Under-17 Rugby League Premiership Team
(L-R) Mark Stephen Bradford is in the second row, third from the left
(**Note**: Some had exchanged their jersey with the losing team)
(Private Source)

Recipients of the Australia Defence Medal in 2008
Author, second row, extreme right
(Private Source)

ABBREVIATIONS

7RAR	7th Battalion, Royal Australian Regiment
ADF	Automatic Direction Finder
AGCC	Arthur Gorrie Correctional Centre
AHS	Australian Hospital Ship
ASA	Air Safety Authority
AWU	Australian Workers' Union
BOM	Bureau of Meteorology
CBD	Central Business District
CDO	Civil Defence Organisation
CIB	Criminal Investigation Branch
CJC	Criminal Justice Commission
CMF	Citizens Military Forces
CO	Commanding Officer
CSM	Company Sergeant Major
DCA	Department of Civil Aviation
DME	Distance Measuring Equipment
ESP	Extrasensory perception
IEF	Information Engineering Facility
MBTI	Myers-Briggs Type Indicator
MEC	Middle East Command
NQPGC	North Queensland Police Golf Championships
PAF	Permanent Air Force
PCT	Porphyria Cutanea Tarda
QATB	Queensland Ambulance Transport Brigade
QC	Queen's Counsel
QPF	Queensland Police Force
QPS	Queensland Police Service
QT	Queensland Transport
RAAF	Royal Australian Air Force
RAF	Royal Air Force
RCIADIC	Royal Commission into Aboriginal Deaths in Custody
RDO	Regional Duty Officer
RQR	Royal Queensland Regiment
RSL	Returned and Services League of Australia

SES	State Emergency Service
STD	Subscriber Trunk Dialling
TRAILS	Transport Registration and Integrated Licensing System
UHF	Ultra High Frequency
VHF	Very High Frequency
WTMD	Walk-Through Metal Detector

ENDNOTES

INTRODUCTION

1. Blue wall of silence, *Wikipedia*, viewed August 3, 2021.
2. Aircraft Accident Investigation of Cessna 402 VH-RIZ on January 28, 1970, report, *Department of Civil Aviation*, February 4, 1971, AS/701/1004.
3. Officer complains of police vendetta, *The Canberra Times*, April 27, 1988, page 7.
4. The Fitzgerald Inquiry, *Crime and Corruption Commission, Queensland*, viewed July 9, 2021.
5. From the CJC to the CCC: an overview, *Crime and Corruption Commission, Queensland*, viewed August 6, 2022.
6. Four days, three nights on Bell Peak North, *The Weekend Post*, February 13, 2010, pages 36, 37.
7. Ray Hickling: The North Bell Peak Aircraft Crash 28/01/1970, *Mulgrave Shire Historical Society Inc*, September 2009, Bulletin No. 322, ISSN-0155-4808.
8. Ray Hickling: The North Bell Peak Aircraft Crash 28/01/1970, *Mulgrave Shire Historical Society Inc*, October 2009, Bulletin No. 323, ISSN-0155-4808.
9. Kevin M8: Combined memories of Ray Hickling, Alan Broughton, and Kevin Murgatroyd: Bell Peak North Plane Crash 28 January 1970, *ExplorOz*, viewed July 29, 2021.

1.   EARLY BEGINNINGS

1. Birth Record of Neil Raymond Bradford, 1946, *Registrar of Birth, Deaths and Marriages QLD*, 35207/1946.
2. Ancestry DNA Review 2021, *DNA Weekly*, viewed June 27, 2021.
3. Ring a Ring o' Roses, *Wikipedia*, viewed November 1, 2022.
4. Rounders, *Wikipedia*, viewed November 1, 2022.
5. Autism, *healthdirect*, viewed July 6, 2021.
6. Bradford, Neil Raymond. *Voices from The Past: Law Enforcement on the Central Highlands*, Boolarong Press, Brisbane, 2013, pages 1-2, 69-70, 279, 292.

7.   Mackay Notes, *The Townsville Daily Bulletin*, April 26, 1928, page 5.

8.   Our History, *Paul Hopkins Medical Clinic*, viewed January 3, 2023.

9.   Hospitals' Serious Problems, *The Cairns Post*, January 14, 1948, page 5.

10. Thanks, *The Daily Mercury*, November 3, 1948, page 2.

11. Death Record of Paul William Hopkins, *Registrar of Birth, Deaths and Marriages QLD*, 1965/B/72382.

12. Mackay Forms Child Minding Association, *The Morning Bulletin*, May 23, 1947, page 3.

13. Department of Defence to N. R. Bradford, letter, November 3, 2008, DHA 08/282732.

14. RAAF Base Amberley, *Royal Australian Air Force*, viewed June 27, 2021.

15. Moreton Island National Park, *Wikipedia*, viewed June 27, 2021.

16. Vera Lynn: The White Cliffs of Dover, *CUNY Academic Commons*, viewed June 27, 2021.

17. Lincoln bombers at the RAAF Base Amberley, Queensland, 1951, *National Library of Australia*, viewed June 27, 2021.

18. Sinking of the Centaur, *Australian War Memorial*, viewed June 27, 2021.

19. World War II, *Wikipedia*, viewed June 27, 2021.

20. Queensland Plan of Development, *The Daily Mercury*, February 26, 1946, page 2.

21. Humpybong State School, *Queensland Government*, viewed June 27, 2021.

22. Bay hotel sold to Victorian, *The Sunday Mail*, February 19, 1950, page 3.

23. Limevale, Queensland, *Wikipedia*, viewed June 27, 2021.

24. Working Safely with Phenol, *University of Queensland*, viewed July 16, 2021.

25. Eidetic memory, *Wikipedia*, viewed December 15, 2022.

26. Arsey, *Oxford Learner's Dictionaries*, viewed December 18, 2022.

27. Dobber, Aussie Slang Dictionary, viewed December 18, 2022.

28. Criminal Code 1899 - Section 69: Going armed so as to cause

fear, *Queensland Consolidated Acts*, viewed December 18, 2022.

2.   TOUGH TIMES

1.   Great Wall of China, *Wikipedia*, viewed June 30, 2021.

2.   Long paddock, *lexico*, viewed July 6, 2021.

3.   Guinea grass, *Queensland Government*, viewed July 6, 2021.

4.   Coastal Taipan, *Queensland Museum*, viewed June 30, 2021.

5.   Bradford, Neil Raymond. *Voices from The Past: Law Enforcement on the Central Highlands*, Boolarong Press, Brisbane, 2013, page 320.

6.   Crocodile tragedy recalled, *The Daily Mercury*, January 2, 1981, pages 3, 8.

7.   A Survey & Some Opinions, *The Sydney Mail*, June 24, 1935, page 6.

8.   Mackay claims croc record, *The Townsville Daily Bulletin*, May 16, 1951, page 2.

9.   It's real all right: Man claims historic photo of world-record 10 Metre crocodile caught in a Queensland river is true – and says his father paid sixpence to see it at a pub, *Daily Mail Australia*, viewed July 6, 2021.

10.   Porphyria, *healthdirect*, viewed July 6, 2021.

11.   Autism, *healthdirect*, viewed July 6, 2021.

12.   Common tree snake, *Queensland Government*, viewed July 1, 2021.

13.   Neil Bradford, certificate, *Sarina and District All School Sports*, Boys' Footrace 75 Yards (1946), 1959.

14.   Neil Bradford, certificate, *Sarina and District All School Sports*, Championship – C. A. Cummings Cup – Boys' 100 Yards 1946 (12.8 seconds), 1959.

15.   Neil Bradford, certificate, *Sarina and District All School Sports*, Boys' Championship 100 Yards 1946, 1960.

16.   Neil Bradford, certificate, *Sarina and District All School Sports*, Senior High Jump 1946/47, 1960.

17.   Neil Bradford, certificate, *Sarina and District All School Sports*, Senior Broad Jump 1946/48, 1960.

18.   Neil Bradford, certificate, *Sarina and District All School Sports*, Open Hurdle 1946/48, 1960.

19. Pre-Decimal Inflation Calculator, *Reserve Bank of Australia*, viewed July 6, 2021.

20. Barramundi – north-east coast monitoring & Barramundi – central-east coast, *Queensland Government*, viewed July 6, 2021.

21. World War I, *Wikipedia*, viewed July 6, 2021.

22. Cape Palmerston National Park, *Queensland Government*, viewed July 2, 2021.

23. Darumbal language, *Wikipedia*, viewed July 6, 2021.

24. Wally Taylor achieved national acclaim, *The Courier Mail*, viewed July 17, 2021.

3.   NEW BEGINNING

1. Citizen Military Forces, *Australian War Memorial*, viewed July 3, 2021.

2. Douglas Bradford, *Australian Army*, Attestation Form, May 6, 1942.

3. 42nd Battalion (Australia), *Wikipedia*, viewed July 3, 2021.

4. Neil Raymond Bradford, *Australian Army*, Record of Service, August 5, 2002.

5. Neil Raymond Bradford, *Queensland Police Service*, Personal Details, Qualifications, and Experience, August 15, 1997.

6. 31st Battalion, Royal Queensland Regiment, *Wikipedia*, viewed July 3, 2021.

7. 51st Battalion, Far North Queensland Regiment, *Wikipedia*, viewed July 3, 2021.

8. Eidetic memory, *Wikipedia*, viewed December 15, 2022.

9. Shoalwater Bay Training Area, Queensland, *Australian Government*, viewed July 3, 2021.

10. Neil Raymond Bradford, *Queensland Police Service*, Details of Service, August 15, 1997.

11. Neil Raymond Bradford, *Queensland Police Service*, assessed in horsemanship, August 15, 1997.

12. Neil Raymond Bradford, *Queensland Police Service*, assessed in boat rowing, August 15, 1997.

13. Oath of Office, *Queensland Police Museum*, 1966.

4.   GORDONVALE FLOOD

1.   Neil Raymond Bradford, *Queensland Police Service*, Personal Details, Qualifications, and Experience, August 15, 1997.

2.   Moonlight State: The honest cop who helped blow the whistle on Australia's most corrupt police force, *Four Corners*, viewed June 5, 2021.

3.   Kevin M8: Combined memories of Ray Hickling, Alan Broughton, and Kevin Murgatroyd: Bell Peak North Plane Crash 28 January 1970, *ExplorOz*, viewed July 29, 2021.

4.   Jack Pizzey, *Wikipedia*, viewed July 9, 2021.

5.   Herbert: Lewis was involved, *The Canberra Times*, December 13, 1989.

6.   Whitrod, Ray. *Before I Sleep: Memoirs of a Modern Police Commissioner*, University of Queensland Press, Brisbane, 2001, page 139,147-150,157.

7.   Queensland Police Service, *Wikipedia*, viewed December 24, 2022.

8.   Electrical Safety, *Queensland Government*, viewed July 9, 2021.

9.   Flooding and electricity, *Scottish & Southern Electricity Networks*, viewed July 9, 2021.

10.   Bellenden Ker Range, *Wikipedia*, viewed July 9, 2021.

11.   Flood Warning System for the Mulgrave and Russell Rivers, *Australian Government*, viewed July 9, 2021.

12.   Peter Baddiley to Neil Bradford re Gordonvale flood in 1967, email, June 25, 2010.

13.   Gordon Cotterill to Neil Bradford re Gordonvale flood in 1967, letter, December 29, 2010.

5.   WALL OF SILENCE

1.   Neil Raymond Bradford, *Technical Correspondence* School, CN644 Certificate in Police Studies, December 23, 1987.

2.   Neil Raymond Bradford, *James Cook University of North Queensland*, Degree of Bachelor of Community Welfare, April 8, 1995.

3.   Francis Erich (Frank) Bischof, *Australian National University*, viewed December 24, 2022.

4.   Croydon, Queensland, *Wikipedia*, viewed June 1, 2022.

5.   Death of Marian Noland, *QLD Births, Deaths, Marriages, and Di-*

vorces, 1909/C866.

6. Death of Charles James Noland, *QLD Births, Deaths, Marriages, and Divorces*, 1912/C978.

7. Marion Parker Noland, *Australia, Electoral Rolls*, 1905, Croydon – Kennedy Division.

8. Extrasensory perception, *Wikipedia*, viewed June 1, 2022.

9. Autism and Theory of Mind in Practice, *Psychreg*, viewed December 24, 2022.

10. Yellow Submarine, *The Beatles*, viewed July 11, 2021.

11. Commendation awarded to Constable B J V Downs on June 3, 1969, *Queensland Police Gazette*, July 19, 1969, page 584.

12. Neil Raymond Bradford, *Australian Army*, Record of Service, August 5, 2002.

13. Seaview Range, *Wikipedia*, viewed July 11, 2021.

14. Wondecla, Queensland, *Wikipedia*, viewed July 11, 2021.

15. Atherton Tableland, *Wikipedia*, viewed July 11, 2021.

16. Blue wall of silence, *Wikipedia*, viewed August 3, 2021.

17. Welcome to Pyramid Highleigh No. 161, *United Grand Lodge of Queensland*, viewed July 12, 2021.

18. Officer complains of police vendetta, *The Canberra Times*, April 27, 1988, page 7.

19. The Fitzgerald Inquiry, *Crime and Corruption Commission*, viewed July 9, 2021.

20. Policing Queensland timeline 1864 – 2014, *Queensland Police Service*, viewed December 24, 2022.

6.   FATAL FLIGHT

1. Aircraft Accident Investigation of Cessna 402 VH-RIZ on January 28, 1970, report, *Department of Civil Aviation*, February 4, 1971, AS/701/1004.

2. No. 43 Squadron RAF, *Wikipedia*, viewed July 12, 2021.

3. Joanne Fletcher to Neil Bradford re Patrick Hill, emails, August 24, August 31, December 22 & 23, 2020.

4. Searchers Climb to Wreckage of Cessna, *The Cairns Post*, January 30, 1970, page 1.

5. Efforts to recover 2 men's bodies: Plane crash victims, *The Cairns Post*, January 31, 1970, page 1.

6. Distance measuring equipment (aviation), *Wikipedia*, viewed July 13, 2021.

7. Values of Country, *Djunbunji Land & Sea Program*, viewed July 13, 2021.

8. Ray Hickling to Neil Bradford re aircraft accident on Bell Peak North, *letter*, February 23, 2010.

7.   SEARCH AND RECOVERY

1. Aircraft Accident Investigation of Cessna 402 VH-RIZ on January 28, 1970, report, *Department of Civil Aviation*, February 4, 1971, AS/701/1004.

2. Joan Starr: The Day We Climbed Bell Peak, *Weekender*, October 18, 1973, pages 11-13.

3. Ray Hickling: The North Bell Peak Aircraft Crash 28/01/1970, *Mulgrave Shire Historical Society Inc*, September 2009, Bulletin No. 322, ISSN-04155-4808.

4. Searchers Climb to Wreckage of Cessna, *The Cairns Post*, January 30, 1970, page 1.

5. Kitchen furniture floated from wall to wall, *Australian Women's Weekly*, April 5, 1967, page 9.

6. RAAF in flood rescues, *RAAF News*, April 1, 1967, page 3.

7. Ray Hickling to Neil Bradford re aircraft accident on Bell Peak North, *letter*, February 23, 2010.

8. Policing Queensland timeline 1864 – 2014, *Queensland Police Service*, viewed December 24, 2022.

9. Kevin M8: Combined memories of Ray Hickling, Alan Broughton, and Kevin Murgatroyd: Bell Peak North Plane Crash 28 January 1970, *ExplorOz*, viewed July 29, 2021.

10. Blue wall of silence, *Wikipedia*, viewed August 3, 2021.

8.   FORGOTTEN HEROES

1. Values of Country, *Djunbunji Land & Sea Program*, viewed July 29, 2021.

2. Ray Hickling: The North Bell Peak Aircraft Crash 28/01/1970, *Mulgrave Shire Historical Society Inc*, September 2009, Bulletin No. 322, ISSN-0155-4808.

3. Joan Starr: The Day We Climbed Bell Peak, *Weekender*, October 18, 1973, pages 11-13.

4. Searchers Climb to Wreckage of Cessna, *The Cairns Post*, January 30, 1970, page 1.

5. Kevin M8: Combined memories of Ray Hickling, Alan Broughton, and Kevin Murgatroyd: Bell Peak North Plane Crash 28 January 1970, *ExplorOz*, viewed July 29, 2021.

6. Policing Queensland timeline 1864 – 2014, *Queensland Police Service*, viewed December 24, 2022.

7. Ray Hickling: The North Bell Peak Aircraft Crash 28/01/1970, *Mulgrave Shire Historical Society Inc*, October 2009, Bulletin No. 323, ISSN-0155-4808.

8. Copaifera langsdorffii, *Wikipedia*, viewed August 1, 2021.

9. An indication of conditions at Bell Peak North on the night of 29th January 1997, estimation, *Bureau of Meteorology, Australian Government*, May 20, 2010.

10. Lance Sergeant Robert James Wallace, World War Two Service, certificate, *Australian Army*, Q39545.

11. 31st/51st Battalion (Australia), *Wikipedia*, viewed August 2, 2021.

12. Kokoda Track, *Wikipedia*, viewed August 2, 2021.

13. Letter to the Editor by Kevin Murgatroyd: Article concerning the Bell Peak expedition, *The Cairns Post*, 2010.

9. MISSION IMPOSSIBLE

1. Policing Queensland timeline 1864 – 2014, *Queensland Police Service*, viewed December 24, 2022.

2. Efforts to recover 2 men's bodies: Plane crash victims, *The Cairns Post*, January 31, 1970, page 1.

3. Ray Hickling: The North Bell Peak Aircraft Crash 28/01/1970, *Mulgrave Shire Historical Society Inc*, October 2009, Bulletin No. 323, ISSN-0155-4808.

4. Searchers Climb to Wreckage of Cessna, *The Cairns Post*, January 30, 1970, page 1.

5. Civil Aviation Amendment Order (No. R2) 2004, *Civil Aviation Safety Authority*, December 2, 2004.

6. Gordon Cotterill to Neil Bradford re Benedetti family, *letter*, December 29, 2010.

7. Kevin M8: Combined memories of Ray Hickling, Alan Brough-

ton and Kevin Murgatroyd: Bell Peak North Plane Crash 28 January 1970, *ExplorOz*, viewed July 29, 2021.

10. SAFELY EXTRACTED

1. Efforts to recover 2 men's bodies: Plane crash victims, *The Cairns Post*, January 31, 1970, page 1.
2. Civil Aviation Amendment Order (No. R2) 2004, *Civil Aviation Safety Authority*, December 2, 2004.
3. Ray Hickling to Neil Bradford re aircraft accident on Bell Peak North, *letter*, February 23, 2010.
4. Lisa Jones (Queensland Police Museum) to Neil Bradford re Favourable Records, *email*, August 2, 2021.
5. Blue wall of silence, *Wikipedia*, viewed August 3, 2021.
6. Kevin M8: Combined memories of Ray Hickling, Alan Broughton and Kevin Murgatroyd: Bell Peak North Plane Crash 28 January 1970, *ExplorOz*, viewed July 29, 2021.
7. Ray Hickling: The North Bell Peak Aircraft Crash 28/01/1970, *Mulgrave Shire Historical Society Inc*, October 2009, Bulletin No. 323, ISSN-0155-4808.

11. GREEN MAFIA

1. Four days, three nights on Bell Peak North, *The Weekend Post*, February 13, 2010, pages 36, 37.
2. Letter to the Editor by Graham Morrisson: Article took a swipe at police sergeant, *The Cairns Post*, 2010.
3. Blue wall of silence, *Wikipedia*, viewed August 3, 2021.
4. Ronald George Morrison (Roll of Honour), *Queensland Retired Police Association*, 11.08.2014.
5. Letter to the Editor by Kevin Murgatroyd: Article concerning the Bell Peak expedition, *The Cairns Post*, 2010.
6. Ray Hickling: The North Bell Peak Aircraft Crash 28/01/1970, *Mulgrave Shire Historical Society Inc*, October 2009, Bulletin No. 323, ISSN-0155-4808.
7. Whitrod, Ray. *Before I Sleep: Memoirs of a Modern Police Commissioner*, University of Queensland Press, Brisbane, 2001, page 138-142,146,160.
8. Joh Bjelke-Petersen, *Wikipedia*, viewed December 24, 2022.
9. Thomas Hiley, *Wikipedia*, viewed December 24, 2022.

10. Death of Honourable Sir Thomas Alfred Hiley, *Queensland Parliament*, Motion of Condolence appearing in Hansard, Volume 316.

11. Wayne Goss, *Wikipedia*, viewed December 24, 2022.

12. Neil Raymond Bradford, *Technical Correspondence* School, CN644 Certificate in Police Studies, December 23, 1987.

13. Gordon Cotterill to Neil Bradford re aircraft accident on Bell Peak North, *letter*, April 30, 2010.

14. Ian Wallace to Neil Bradford re the Bells Peak Tragedy, *letter*, March 5, 2010.

15. Ray Hickling to Neil Bradford re aircraft accident on Bell Peak North, *letter*, February 23, 2010.

16. Officer complains of police vendetta, *The Canberra Times*, April 27, 1988, page 7.

12. FALSELY ACCUSED

1. Cyclone Althea, *Wikipedia*, viewed December 24, 2022.

2. Leslie James (Les) Bardwell, *Australian National University*, viewed December 24, 2022.

3. Escaped murderer recaptured, *The Canberra Times*, January 7, 1976, page 7.

4. Labourer Facing Murder charge, *The Canberra Times*, December 25, 1959, page 1.

5. Lived in House with Skeletons, *The Canberra Times*, December 24, 1959, page 3.

6. Prisoner charged, *The Canberra Times*, March 11, 1976, page 6.

7. Committed for trial, *The Canberra Times*, March 12, 1976, page 6.

8. Whitrod, Ray. *Before I Sleep: Memoirs of a Modern Police Commissioner*, University of Queensland Press, Brisbane, 2001, page 152,184.

9. The Fitzgerald Inquiry Report, *Crime and Corruption Commission*, viewed July 9, 2021.

10. Qld head of police resigns, The Canberra Times, November 16, 1976, page 3.

11. New head for Qld Police, *The Canberra Times*, November 23, 1976, page 3.

12.   Inland taipan, *Wikipedia*, viewed August 23, 2021.

13.   Neil Raymond Bradford, *Queensland Police Service*, Details of Service, August 15, 1997.

14.   Pity the Policeman, *Truth*, July 17, 1910, page 9.

15.   William Geoffrey Cahill, *Wikipedia*, viewed December 28, 2022.

16.   Myers-Briggs Type Indicator, *Wikipedia*, viewed December 28, 2022.

17.   Autism, *healthdirect*, viewed July 6, 2021.

13. THE JOKE

1.   Neil Raymond Bradford, *Queensland Police Service*, Personal Details, Qualifications, and Experience, August 15, 1997.

2.   Murphy, M J. *Tony Murphy: An Honest Cop*, Watson Ferguson & Company, Brisbane, 2015, pages 36,37.

3.   Joh, police files and paper bags, *The Canberra Times*, December 7, 1988, page 1.

4.   Vincenzo Bellino v Australian Broadcasting Corporation, 28 March 1996, *High Court of Australia*, Defamation (1996) 185 CLR 183, viewed August 14, 2021.

5.   Sergeant 1/c N. R. Bradford, letter, unsuccessful in obtaining sufficient percentage at the 4th Commissioner Officer's Qualifying Course Part 1, *Queensland Police Department*, May 5, 1985.

6.   Money turned 'white', *The Canberra Times*, August 4, 1988, page 5.

7.   Whitrod, Ray. *Before I Sleep: Memoirs of a Modern Police Commissioner*, University of Queensland Press, Brisbane, 2001, page 146.

8.   Cairns' lawyer is Mr Big, inquiry told, The Canberra times, December 4, 1987, page 3.

9.   The Fitzgerald Inquiry, *Crime and Corruption Commission*, viewed July 9, 2021.

10.   Policeman called a liar in Qld corruption hearing, *The Canberra times*, December 11, 1987, page 10.

11.   Bill Gunn (Queensland politician, born 1920), *Wikipedia*, viewed December 29, 2022.

12.   Tony Fitzgerald, *Wikipedia*, viewed December 29, 2022.

13.   Senior Sergeant N. R. Bradford, letter, *Queensland Police Depart-*

ment, successfully completed the Special Commissioned Officer's Qualifying Course, March 10, 1988.

14. 60 years since Mackay plane crash tragedy, *The Courier Mail*, June 6, 2020.

15. The Good, the Bad and the Ugly, *Wikipedia*, viewed August 12, 2021.

16. $16,000 bribe 'for police,' *The Canberra Times*, July 26, 1989, page 6.

17. Judge says Fitzgerald agents used threats, *The Canberra Times*, August 2, 1989, page 1.

18. Paul de Jersey, *Wikipedia*, viewed August 13, 2021.

14. GAME OVER

1. Neil Raymond Bradford, *Queensland Police Service*, Personal Details, Qualifications, and Experience, August 15, 1997.

2. State police receive last imperial honours, *The Courier-Mail*, May 26, 1990, page 7.

3. Royal Commission into Aboriginal Deaths in Custody, *Wikipedia*, viewed December 30, 2022.

4. Speaker of the Legislative Assembly of Queensland, *Wikipedia*, viewed December 30, 2022.

5. Myers-Briggs Type Indicator, *Wikipedia*, viewed December 28, 2022.

6. Adopt a Cop, *Queensland Police Service*, viewed December 30, 2022.

7. Whitrod, Ray. *Before I Sleep: Memoirs of a Modern Police Commissioner*, University of Queensland Press, Brisbane, 2001, page 147-150,157.

8. Inspector Neil Bradford, reference, from Bill Jordan, Director of Corporate Projects, Queensland Transport, November 17, 1944.

9. Doctor Peter Rossberg to Neil Raymond Bradford, letter, diagnosed with Porphyria Cutanea Tarda (PCT), September 10, 1998.

10. Charles Appleton to Neil Raymond Bradford, letter, PCT in remission, June 15, 2000.

11. Everything You Should Know About Porphyria Cutanea

Tarda, *healthline*, viewed December 31, 2022.

12. Commission of inquiry into Queensland police culture and responses to domestic violence report handed down, *Australian Broadcasting Corporation*, viewed January 6, 2023.

CONCLUSION

1. Take our quick autism test, *Clinical Partners*, viewed December 31, 2022.

2. Police Long Service and Good Conduct Medal, *Wikipedia*, viewed December 31, 2022.

3. National Police Service Medal, *Australian Government*, viewed December 31, 2022.

4. Queensland Police Service Medal, *Queensland Police Service*, viewed December 31, 2022.

5. Australian Defence Medal, *Australian Government*, viewed December 31, 2022.

BIBLIOGRAPHY

Books

Bradford, Neil Raymond. *Voices from The Past: Law Enforcement on the Central Highlands*, Boolarong Press, Brisbane, 2013.

Murphy, M J. *Tony Murphy: An Honest Cop*, Watson Ferguson & Company, Brisbane, 2015

Whitrod, Ray. *Before I Sleep: Memoirs of a Modern Police Commissioner*, University of Queensland Press, Brisbane, 2001.

Newspapers

Australian Women's Weekly
Daily Mail Australia
RAAF News
Royal Australian Air Force
The Cairns Post
The Canberra Times
The Daily Mercury
The Morning Bulletin
The Sunday Mail
The Townsville Daily Bulletin
The Weekend Post
Truth
Weekender

Online Publications

31st Battalion, Royal Queensland Regiment, *Wikipedia*, viewed July 3, 2021.

31st/51st Battalion (Australia), *Wikipedia*, viewed August 2, 2021.

42nd Battalion (Australia), *Wikipedia*, viewed July 3, 2021.

51st Battalion, Far North Queensland Regiment, *Wikipedia*, viewed July 3, 2021.

Adopt a Cop, *Queensland Police Service*, viewed December 30, 2022.

Ancestry DNA Review 2021, *DNA Weekly*, viewed June 27, 2021.

Arsey, *Oxford Learner's Dictionaries*, viewed December 18, 2022.

Atherton Tableland, *Wikipedia*, viewed July 11, 2021.

Australian Defence Medal, *Australian Government*, viewed December 31, 2022.

Autism and Theory of Mind in Practice, *Psychreg*, viewed December 24, 2022.

Autism, *healthdirect*, viewed July 6, 2021.

Barramundi – north-east coast monitoring & Barramundi – central-east coast, *Queensland Government*, viewed July 6, 2021.

Bellenden Ker Range, *Wikipedia*, viewed July 9, 2021.

Bill Gunn (Queensland politician, born 1920), *Wikipedia*, viewed December 29, 2022.

Blue wall of silence, *Wikipedia*, viewed August 3, 2021.

Cape Palmerston National Park, *Queensland Government*, viewed July 2, 2021.

Citizen Military Forces, *Australian War Memorial*, viewed July 3, 2021.

Coastal Taipan, *Queensland Museum*, viewed June 30, 2021.

Commission of inquiry into Queensland police culture and responses to domestic violence report handed down, *Australian Broadcasting Corporation*, viewed January 6, 2023.

Common tree snake, *Queensland Government*, viewed July 1, 2021.

Copaifera langsdorffii, *Wikipedia*, viewed August 1, 2021.

Criminal Code 1899 - Section 69: Going armed so as to cause fear, *Queensland Consolidated Acts*, viewed December 18, 2022.

Croydon, Queensland, *Wikipedia*, viewed June 1, 2022.

Cyclone Althea, *Wikipedia*, viewed December 24, 2022.

Darumbal language, *Wikipedia*, viewed July 6, 2021.

Distance measuring equipment (aviation), *Wikipedia*, viewed July 13, 2021.

Dobber, Aussie Slang Dictionary, viewed December 18, 2022.

Eidetic memory, *Wikipedia*, viewed December 15, 2022.

Electrical Safety, *Queensland Government*, viewed July 9, 2021.

Everything You Should Know About Porphyria Cutanea Tarda, *healthline*, viewed December 31, 2022.

Extrasensory perception, *Wikipedia*, viewed June 1, 2022.

Flood Warning System for the Mulgrave and Russell Rivers, *Australian Government*, viewed July 9, 2021.

Flooding and electricity, *Scottish & Southern Electricity Networks*, viewed July 9, 2021.

Francis Erich (Frank) Bischof, *Australian National University*, viewed December 24, 2022.

From the CJC to the CCC: an overview, *Crime and Corruption Commission, Queensland*, viewed August 6, 2022.

Great Wall of China, *Wikipedia*, viewed June 30, 2021.

Guinea grass, *Queensland Government*, viewed July 6, 2021.

Humpybong State School, *Queensland Government*, viewed June 27, 2021.

Inland taipan, *Wikipedia*, viewed August 23, 2021.

Jack Pizzey, *Wikipedia*, viewed July 9, 2021.

Joh Bjelke-Petersen, *Wikipedia*, viewed December 24, 2022.

Kevin M8: Combined memories of Ray Hickling, Alan Broughton, and Kevin Murgatroyd: Bell Peak North Plane Crash 28 January 1970, *ExplorOz*, viewed July 29, 2021.

Kokoda Track, *Wikipedia*, viewed August 2, 2021.

Leslie James (Les) Bardwell, *Australian National University*, viewed December 24, 2022.

Limevale, Queensland, *Wikipedia*, viewed June 27, 2021.

Lincoln bombers at the RAAF Base Amberley, Queensland, 1951, *National Library of Australia*, viewed June 27, 2021.

Long paddock, *lexico*, viewed July 6, 2021.

Moonlight State: The honest cop who helped blow the whistle on Australia's most corrupt police force, *Four Corners*, viewed June 5, 2021.

Moreton Island National Park, *Wikipedia*, viewed June 27, 2021.

Myers-Briggs Type Indicator, *Wikipedia*, viewed December 28, 2022.

National Police Service Medal, *Australian Government*, viewed December 31, 2022.

No. 43 Squadron RAF, *Wikipedia*, viewed July 12, 2021.

Our History, *Paul Hopkins Medical Clinic*, viewed January 3, 2023.

Paul de Jersey, *Wikipedia*, viewed August 13, 2021.

Police Long Service and Good Conduct Medal, *Wikipedia*, viewed December 31, 2022.

Policing Queensland timeline 1864 – 2014, *Queensland Police Service*, viewed December 24, 2022.

Porphyria, *healthdirect*, viewed July 6, 2021.

Pre-Decimal Inflation Calculator, *Reserve Bank of Australia*, accessed July 6, 2021.

Queensland Police Service Medal, *Queensland Police Service*, viewed December 31, 2022.

Queensland Police Service, *Wikipedia*, viewed December 24, 2022.

Ring a Ring o' Roses, *Wikipedia*, viewed November 1, 2022.

Rounders, *Wikipedia*, viewed November 1, 2022.

Royal Commission into Aboriginal Deaths in Custody, *Wikipedia*, viewed December 30, 2022.

Seaview Range, *Wikipedia*, viewed July 11, 2021.

Shoalwater Bay Training Area, Queensland, *Australian Government*, viewed July 3, 2021.

Sinking of the Centaur, *Australian War Memorial*, viewed June 27, 2021.

Speaker of the Legislative Assembly of Queensland, *Wikipedia*, viewed December 30, 2022.

Take our quick autism test, *Clinical Partners*, viewed December 31, 2022.

The Fitzgerald Inquiry, *Crime and Corruption Commission, Queensland*, viewed July 9, 2021.

The Good, the Bad and the Ugly, *Wikipedia*, viewed August 12, 2021.

Thomas Hiley, *Wikipedia*, viewed December 24, 2022.

Tony Fitzgerald, *Wikipedia*, viewed December 29, 2022.

Values of Country, *Djunbunji Land & Sea Program*, viewed July 13, 2021.

Vera Lynn: The White Cliffs of Dover, *CUNY Academic Commons*, viewed June 27, 2021.

Vincenzo Bellino v Australian Broadcasting Corporation, 28 March 1996, *High Court of Australia*, Defamation (1996) 185 CLR 183, viewed August 14, 2021.

Wally Taylor achieved national acclaim, *The Courier Mail*, viewed July 17, 2021.

Wayne Goss, *Wikipedia*, viewed December 24, 2022.

Welcome to Pyramid Highleigh No. 161, *United Grand Lodge of*

Queensland, viewed July 12, 2021.

William Geoffrey Cahill, *Wikipedia*, viewed December 28, 2022.

Wondecla, Queensland, *Wikipedia*, viewed July 11, 2021.

Working Safely with Phenol, *University of Queensland*, viewed July 16, 2021.

World War I, *Wikipedia*, viewed July 6, 2021.

World War II, *Wikipedia*, viewed June 27, 2021.

Yellow Submarine, *The Beatles*, viewed July 11, 2021.

Publications

Queensland Police Gazette

INDEX

$5,000 (cash), 230

15-year-old girl, 233

31st Battalion, 120, 164

42nd Battalion, 65

51st Battalion, 120

7th Battalion, Royal Australian Regiment, 121, 125

Abertawe Kennels, 200

Accounts Section, 231

accused (falsely), 1, 189, 207

Acting District Officer (author), 223, 239

Acting Inspector (author), 238, 267, 268

Acting Sergeant First Class (author), 221

Acting Superintendent, 253, 259, 260

Addison, Elwynn Kenneth (Ken) Sub-Inspector, 223

Aden, 126

Administration Branch, 92, 241, 251

Adopt-a-Cop, 255

Ahern, Mary, 34

Air Navigation Regulation 34(1), 127

Air Safety Authority, 142, 143, 170, 174

aircraft accident (fatal), 1, 2, 131, 139, 238

Alderley, 252

Alfa Romeo Sedan, 257

allegation (Cairns and Innisfail), 232

allegation (senior Non-Commissioned Officer), 233

Alligator Creek, 18, 37

Alligator Creek State School, 20

Aloomba, 103, 118, 126, 130, 137, 153

Aloomba Hotel, 193, 195

altered (report), 2

amateur boxing, 52

Amberley, 10

anaesthetist, 266

Andergrove, 6, 15, 16, 17, 33

Anderson Road, 102, 103

Anderson, Bob, 144, 162, 170

Angelino, Emelio, 144, 151, 162, 170

Angelino, Lou, 174

Annat, Don, 131, 132, 139, 140, 182

apology (Assistant Commissioner), 265

apology (colleagues), 211

appendix, 63, 266

arguments (parents), 18, 62

army training area, 72

Arsey Joe, 20

Arthur Gorrie Correctional Centre, 233

ASA investigators, 142, 158, 161, 176, 178, 179, 181, 182

Ashmore, Regional Brian (Lurch) Superintendent, 249, 251, 256

Ashton-Shorter, H. L. Doctor, 8

Atherton Tablelands, 115, 117, 120

Athleticism
  broad jumping, 43
  bullock riding, 49
  golf, 240, 266
  high jumping, 43
  hurdles, 43
  relay teams, 43
  roughriding horses, 50
  rugby league, 43
  running, 16, 20, 43
  swimming, 19
Auditor-General's Department, 97
Australian Army, 65, 156, 157, 165
Australian Defence Medal, 277
Australian hornets, 145
Australian Hospital Ship, 10
Australian Workers' Union, 62
autism, 2, 5, 8, 11, 16, 20, 21, 23, 25, 26, 32, 35, 41, 64, 76, 91, 94, 117, 201, 204, 224, 225, 264, 265, 276, 277
autism (years of denial), 7
autism online test, 276
Automatic Direction Finder, 128
Aviation Protection Officer, 208, 275
AWU representative, 121, 201
Babinda (police), 117
Bachelor of Community Welfare degree, 250
backward, 51
Bailey, George, 49
Bailiff, 202
baked beans, 72
Baker's Creek, 51, 209

Ballera, 275
bandicoot, 99
bank account, 61
bank clerk, 218, 219, 235
Bank of New South Wales, 217, 218
Bankstown, 127
Banyo Physiotherapy, 254, 257, 270, 271
Banyo Police Station, 254, 260, 271
barber, 231
Bardon Police Station, 76, 254
Bardwell, Leslie James (Les) Inspector, 206
Barlow, Sub-Inspector, 75
Barnes Creek Road, 17
barracks (Yukan), 60
barramundi, 49, 72
Bathurst, 116
Bauer, Norwin William (Norm) Commissioner, 112
Baulch, Stan, 102, 103
beat duty, 76
Beat Sergeant, 76
Bedford, Alice Rebecca, 15
Bedford, Cecil Herbert (Pop), 6, 15, 33
Bedford, Cecil William Joseph (Bill), 64
Bedford, Iris Neta Annie. *See* Iris Neta Annie Turner
Bedford, Margaret Isabella. *See* Margaret Isabella Bradford
behaviour (consistency), 4
Beijing, 33
Bell Peak Motel, 176

Bell Peak North, 1, 67, 94, 123, 126, 129, 130, 132, 137, 138, 139, 140, 141, 142, 144, 145, 146, 150, 151, 153, 155, 160, 162, 163, 164, 165, 169, 170, 174, 176, 177, 178, 179, 180, 181, 182, 183, 187, 188, 193, 194, 195, 196, 197, 215

Bell, Peter, 141, 144, 146, 151, 162, 170, 188

Bellenden Ker Range, 171

Bellino, Vincenzo (Vince), 231

Belvedere Hotel, 11

Belyando, 202

bender, 48

Benedetti (daughter of Savino and Lena Benedetti), 175

Benedetti, Lena, 175

Benedetti, Savino, 175

Bennett Road, 103, 122, 130

Bessie Point, 200

best man, 74

better (than others), 70

Bianchi, Arthur Gordon (AGB) Inspector, 205, 208

Big Smoke, 72, 250

Bischof, Francis Erich (Frank) Commissioner, 95, 97, 112, 114, 122, 217

bivouacs, 65

Bjelke-Petersen, Johannes (Joh) Sir, 190, 221

black (book), 232

Black Nugget Hotel/Motel, 205

blazed (trees), 142, 143

blind date, 66, 67, 74

blood blister, 20

boat rower (experienced), 102

Boccalatte, Bill, 89

Boccalatte, Lena, 89

Bodgie boots, 75

body bags, 156, 178

boiled bacon, 72

books (black and red), 232

Boondall Wetlands, 261

Bopf, Charles (Charlie) Regional Superintendent, 223

Bosca Asti Spumante, 175

Bougainville Campaign in 1944-45, 164

Boyle, Tom Inspector, 70, 71

Bradford, Albert Edward (Ned), 41, 43

Bradford, Arnold, 3, 29

Bradford, Christopher, 114, 115, 124, 141

Bradford, Douglas (Doug), 52, 60, 61, 64, 65, 66, 68, 69, 70, 205

Bradford, Ernie, 68

Bradford, Evelyn, 61

Bradford, George Edward (Bunny), 43

Bradford, Ivan, 68

Bradford, James (Slim), 31, 32, 60

Bradford, Les, 68

Bradford, Margaret Isabella, 3, 28

Bradford, Marjorie May (Marj). *See* Marjorie May (Marj) Petersen

Bradford, Mark Stephen, 100, 104, 110, 115, 124, 141, 275, 276, 278

Bradford, Neil Raymond, 28, 30, 54, 56, 57, 58, 59, 79, 80, 81, 82, 83, 84, 85, 86, 87, 110, 111, 124, 144, 147, 151, 154, 155, 184, 187, 227, 228, 243, 244, 245, 246, 247, 248, 270, 271, 272, 273, 274, 278, 279

Bradford, Patricia Frances, 24, 66, 68, 70, 72, 73, 74, 82, 88, 93, 99, 100, 101, 103, 104, 110, 115, 122, 141, 175, 176, 187, 189, 200, 203, 205, 206, 208, 216, 225, 232, 241, 254, 255, 256, 257, 261, 262, 276, 277, 278

Bradford, Stanley Septimus (Stan), 42, 43, 44

breeder (canine), 200, 201

bribes (taken by Regional Superintendent, Cairns), 235

bridesmaid, 74

briefcase, 230, 231

Brisbane, 10, 72, 73, 88, 95, 114, 127, 206, 216, 218, 219, 222, 225, 231, 238, 240, 241, 249, 254, 275, 276

Brisbane Airport, 32, 208

Brisbane Police District, 78

Brisbane Water Police, 102

Brody, Janos Doctor, 93

Broughton, Alan, 94, 140, 141, 144, 146, 151, 158, 179, 180, 181, 182, 184, 185, 188, 189

Bruce Highway, 98, 99, 112, 113, 117, 204

Brumbies, 50

Bruton, Pat, 47, 71

Bryce, Thomas (Tom), 104

bulldoze, 250, 256

burden (on family), 9, 17, 19, 21, 25, 51

Bureau of Meteorology, 103, 164, 168

burglar alarm, 76

Bush Pilots' Airways, 137

Business Community, 255

Business Development phase, 267

business practices, 267

C. A. Cumming's Cup, 43

Cahill, William Geoffrey Commissioner, 222

Cairns, 1, 88, 95, 96, 101, 115, 117, 126, 127, 128, 208, 230, 231, 232, 235, 249, 265, 276, 278

Cairns Police District Headquarters, 230

Cairns Police Division, 204

Cairns Police Station, 123, 137, 138, 141, 169, 219, 223, 230, 231

Cairns Regional Airport, 123, 128, 134, 135, 139, 169

Cairns Traffic Branch, 204

calf, 35

Campbell Creek, 132, 137, 140, 171, 189, 193, 194, 195, 196

Campbell Creek Falls, 189

Campbell, Sir Walter Governor, 251

camps (army), 65, 72

Cannon Park Racecourse, 191

Cape Moreton Lighthouse, 10

Cape Palmerston National Park, 50

Car 54, 249

cardiac arrest, 266

cargo net, 172, 173, 174, 177, 178, 179, 182, 183, 193

Carina Close, 230

Carlon's Hotel, 74

Carmila, 14

Carr, Albert, 44, 49, 50

Cassidy, John, 132, 139, 140, 193

cast net, 210

Catchments
Goldsborough, 98, 103
Little Mulgrave, 98, 103

Catholic, 112, 193

ceiling, 231

ceiling (Regional Superintendent's office), 231

Centaur, 10

Central Traffic Support Group, 258, 259, 260, 264

Cessna 402 (plane), 126, 127, 130, 133, 215

chainsaw, 171, 172, 173

chalk and cheese, 196

Chalk, Gordon, 96

Charge of the Light Horse Brigade, 94

Chelmer Police College, 191, 216, 223, 232, 261

Chemicals (beer), 119

child abuse, 5, 13, 16, 18, 19, 21, 22, 23, 25, 35, 36, 39, 42, 45, 73

chopping axe, 171, 172, 173

Christmas (1968), 118

Christmas Eve (1971), 204

Churchill, Malcolm John (Mal) Sergeant, 240

Citizens Military Forces, 65, 69, 72, 115, 120, 157, 181

Civic Theatre, 23

Civil Defence Organisation, 137

CJC interview, 261, 262

CJC investigators, 261, 262

clearing (crash site), 172, 177, 178

Clements, Maria, 115

Clements, William James, 73, 202

Clerical Functions, 96, 220, 221, 222, 223, 230, 260, 262

clerk (Mount Isa), 259

Clerk of the Court, Brisbane, 259

Clinical Partners, 276

Coastal Taipan, 35, 42

cofferdams, 67

collision course (Cessna 402), 129

command and control, 36, 93, 137, 139, 140, 142, 170, 196

Commissioned Officer's Qualifying Course, 232, 235, 237, 261

Commissioned Officer's Qualifying Course (Special), 237

Commissioner Officer (high-ranking), 232

Commissioner's Memorandum (1965), 96, 97, 256

Commonwealth versus State dispute, 170

Company Sergeant Major, 72

complainant (falsely accused by colleagues), 200

complainant's husband, 201, 208

complex (inferiority), 17

Concise Oxford English
Dictionary, 93
concrete pipes, 64
Condie, Donald Malcolm Leslie
(Don) Senior Constable, 205
conduct (consistency), 4
confidential investigations, 234
Consolidated Revenue, 231
*constable who almost put the
Premier through the windscreen*,
222
contact engagements (army), 93
contamination, 158
continuity, 178
Control Tower (Cairns), 128, 129,
130, 131, 137
Copaifera langsdorffii, 164
coronial investigation, 123, 142,
153, 169, 181
corruption (*Joke*), 91, 96, 114, 120,
216, 230, 233, 252
Cotterill, Albert Gordon
(Gordon), 103, 118, 122, 136,
193, 197
Cotterill's farm, 122, 129, 130,
136
counter-allegation (Cairns and
Innisfail), 232
Country Boy, 73, 77, 250
coupling, 177, 178, 183, 185
course panel, 232
cows (farm), 34, 35, 42
crank calls, 276
crash site (aircraft accident), 126,
131, 142, 143, 145, 146, 153,
154, 155, 156, 158, 159, 161,

162, 163, 169, 170, 176, 181,
182, 193, 194, 195
credible witness, 233
Cremorne Hotel, 17
cricket, 66
Crime Investigation Course, 216,
228
Criminal Justice Commission, 2,
252, 261
crocodile, 18, 22, 37, 38, 39, 45, 68
crocodile (monster), 38
crocodile (thirty-two feet and
nine inches), 38
crocodile eggs, 38
Cromer Private Hospital, 6, 7, 8
crosscut saw, 33
Croydon, 115, 116
Cunninghams Gap, 14
Cyclone Althea, 204
Cyprus, 126
dagger eyes (doctor), 63
dagger eyes (Tony Murphy), 230
dairy farm, 6, 15, 16, 33
Dalton Road, 118
dangerous driving causing
death, 114
database (whole-of-
government), 266
DCA Engineer, 182, 185
De Jersey, Paul, 241
dead wood, 250
debriefing, 1, 193
declaration, 138, 196
deep thinker, 44
Deeral, 117
demotion, 2, 222, 242, 252, 263

Department of Civil Aviation,
123, 127, 129, 130, 132, 139,
140, 142, 143, 145, 153, 155,
157, 158, 159, 161, 162, 169,
170, 171, 172, 173, 174, 176,
177, 179, 181, 194, 195, 196
Department of Transport, 259
Deputy High Bailiff, 202
descent (Cessna 402), 128
Design and Construction phase,
267
Detective Inspector, 261
Detective Superintendent, 261
*Diesel Tree. See Copaifera
langsdorffii*
different, 3, 4, 7, 24, 69, 76, 188,
224, 236, 255, 277
dingoes, 35
Disciplinary Hearing, 262
Disciplinary Officer, 97, 234, 252,
259, 263
disruptive behaviour, 17
Distance Measuring Equipment,
128
District Officer (acting), 241
District Superintendent of
Traffic, 259, 260, 264
DNA, 3, 24
dobber, 23, 222
dogs (wild), 194
double life (lived), 17
Downs, Barry Joseph Vincent
(Barry) Constable, 112, 120,
137, 144, 146, 151, 154, 155,
156, 160, 161, 162, 175, 181
Drawbridge, Bruce John, 211,
212, 213, 214, 215, 216

drink-driving, 203
drum (44-gallon – aircraft
accident), 179
drum (44-gallon - flood), 99
Drummond, Stewart Rutherford,
126
drunkenness, 25, 71
Dunk Island, 128, 134
Dunlop (water drop), 157, 171
Dunster, Keith, 70
duplex (Tony Murphy), 230
Duty Sergeant, 73
Dwyer, Michael Maxwell (Max)
Magistrate, 203
Education
*Batchelor of Community Welfare
degree*, 113
Certificate in Police Studies, 113,
191
Crime Investigation Course,
191
*Fundamentals of Information
Processing*, 113
Map Reading, 65
Qualified - Constable First
Class, 192
Qualified - Senior Sergeant,
235
Qualified - Sergeant First
Class, 230
Qualified - Sergeant Second
Class, 222
Senior level, 113
Signaller's course, 65
Special Commissioned
Officer's Qualifying Course,
237

eidetic memory, 18, 67

elderly woman, 261

Emotion
  not present, 12, 15
  present, 13, 15

Empire Games, 52

endoscopic sinus surgery, 266

Eton Range, 208, 220

Eureka, 6, 15, 16

European Carp, 12

examination papers (shredded), 233, 261

examinations (police), 192

Executive Council, 241

Executive Officer, 263

explosion (wood stove), 23, 24

extraction (bodies), 178, 184, 194, 196

extramarital affairs, 42, 49, 115

extraordinary strength, 17, 52

Extrasensory perception, 116

Eye contact
  death stare, 32, 33
  freezing, 36
  with others, 19, 33, 36, 66

falsely (accused), 1, 207

Far Beach, 238, 240

Far North Queensland, 231

farmer's spouse, 89, 101

Favourable Record, 180, 197

Fernleigh Dairy, 6

filing cabinet, 234

fingerprinting, 231

fire (Regional Superintendent's office), 231

Fire Brigade, 93, 113, 231

firearm (departmental-issued), 212

firearms licence, 254, 259

fireplace, 176

firing range, 157

fish (stunned), 72

fishing net, 37, 39

Fitzgerald Commission of Inquiry, 2, 92, 122, 191, 220, 221, 231, 232, 233, 235, 236, 237, 239, 250, 251, 256, 260

Fitzgerald investigator, 232, 237, 238, 240

Fitzgerald, Gerald Edward (Tony), 237

Flaggy Rock, 49

flat (Red Hill), 75, 88

flight plan, 128

floodplain, 98, 107

floodwater, 14, 15, 98, 99, 100, 101, 102, 103, 104

fluorescent lights, 92

Forgan Bridge, 17

Fortitude Valley Police District, 97, 249, 253

Fortitude Valley Police Station, 97, 249, 252

Foster, Howard (Head Teacher), 46

foul play, 66

Fouras, Demetrios (Jim), 253

foxes, 12

Gallagher, Jack Constable, 38

Gallon, Eva May, 214

Gallon, Ian, 199, 214

games (silly), 5, 9, 16

Gemfields, 207, 208

Germany, 10

Gillies Range, 99

Gillies Range Road, 91, 94, 113

girlfriend, 52, 66

give way sign, 94

Gleeson, Kevin John (Kevin), 220, 221

Glenella, 16, 26

going armed so as to cause fear, 25, 71

Gold Coast (beaches), 73

Gold Coast (real estate), 232

Golden Gloves, 52, 53

Goodyear (water drop), 157, 171

Gordonvale, 18, 78, 88, 90, 103, 114, 153, 197, 200, 203, 204, 207, 208, 211, 221, 231

Gordonvale Hotel, 193

Gordonvale Memorial Hospital, 104, 114

Gordonvale Police Station, 91, 97, 130, 150, 192, 193, 200

Goss, Wayne Keith Premier, 190

Goss, Wayne Premier, 260

grandstand seat, 178

grappling hook, 210

gravel, 190

Great Dividing Range, 14

Great Wall of China, 33

Green Mafia, 192, 198

grocer, 191

grocer's son, 191

Groundwater, Betty, 206

Groundwater, Kevin Nichol (Kevin) Sergeant, 205, 206, 207, 209

growth spurt, 37, 39

Guard
bodies, 169
crash site, 143, 145, 154, 158, 169

Guinea grass, 35, 42

Gunn, Allan Cameron (Tubby), 91, 95

Gunn, William Angus Manson (Bill) Acting Premier, 237

Guwinmal people, 50

half-brother, 8

Hand signals (Bell Peak North)
all clear, 174
change of procedures, 182
move ahead, 174
move downwards, 174
move upwards, 174
simple hand signals, 182
used by Ray Hickling, 183

handshake (*drooping-lily*), 191

Hannigan, Mick Superintendent, 267

Hansen, Tracey, 99, 100, 101, 103

Harassment
called a *dog* (derogatory), 2, 197
Dirty Dozen, 237
feeling unsafe, 197
Filthy Five, 237
get even with you one day, 234
go out into the cold awhile, 233
I don't like you, 235
not to be trusted, 2
revenge, 101, 234
yes men, 101

Harris, John, 47, 71
hat trick, 66
Hawker De Havilland
    (Australia) Pty Ltd, 127
Head Teacher, 16, 32, 46
Head Typist, 264
Healey, Neil, 122
Heaths Road, 16
Heightened senses
    Extrasensory perception
        (ESP), 116
    hairs standing up (back of
        neck), 35, 212, 217
Helicopter
    army, 67, 120, 173, 174
    Bell 47, 160, 167, 170, 171, 172,
        173, 174
    equipment fell from the quick-
        release hook, 179
    Iroquois, 125, 138, 148, 196
    large, 172, 173, 174, 177, 179
    repairs to quick-release hook,
        179
Hercules, 138, 148
hexamine stove, 143
Hickling, Norman Charles
    (Norman), 130
Hickling, Ray (twelfth wedding
    anniversary), 181
Hickling, Raymond Charles
    (Ray), 94, 122, 130, 131, 132,
        139, 140, 142, 144, 145, 146,
        151, 153, 156, 158, 159, 162,
        163, 165, 169, 170, 171, 172,
        173, 174, 176, 177, 178, 180,
        181, 182, 184, 185, 189, 193,
        195, 197

Hickling's farm, 122, 130, 139
High Range, 65, 157
Highfields, 275
Highleigh Base, 140, 143, 145,
    146, 158, 159, 160, 169, 170,
    171, 172, 193
Hiley Report, 190
Hiley, Thomas Alfred (Tom) Sir,
    190
Hill, Patrick John, 126, 127, 133,
    197
Hill, Patty, 34
Hockings, Ernest Robert (Ernie)
    Detective, 239
Hogget, Ken Sergeant, 223
homeless men, 98, 100, 103
Honda House, 262
Hoochie tent, 143
Hopkins, Paul William Doctor, 7,
    8, 64
Hops (beer), 119
Horan, Ernest (Ernie) Regional
    Superintendent, 220
Hore, Herb Inspector, 131, 137,
    138, 139, 140, 179, 196, 204
horse manure, 190
Housing Commission home, 206
hovering, 171, 172, 173, 177, 178
Howarth, Keith, 131, 137, 139,
    140, 143, 188
howitzer, 157
Hughes, Ted, 137, 144, 151, 160
Humpybong State School, 11
Identity Card, 78
illegal gambling, 90
ill-gotten gains, 231
impenetrable, 194

inappropriate relationship, 233
index book, 234
inferiority complex, 17
infidelity, 89, 90, 91, 92, 101
informant (money paid), 234
Information Engineering
    Facility, 267
Ingham, 159
Inland Taipan, 217
Innisfail, 104, 232, 234
Inspector's clerk, 92, 205, 223
Instrument Flight Rules, 127, 128
Instrument Landing System, 128
Instrument Rating, 127
intercourse, 21
interloper, 259, 268
international terminal, 208
irregularities (report), 264
Japan, 10, 156
Jenkins, William Crossley (Bill),
    88
Joe, 20, 38
Johnston, Roy, 144
Jones, Lisa, 180
Jordan, Bill, 267
Kangaroo Court, 242
Karremal Siding, 31, 34, 35, 42,
    47, 50, 51
Kay, Cecil, 66, 68
Kay, Joyce, 66
kerosene, 24
Kerosene Tree. See Copaifera
    langsdorffii
khaki slouch hat, 92
Khormaksar, 126
Kokoda Track, 165
Koumala, 8, 31, 32, 37, 47, 66

Koumala Hotel, 66
Koumala State School, 32
Kuranda, 123
Lamb, Bob, 44, 48, 49, 51
landing skids, 121, 172, 174
landing zone, 159, 171, 172, 173,
    177, 180
latrine trench, 176
lawn (mowing), 217
left the family at 15 years, 51
Leichhardt Hotel, 38
Lenning, John, 42, 44
Licensing Branch, 225
life (lived double), 17
life-endangering offence, 95, 96
liftman, 34, 47, 48
Limevale, 3, 12, 13, 14, 18
Limevale State School, 12
Lincoln bombers, 10, 29
Lister Private Hospital, 6, 7, 8,
    42, 63, 64, 209, 266
Loloma, 8
long paddock, 34
Lynch, Arthur, 181, 182, 183, 184,
    185, 193
Lynn. Vera, 10
Machan, Tom, 182, 184, 185
machete, 142, 159
Mackay, 3, 12, 13, 14, 17, 18, 26,
    31, 41, 51, 88, 92, 115, 127, 128,
    164, 204, 208, 209, 225, 232,
    235, 237
Mackay Base Hospital, 41, 42,
    209, 210
Mackay Cemetery, 202
Mackay District Hospital, 8
Mackay District/Base Hospital, 6

Mackay Golf Club, 240
Mackay Police District, 238, 240
Mackay Police Station, 70
Magnetic Island, 204
Magpies Under-19 team, 66, 68
Main Roads' police, 206
mainstream society, 233, 236, 251, 255, 277
Maintenance Release, 127
Maitland Road, 89
Malbon Thompson Range, 1, 2, 126, 129, 130, 153, 171
Mandingalbay Yidinji Country, 153
March flies, 145
Margate, 3, 10, 11
Marlborough, 74
Marlin, Brian Anthony (Brian) Detective, 239
Mason, 90, 112
Masonic fraternity, 90, 104, 105, 112, 192
Masonic Pyramid Highleigh Lodge No. 161, 122
McArthur, Nancy, 126, 133
McArthur, William John (Bill) Inspector, 223
McCarthy, Mick Sub-Inspector, 179
McDonnell Constructions, 67
McNamara, Vincent Lloyd (Foggy), 225, 226
McNaughton, Neil Kingdon (Neil) Senior Sergeant, 235
mechanical harvester, 70
Medals
    Australian Defence Medal, 277
    National Police Service Medal, 277
    Police Long Service and Good Conduct Medal, 277
    Queensland Police Service Medal, 277
memorial (Far Beach), 238
Memory
    eidetic, 67
    eidetic memory, 17, 38, 126
    mental image snapshot, 17
    photographic, 67
Meneguzzo, Vittoria, 88
Meneguzzo, Wanda, 88
methylated spirits, 24
Metropolitan North Region, 96, 252, 253, 257, 262, 268
Michaelmas Reef, 118
micro-cassette tape recorder, 120, 240, 257
middens, 50
Middle East Command, 126
Moccasins, 75
Molloy, Tom Sergeant, 73, 75
money (paid to informant), 234
Moranbah, 202, 204, 205, 206, 207, 208, 209, 211
Moreton Bay, 10
Moreton Island, 10
Morris, Jack, 144
Morris, Raymond Frederick (Ray), 118, 122, 179, 193, 194, 195, 197
Morris, Rodney, 144, 145, 151, 160

Morris' farm, 132, 137, 138, 139, 140, 148, 171, 177, 178, 179, 193, 194, 196

Morrisson, Graham, 187

Morrisson, Ronald George (Ron) Sergeant, 112, 113, 114, 118, 120, 121, 131, 132, 137, 139, 141, 142, 143, 144, 148, 169, 175, 179, 180, 187, 188, 190, 191, 192, 195, 197, 201, 205, 208, 211

mortar platoon, 65

mortars (unexploded), 157

mosquito net, 176

mosquitoes, 45, 145, 261

Moss Road, 99, 102

Mount Blackwood, 65

Mount Christian, 34, 38, 50

Mount Isa, 96, 219, 222, 225, 230, 249, 265

Mount Surprise, 115

Mountain View Hotel, 91, 119, 120

Mr Big, 232

Mulgrave River, 89, 98, 103, 107, 175

Mulgrave Shire Historical Society, 172, 173

Mulgrave Sugar Mill, 141, 150, 201, 208

Munro's barracks, 89, 98, 101, 103

Murgatroyd, Kevin, 94, 139, 140, 141, 144, 146, 151, 154, 155, 158, 162, 165, 166, 170, 172, 174, 175, 176, 178, 180, 181, 182, 184, 188, 189, 195

Murphy, Anthony (Tony) Inspector/Regional Superintendent/Assistant Commissioner, 216, 217, 230, 231

Murphy, Vince Sergeant, 97

Murphy's Marauders, 97, 254, 256

Murphy's replacement, 231

mustering, 36, 49

Mutchero Inlet, 103, 153

Myers-Briggs Type Indicator, 223, 255

Myrteza, John, 144, 151, 162, 170

National Australia Bank, 230

National Police Service Medal, 277

Native Mounted Police, 202

Neilly, 251, 253, 262

Nicosia, 126

No. 43 (Fighter) Squadron, 126

Noakes, Max Lyndon (Max) Inspector, 201, 202, 203, 204, 208

Noland, Charles James, 116

Noland, Marian. *See* Maria Clements

Noland, Marion Parker. *See* Maria Clements

non-life-endangering offence, 97

Norman Park, 98

North Brisbane Police District, 252, 256

North Queensland Police Golf Championships, 240

Northern Mafia, 191

Northern Territory, 215

Northerner, 101, 102

Northgate, 254

O'Toole, John Sub-Inspector, 77

Oaky Creek, 12

Oath of Office, 75

Officer in Charge, 235, 236, 237, 240, 262

old-timers, 50

out of the blue, 200, 201

overzealous enforcement, 97, 254, 255, 256, 258

Oxley Golf Club, 265

Oxley Police Academy, 237, 252

Pacific Ocean, 10, 11, 153

Paget, 21, 64

pain (sensitivity), 21

Pannell, Madeline Grace (Madge), v, 66, 67, 70, 73, 88, 205, 225

Pannell, Patricia Frances. *See* Patricia Frances Bradford

Pannell, Walter Joseph Alfred (Wally), v, 66, 67, 205, 232

paper bag (brown), 231

parked dangerously, 257

Parker, Mary Ann, 116

Paul Hopkins Medical Clinic, 8

Peacock, Kevin, 222

Pembroke Welsh Corgi, 200

pencil pusher, 222

peritonitis, 63

Permanent Air Force, 10, 12

personal record, 203

Petersen, Marjorie May (Marj), 7

Petrie Terrace, 72

phenol, 17

photographic memory, 67

photographing, 231

Pickanjinnie, 211, 215

Pindi Pindi, 37

Pine Creek Road, 200

Pioneer River, 17, 38

Pitman, Brian Alan (Barney) Superintendent, 241, 251

Pizzey, Jack, 94, 98, 104

Plane Creek Sugar Mill, 34, 47

planting (sugarcane), 33, 34

Pluto, 26

police contingent, 179, 180, 181

Police Depot, 71, 72, 73, 74, 75, 95, 117, 202, 216

police force (joining), 8

Police Long Service and Good Conduct Medal, 252, 277

police notebook, 144, 182

Police Reserve, 187, 222

Police Union, 192

policy, orders, and procedures, 262

Porphyria Cutanea Tarda, 41, 63, 268

Porter, Madeline Grace (Madge). *See* Madeline Grace (Madge) Pannell

post-mortem, 93

postnatal depression, 18

pound-man, 202

powdered scrambled eggs, 72

power struggle, 137

preferential treatment, 263

prescribed medication (reactions), 64

Princess Theatre, 23

principles, 2, 165, 195

Probationary, 1, 73, 75, 254

Project Team (1991), 96, 262

promotion, 235

Proserpine, 88

prostitution, 21, 90

Protestant equivalent, 192, 198

publican, 21, 37, 41, 92, 119, 120

Putt, William Cowan (Bill), 91,
    95, 98, 104, 111

Pyramid Highleigh Lodge, 90,
    197, 198

Pyramid Siding Road, 102

Qantas Airways, 126

Queensland Ambulance
    Transport Brigade, 93, 113,
    145, 147, 164

Queensland Police Force, 1, 76,
    123, 130, 137, 138, 139, 141,
    142, 145, 161, 170, 181, 191,
    195, 196, 221, 224, 225, 241, 250

Queensland Police Museum, 180

Queensland Police Service, 96,
    189, 264, 266, 267, 268, 269, 275

Queensland Police Service
    Medal, 277

Queensland Policeman's
    Manual, 123, 169

Queensland Transport, 266

quick-release hook, 172, 173, 177,
    179

rabbits, 12, 200, 231

Radio
    UHF, 123, 139, 145, 161, 169
    VHF, 65, 142, 145, 169, 170,
        181

Radio Maintenance Section, 123,
    138, 169

radio operator, 118, 137, 141, 213

railmotor, 32, 34, 35

railway bridge, 98

Railway residence, 254

Railway yard, 257

reactions (prescribed
    medication), 63, 64, 209, 266

real-estate purchases, 232

Reason, Evan Arthur (Nifty)
    Sergeant, 205

Records of Interview, 112

Recruitment Section, 219, 235

red (book), 232

Redcliffe Peninsula, 3, 10

Reeves, Coral Elaine, 212, 214

Regional Duty Officer, 252, 255,
    257, 259, 268

Regional Superintendent's office
    (Cairns), 231

relationships (long-term), 1, 66

remains (pilot and passenger),
    126, 168

Report (author's)
    altered, 2, 272, 273
    declaration, 263
    irregularities, 264
    re-typing, 265
    submitted, 262, 263

Returned and Services League of
    Australia, 225

re-typing, 265

revocation, 258

revolver (carried illegally), 90

revolver (departmental), 238

Rex, 89, 99, 100, 103, 200

ridge, 140, 141, 142, 144, 154, 155,
    158, 159, 160, 165, 179, 180,
    181, 182, 196

rigger, 67

rigger's offsider, 67, 173

ring (heirloom), 194

Ring-a-ring o' roses, 5

ringbarking, 33

Riseham, Alice Rebecca. *See*
    Alice Rebecca Bedford

Robertson, Benjamin Harold
    (Ben) Regional
    Superintendent, 236

Robertson, Duncan Doctor, 8, 63,
    64

Rockhampton, 74, 206, 236

Rocky Dam Creek, 37, 38, 55

Rocla Pipes, 64

rodeo, 41, 43, 45, 49, 50, 52, 61,
    66, 69

Rodger, Robert Stevenson (Bob),
    95, 221, 252, 253, 261, 265, 269

Roma, 211, 218

Roma Street Police
    Headquarters, 263

Roma Street Police Station, 76,
    77, 78, 249

Ross River Fever, 261

rounders, 5, 22

Royal Air Force, 126

Royal Australian Air Force, 10,
    47, 196

Royal Commission (2022), 206,
    269

Royal Commission into
    Aboriginal Deaths in Custody,
    253

Royal Queensland Regiment, 65

rugby league, 41, 52, 66, 69, 115

rumourmongers, 241

running, 5

Russell Heads, 103, 126, 153

Russell River, 103

Saddle Mountain, 123, 139, 145,
    161, 169

safe, 230

Sandy Creek, 67

Santos, 275

Sarina, 6, 20, 31, 34, 41, 47, 52, 63,
    72, 74, 88, 205, 206, 208

Sarina and District All School
    Sports, 46

Sarina Police Station, 71

Sarina Pony Club, 52

sawyer, 202

Scholarship Examination, 46

school sports, 43

schoolteacher bushwalkers, 141,
    144, 159, 195

schooner, 66

Schwenke, Alan Charles (Alan),
    90, 118, 122

Scientific Section, 206

scorpions, 145

Search and Recovery mission, 2,
    94, 130, 131, 132, 137, 138, 139,
    141, 142, 144, 155, 161, 162,
    169, 170, 179, 180, 187, 189,
    194, 195, 196, 197

Search and Recovery party, 141,
    194

Seaview Range, 65, 67, 120, 157,
    159, 181

Second World War, 10, 156

Section 6.1.3 of the Police Service
    Code of Conduct, 263

Security Officer, 275

semi-trail driver, 114

semi-trailer, 113

Senior Commercial Pilot Licence,
127

senior Non-Commissioned
Officer, 97, 233, 234, 263, 265

Sensitivity
doubts (parentage), 3, 31
Extrasensory perception
(ESP), 116
hairs standing up (back of
neck), 35, 212, 217
light, 4, 6, 92
loner, 9, 20, 22, 224
pain, 17, 21, 23
sleep, 46
smell, 17, 46, 93
sound, 4, 6, 18
subtle as a train smash, 95, 221
suicidal thoughts, 37
watch my back, 202

sensory capabilities, 263

Sexton, 202

Shamrock Hotel, 26

Shandy, 11

shark, 18, 68

Shed
railway, 98, 100, 103
tennis courts, 98, 100

Sheddon, Colin (pilot), 137, 146

shelter (Bell Peak North), 163,
176

shelter (during food drop), 157

Shinfield, 31, 60

Shoalwater Bay, 72

shoot (to kill), 238

shotgun, 206, 220

shovel, 176

sick leave, 209, 261

signaller (CMF), 138

signature, 261

silly games, 5, 9, 16

Silverwater Detention Centre,
213

Simons, Adrian, 104

Simons, Jean, 104

Simons, Tom, 104

siren (air-raid), 10

sister-in-charge, 210

sister-in-law. *See* complainant

six-of-the-best, 32

Sleep
disorders, 6
eyes open, 24
talking, 46
tiredness and fatigue, 21, 23,
24
walking, 6

sleeping bags, 173, 176

small books (black and red), 232

Smith, Cedric Magistrate, 114,
117

smitten, 66

smoko, 144, 145

Snowdon of Abertawe. See Snowy

Snowy, 200, 227

Socializing
alienated, 22
blamed for doing something,
22
colleagues, 91
deep thinker, 32
excluded, 22
other children, 22

quiet one, 32
    small talk, 21, 32
solicitor named *Mr Big*, 232
southpaw, 39, 53
souvenire, 159
Speaker's nephew, 253, 254, 258
speeding vehicle (Drawbridge),
    211
spiteful, 123, 145, 161, 169
spotter (plane), 137
Starr, Joan, 137, 144, 146, 152,
    154, 155, 159, 160, 161, 162
State Emergency Service, 196
State Traffic Support Group, 267
Steene, Francis James (Frank),
    137, 144, 151, 154, 155, 156, 160
stepdaughter, 18
stepfather, 18
stigmatization, 64
stockmen, 50
storm surge, 204
strange, 224, 236, 251, 267, 268,
    275
stringent vetting, 252
Stroud, Gary, 101, 102, 103, 104
stupid, 51
subconscious, 1
Subscriber Trunk Dialling, 225
Sugarcane Inspector, 208
sugarcane knife, 62, 142, 159
Superintendent (Cairns), 232,
    233, 234
Superintendent's office, 230, 264
supplying details in writing, 263
surplus, 267
Sydney, 127
Sydney CIB, 213

tainted pasts, 261
Taipan, 35, 89, 99, 100, 181
talking (sleep), 23
Tapsall, Colin Constable, 123,
    169
tarpaulin, 173, 176, 194, 195
Taylor, Lawrie, 52
Taylor, Ollie, 52
Taylor, Wally, 52
Tedlands (side-creek), 37, 39, 44,
    55, 56
Tedlands' cattle property, 38, 49
telephone call (from son), 238
temporary army camp (Bell Peak
    North), 176
Texas, 13, 267
The Good, the Bad, and the Ugly,
    238
Thomason, Jim, 140
Thomason, Reta, 140, 174
Thomason's farm, 139, 140, 141,
    142, 151, 160, 171, 178, 181,
    182, 183, 189, 193, 196
Thomson, Joanne, 126
ticket (give way), 95
ticket (speeding), 96
Tiger leeches, 145
tomahawk, 142, 159
Toowoomba, 96, 99, 275
Tovell, Ted, 178, 182, 184, 185
Town Hall, 9
Townsville, 51, 104, 128, 204, 223
track (from Thomason's farm),
    142
traffic bridge, 98
traffic duties (competent), 179,
    204

transferred (in disgrace), 2, 197
Transport Registration and Integrated Licensing System, 266
Trinity Inlet, 118
Truman, John Henry (John), 217, 219
Tuckett, Mary, 37, 55
Tuckett, Thelma, 37, 55
Turner, Iris Neta Annie, 15
Turner, William Henry (Bill), 15
Turnors Paddock, 34, 47, 50
Turrawan Private Hospital, 266
typewriter (altered report), 264
Typing Pool, 264
U-bolt, 174
uncoupling, 173, 174, 177, 183
unique (personality), 223, 225, 236, 255
units (Tony Murphy), 230
University of Queensland, 224
unlawful use of a motor vehicle, 117
vendetta, 123, 145, 161, 169
verbatim, 208
vetting (stringent), 252
Vienna sausages, 72
Vietnam, 121, 196
voluntary (retirement), 238
von Snarski, Barrie Ronald, 238
Wacol, 233
wagons (sugarcane), 173
wait-a-while vines, 145
walked out (Commissioned Officer's Qualifying Course), 237
Walker, Keith, 137, 144, 160

walking (sleep), 23
Walk-Through Metal Detector, 275
Wallace, Ian, 196, 199
Wallace, Patricia, 151, 152, 166, 168
Wallace, Robert James (Bob), 93, 137, 144, 151, 154, 155, 156, 157, 162, 163, 164, 165, 170, 194, 196, 265
wall-of-silence, 1, 122, 141, 180, 183, 188, 190, 197, 200, 201, 204
Wallumbilla, 209, 211, 213, 218, 219, 235
Walshs Pyramid, 99, 101, 107
Ward, Colin Sergeant, 123, 169
war-games exercise, 120
Waria, Buddy, 144, 151, 160, 161
Warr (Ward), Robert, 116
Warr, Maria. *See* Maria Clements
Warrego Highway, 211, 213, 215, 216, 217
wasps, 145, 161
Weapons proficiency
·38 calibre revolver, 72
M60 machine gun, 72
Owen submachine gun, 72
Rifleman, 72
SLR rifle, 72
three-inch mortars, 72
Weis' Restaurant, 221
West Plane Creek, 20, 31
Western Australia, 18, 68
whiplash injury, 209
Whippet utility, 13
whiskey, 175, 176
White Cliffs of Dover, 10, 11

White Lace Motor Inn, 241

white paper, 267

Whiterock, 230

Whitrod, Mavis, 189

Whitrod, Raymond Wells (Ray) Commissioner, 96, 101, 189, 191, 192, 197, 198, 216, 217, 223, 232, 250, 256, 260

Whitrod's policy, 96, 256

whole-of-government database, 266

wife's employer, 263

winch, 172, 173, 174, 177

Winfield, June, 122

Winfield, William Bryce (Bill), 122

wire rope, 172, 173, 174, 177, 178, 179

witness (credible), 233

Wondecla, 120

woodcutters, 33

Woody Point, 11

World War One, 50

World War Two, 65, 164, 165

wreckage, 137, 142, 146, 153, 154, 155, 159

Yarrabah, 126

Yellow Submarine, 118

Youngberry, Barry John (John) Superintendent, 253

Yukan, 52, 60, 64

Zillmere Police Station, 265

www.ingramcontent.com/pod-product-compliance
Lightning Source LLC
Chambersburg PA
CBHW052354030726

47599CB00014B/1057